To my family

INDEX

Chapter One

Chapter Two

Chapter Three

Once upon a time

On a cold and blustery evening in December 1989, Huthaifa Azzam, the teenage son of the legendary Jordanian-Palestinian mujahideen leader Sheikh Abdullah Azzam, went to the airport in Peshawar, Pakistan, to welcome a group of young men. All were new recruits, largely from Jordan, and they had come to fight in a fratricidal civil war in neighboring Afghanistan—an outgrowth of the CIA-financed jihad of the 1980s against the Soviet occupation there.

The men were scruffy, Huthaifa mused as he greeted them, and seemed hardly in battle-ready form. Some had just been released from prison; others were professors and sheikhs. None of them would prove worth remembering—except for a relatively short, squat man named Ahmad Fadhil Nazzal al-Khalaylah. He would later rename himself Abu Musab al-Zarqawi.Once one of the most wanted men in the world, for whose arrest the United States offered a $25 million reward, al-Zarqawi was a notoriously enigmatic figure—a man who was everywhere yet nowhere.

Huthaifa Azzam bridges both worlds. He first went into battle at the age of fifteen, fighting against the Soviets in Afghanistan with his father and Osama bin Laden (to whom his father was a spiritual mentor); three years later, on that December night at the Peshawar airport, he met al-Zarqawi for the first time. The two Azzams and bin Laden had fought against the Soviets in the early days of the jihad; al-Zarqawi would fight in the war's second phase, after the Soviets had pulled out. Both Huthaifa Azzam and al-Zarqawi would eventually leave Afghanistan to pursue two very different lives, but their paths would once again cross on the battlefields of jihad in Iraq, after the U.S. invasion of 2003.

A self-described jihadist—one who believes in struggle, or, more loosely, holy war—Azzam now lives in the Jordanian capital, Amman, where he is at work on a doctorate in classical Arabic literature, but he moves routinely between Jordan and Iraq. Abu Musab al-Zarqawi, barely forty and barely literate, a Bedouin from the Bani Hassan tribe, was until recently almost unknown outside his native Jordan. Then, on February 5, 2003, Secretary of State Colin Powell catapulted him onto the world stage. In his address to the United Nations making the case for war in Iraq, Powell identified al-Zarqawi—mistakenly, as it turned out—as the crucial link between al-Qaeda and Saddam Hussein's regime. Subsequently, al-Zarqawi became a leading figure in the insurgency in

Iraq—and in November of last year, he also brought his jihadist revolution back home, as the architect of three lethal hotel bombings in Amman.

His notoriety grew with every atrocity he perpetrated, yet Western and Middle Eastern intelligence officials remained bedeviled by a simple question: Who was he? Was he al-Qaeda's point man in Iraq, as the Bush administration argued repeatedly? Or was he, as a retired Israeli intelligence official told not long ago, a staunch rival of bin Laden's, whose importance the United States exaggerated in order to validate a link between al-Qaeda and pre-war Iraq, and to put a non-Iraqi face on a complex insurgency?

Bin Laden and Zarqawi had little in common: bin Laden, like most of his inner circle, is a university graduate from an influential family; al-Zarqawi, like many who follow him, was from an anonymous family (even though they are members of a significant tribe) and an anonymous town—a man who was fired from a job as a video-store clerk and whose background included street gangs and, according to Jordanian intelligence officials, prison for sexual assault. He was a ruthless self-promoter who, U.S. officials claim, killed or wounded thousands of people in three years (2003-2006)—in suicide bombings, mass executions, and beheadings that have been videotaped. He developed a mythic aura of invulnerability. But he was not the terrorist mastermind that he was often claimed to be.

Zarqa is a shambolic industrial city of some 850,000 people, a sprawl of factories, open fields, and dust. Twenty-five miles northeast of Amman, it is Jordan's third-largest city, and one of its most militant. For years it has been a magnet for Islamic activists. Along with the cities of Irbid and Salt, it has sent the largest number of Jordanian volunteers to fight abroad, first in Afghanistan and now in Iraq. Al-Zarqawi was born and raised in the al-Masoum neighborhood of Zarqa's old city, which sprawls somewhat haphazardly into the al-Ruseifah Palestinian refugee camp. (More than 60 percent of Jordan's 5.9 million inhabitants are Palestinian, as are some 80 percent of the inhabitants of old Zarqa.)

Until his death, al-Zarqawi kept a home on a quiet lane in Zarqa. It was indistinguishable from its neighbors—a two-story white stucco building surrounded by a whitewashed wall. The house was empty,; al-Zarqawi's sisters, who still live in Zarqa, would come by to look after it.

The first of al-Zarqawi's two wives had lived in the house until recently. She was his cousin, whom he had married when he was twenty-two. They had four children, two boys and two girls. But not long before my visit, al-Zarqawi had sent an unknown man to drive them across the border to be with him in Iraq. His second wife, a Jordanian-Palestinian whom he had married in Afghanistan, and with whom he has a son, was reported to be with him in Iraq as well. Al-Zarqawi's mother, Omm Sayel, whom he adored—and who had traveled to Peshawar with him when he joined the jihad—died of leukemia in 2004; although he was the most wanted man in Jordan at the time of her death, al-Zarqawi returned to Zarqa in disguise to attend her funeral.

Afganistan

Al-Zarqawi was based initially in the border town of Khost, which, after both the Americans and the Soviets had left Afghanistan, was the site of intense and heavily contested battles between the mujahideen and the pro-Soviet Najibullah regime. At the beginning, al-Zarqawi had not been a fighter but had tried his hand at being a journalist. He had worked as a reporter for a small jihadist magazine, Al-Bonian al Marsous.

"He was an ordinary guy, an ordinary fighter, and didn't really distinguish himself," Huthaifa Azzam said of al-Zarqawi's first time in Afghanistan. "He was a quiet guy who didn't talk much. But he was brave. Zarqawi doesn't know the meaning of fear. He's been wounded five or six times in Afghanistan and Iraq. He seems to intentionally place himself in the middle of the most dangerous situations. He fought in the battles of Khost and Kardez and, in April 1992, witnessed the liberation of Kabul by the mujahideen. A lot of Arabs were great commanders during those years. Zarqawi was not. He also wasn't very religious during that time. In fact, he'd only 'returned' to Islam three months before coming to Afghanistan. It was the Tablighi Jamaat [a proselytizing missionary group spread across the Muslim world] who convinced him—he had thirty-seven criminal cases against him by then—that it was time to cleanse himself."

His second time in Afghanistan was far more important than the first. But the first was significant in two ways. Zarqawi was young and impressionable; he'd never been out of Jordan before, and now, for the first time, he was interacting with doctrinaire Islamists from across the Muslim world, most of them brought to Afghanistan by the CIA. It was also his first exposure to al-Qaeda. He didn't meet bin Laden, of course, but he trained in one of his and Abdullah Azzam's camps: the Sada camp near the Afghan border inside Pakistan. He trained under Abu Hafs al-Masri." (The reference was to the nom de guerre of Mohammed Atef, an Egyptian who was bin Laden's military chief and, until he was killed in an American air strike in Afghanistan in November 2001, the No. 3 official in al-Qaeda.)

Abu Muntassir Bilah Muhammad is another jihadist who spent time fighting in Afghanistan and who would later become one of the co-founders of al-Zarqawi's first militant Islamist group. "Zarqawi arrived in Afghanistan as a zero, a man with no career, just floundering about. He trained and fought and he came back to Jordan with ambitions and dreams: to carry the ideology of jihad. His first ambition was to reform Jordan, to set up an Islamist state. And there was a cachet involved in fighting in the jihad. Zarqawi returned to Jordan with newfound respect. It's not so much what Zarqawi did in the jihad—it's what the jihad did for him."

With an eye to the future, al-Zarqawi also used the jihad years to begin the process of cultivating friendships that would eventually lead to the formation of an international support network for his activities. Particularly when he was in Khost, his primary friendships were with the Saudi fighters and others from the Gulf. Some of them were millionaires. There were even a couple of billionaires.

But perhaps as important as anything else, it was in Afghanistan that al-Zarqawi was introduced to Sheikh Abu Muhammad al-Maqdisi (whose real name is Isam Muhammad Tahir al-Barqawi), a revered and militant Salafist cleric who had moved to Zarqa following the mass expulsion of Palestinians from Kuwait in the aftermath of the Gulf War. The Salafiya movement originated in Egypt, at the end of the nineteenth century, as a modernist Sunni reform movement, the aim of which was to let the Muslim world rise to the challenges posed by Western science and political thought. But since the 1920s, it has evolved into a severely puritanical school of absolutist thought that is markedly anti-Western and based on a literal interpretation of the Koran.

Today's most radical Salafists regard any departure from their own rigid principles of Islam to be heretical; their particular hatred of Shiites—who broke with the Sunnis in 632 A.D. over the question of succession to the Prophet Muhammad, and who now constitute the majority in Iran and Iraq—is visceral. Over the years, al-Maqdisi embraced the most extreme school of Salafism, closely akin to the puritanical Wahhabism of Saudi Arabia, and in the early

1980s he published The Creed of Abraham, the single most important source of teachings for Salafist movements around the world.

Al-Zarqawi and al-Maqdisi left Afghanistan in 1993 and returned to Jordan. They found it much changed. In their absence the Jordanians and the Israelis had begun negotiations that would lead to the signing of a peace treaty in 1994; the Palestinians had signed the Oslo Accords of 1993; and the Iraqis had lost the Gulf War. Unemployment was up sharply, the result of a privatization drive agreed to with the International Monetary Fund, and Jordanians were frustrated and angry. The Muslim Brotherhood—the kingdom's only viable opposition political force, which had agreed to support King Hussein in exchange for being allowed to participate in public and parliamentary life—appeared unable to cope with the rising disaffection. Small underground Islamist groups had therefore begun to appear, composed largely of men who had fought in the Afghan jihad, and who were guided by the increasingly loud voices of militant clerics who felt the Muslim Brotherhood had been co-opted by the state.

After the two men returned home, al-Maqdisi toured the kingdom, preaching and recruiting, and al-Zarqawi sought out Abu Muntassir, who had already acquired a standing among Islamic militants in Jordan. Despite their enthusiasm, al-Zarqawi, al-Maqdisi, and Abu Muntassir did not appear to be natural revolutionaries. Their first operation was in Zarqa, in 1993, when al-Zarqawi dispatched one of their men to a local cinema with orders to blow it up because it was showing pornographic films. But the hapless would-be bomber apparently got so distracted by what was happening on the screen that he forgot about his bomb. It exploded and blew off his legs.

In another botched operation, al-Maqdisi (according to court testimony that he denied) gave al-Zarqawi seven grenades he had smuggled into Jordan, and al-Zarqawi hid them in the cellar of his family's home. Al-Maqdisi was already under surveillance by Jordan's intelligence service by that time, because of his growing popularity. The grenades were quickly discovered, and the two men, along with a number of their followers, found themselves for the first time before a state security court. Al-Zarqawi told the court that he had found the grenades while walking down the street. The judges were not amused. They convicted him and al-Maqdisi of possessing illegal weapons and belonging to a banned organization. In 1994, al-Zarqawi was sentenced to fifteen years in prison. He would flourish there.

Al-Zarqawi embraced prison life in the extreme—as he appears to have embraced everything. According to fellow inmates of his, his primary obsessions were recruiting other prisoners to his cause, building his body, and, under the tutelage of al-Maqdisi, memorizing the 6,236 verses of the Koran. He was stern, tough, and unrelenting on anything that he considered to be an infraction of his rules, yet he was often seen in the prison courtyard crying as he read the Koran.

He was fastidious about his appearance in prison—his beard and moustache were always cosmetically groomed—and he wore only Afghan dress: the shalwar kameez and a rolled-brim, woolen Pashtun cap. Islamists flocked to him. He attracted recruits; some joined him out of fascination, others out of curiosity, and still others out of fear. In a short time, he had organized prison life at Swaqa like a gang leader.

There were also confrontations and altercations with prison officials and guards. Whether al-Zarqawi was ever tortured is a matter of dispute: some of his followers say he was; Jordanian government officials, perhaps predictably, say he was not.Al-Zarqawi controlled not only his followers but also the ward's television sets. No one could really watch them, however, since he had covered them with black cloth to prevent the display of female forms. All the inmates could do was listen—and only to the evening news at eight o'clock.

Al-Zarqawi and al-Maqdisi's Bayat al-Imam continued to grow, both inside prison and in Zarqa, Irbic, and Salt. Al-Zarqawi used his Bedouin credentials to good effect, as his own profile began to ascend. His Bani Hassan tribe is one of the Middle East's most prominent, and its tribal lands spill across the borders dividing Jordan, Syria, and Iraq. In Jordan, many of its members hold high-level positions in the government, the army, and the intelligence service. As a result, many of the prisoners, and many of Swaqa's guards, deferred to al-Zarqawi. Al-Maqdisi, a Palestinian, was also accorded special treatment, but largely as a result of his links to al-Zarqawi and the Bani Hassan. Between mentor and pupil, the roles had subtly begun to shift inside the prison walls.

As al-Zarqawi recruited, al-Maqdisi preached, and using the Internet, they broadcast their message of jihad across three continents. Sheikh Abu Qatada, a Palestinian cleric who is one of Salafism's leading ideologues, was also one of al-Maqdisi's closest friends. The two men had been together in Kuwait, then in Zarqa, then Afghanistan. Abu Qatada, after leaving Afghanistan, had moved to London (where he is currently under arrest, awaiting possible deportation to

Jordan). Now al-Maqdisi's religious tracts were smuggled out of Swaqa by prisoners' wives and mothers, with help from sympathetic prison guards, and they were sent on to Abu Qatada, who posted them on the Web sites of Salafists and jihadists throughout Europe, the Middle East, and the Persian Gulf.

Al-Zarqawi's own religious views became increasingly severe, as did his intolerance of anyone he believed to be an infidel. Al-Maqdisi sometimes angrily disagreed with him. It was the first portent of what lay ahead. Al-Zarqawi began to eclipse his mentor in prison, and would continue to do so over the coming years, but their final, and public, break did not occur until November 2005, when, on Al-Jazeera, al-Maqdisi criticized his former protégé for the hotel bombings in Amman. Nevertheless, despite their prison disagreements, al-Maqdisi, from time to time, permitted al-Zarqawi to draft his own religious tracts. Abu Muntassir who would also later break with al-Zarqawi was his editor.

In May of the following year (1999), Jordan's King Abdullah II—newly enthroned after the death of his father, King Hussein—declared a general amnesty, and al-Zarqawi was released from Swaqa. He had made effective use of his time there. As he had done nearly a decade before—when he befriended wealthy Saudi jihadists in Khost—he had expanded his reach and his appeal during his prison years. Among the fellow inmates he had converted to Salafism and brought into the Bayat al-Imam were a substantial number of prisoners from Iraq.

After returning for a few months to Zarqa, al-Zarqawi left again and traveled to Pakistan. He may or may not have known that Jordan was about to declare him a suspect in a series of foiled terrorist attacks intended for New Year's Eve of 1999. The plan, which became known as the "Millennium Plot," involved the bombing of Christian landmarks and other tourist sites, along with the Radisson Hotel in Amman. Had it succeeded, it would have been al-Zarqawi's first involvement in a major terrorist attack.

Whatever the case, al-Zarqawi planned ahead before he left for Pakistan. He arrived bearing a letter of introduction from Abu Kutaiba al-Urduni, one of Jordan's most significant leaders during the jihad in Afghanistan. Al-Urduni had been a key deputy to—and the chief recruiter inside Jordan for—Sheikh Abdullah Azzam, Huthaifa Azzam's father. Having worked for years in Peshawar as the leader of the Service Office, or the Maktab al-Khidmat, the sheikh had become the pivotal figure in the Pan-Islamic recruitment of volunteers for the jihad.) Al-Urduni's letter was the first endorsement that al-Zarqawi had received from such a senior figure—and the letter was addressed to Osama bin Laden.

In December 1999, al-Zarqawi crossed the border into Afghanistan, and later that month he and bin Laden met at the Government Guest House in the southern city of Kandahar, the de facto capital of the ruling Taliban. According to several different accounts of the meeting, bin Laden distrusted and disliked al-Zarqawi immediately. He suspected that the group of Jordanian prisoners with whom al-Zarqawi had been granted amnesty earlier in the year had been infiltrated by Jordanian intelligence.

Something similar had occurred not long before with a Jordanian jihadist cell that had come to Afghanistan. Bin Laden also disliked al-Zarqawi's swagger and the green tattoos on his left hand, which he reportedly considered un-Islamic. Al-Zarqawi came across to bin Laden as aggressively ambitious, abrasive, and overbearing. His hatred of Shiites also seemed to bin Laden to be potentially divisive—which, of course, it was. Bin Laden's mother, to whom he remains close, is a Shiite, from the Alawites of Syria.

Al-Zarqawi would not recant, even in the presence of the legendary head of al-Qaeda. "Shiites should be executed," he reportedly declared. He also took exception to bin Laden's providing Arab fighters to the Taliban, the fundamentalist student militia that, although now in power, was still battling the Northern Alliance, which controlled some 10 percent of Afghanistan. Muslim killing Muslim was un-Islamic, al-Zarqawi is reported to have said. Unaccustomed to such direct criticism, the leader of al-Qaeda was aghast.

A former Egyptian army colonel who had trained in special operations, al-Adel was then al-Qaeda's chief of security and a prominent voice in an emerging debate gripping the militant Islamist world. Who should the primary target be—the "near enemy" (the Muslim world's "un-Islamic" regimes) or the "far enemy" (primarily Israel and the United States)? Al-Zarqawi was a near-enemy advocate, and although his obsession remained the overthrow of the Jordanian monarchy, he had expanded his horizons slightly during his prison years and had now begun to focus on the area known as al-Sham, or the Levant, which includes Jordan, Syria, Lebanon, and historic Palestine.

As an Egyptian who had attempted to overthrow his own country's army-backed regime, al-Adel saw merit in al-Zarqawi's views. Thus, after a good deal of debate within al-Qaeda, it was agreed that al-Zarqawi would be given $5,000 or so in "seed money" to set up his own training camp outside the western Afghan city of Herat, near the Iranian border. It was about as far away as he could be from bin Laden. Saif al-Adel was designated the middleman.

In early 2000, with a dozen or so followers who had arrived from Peshawar and Amman, al-Zarqawi set out for the western desert encircling Herat. His goal: to build an army that he could export to anywhere in the world. Al-Adel paid monthly visits to al-Zarqawi's training camp; later, on his Web site, he would write that he was amazed at what he saw there. The number of al-Zarqawi's fighters multiplied from dozens to hundreds during the following year, and by the time the forces evacuated their camp, prior to the U.S. air strikes of October 2001, the fighters and their families numbered some 2,000 to 3,000. According to al-Adel, the wives of al-Zarqawi's followers served lavish Levantine cuisine in the camp.

It was in Herat that al-Zarqawi formed the militant organization Jund al-Sham, or Soldiers of the Levant. His key operational lieutenants were mainly Syrians—most of whom had fought in the Afghan jihad, and many of whom belonged to their country's banned Muslim Brotherhood. The Brotherhood's exiled leadership, which is largely based in Europe, was immensely important in recruiting for the Herat camp, although whether it also supplied funds remains under debate. What is clear, however, is that al-Zarqawi's closest aide, a Syrian from the city of Hama named Sulayman Khalid Darwish—or Abu al-Ghadiyah—was considered to be, one of al-Zarqawi's most likely successors.

For Zarqawi, it was the turning point. Herat was the beginning of what he is now. He had command responsibilities for the first time; he had a battle plan. And even though he and bin Laden never got on, he was important to them. Herat was the only training camp in Afghanistan that was actively recruiting volunteers specifically from the Sham. In Herat, he called himself the 'Emir of Sham'!"
At least five times, in 2000 and 2001, bin Laden called al-Zarqawi to come to Kandahar and pay bayat—take an oath of allegiance—to him. Each time, al-Zarqawi refused. Under no circumstances did he want to become involved in the battle between the Northern Alliance and the Taliban. He also did not believe that either bin Laden or the Taliban was serious enough about jihad.

When the United States launched its air war inside Afghanistan, on October 7, 2001, al-Zarqawi joined forces with al-Qaeda and the Taliban for the first time.

He and his Jund al-Sham fought in and around Herat and Kandahar. Al-Zarqawi was wounded in an American air strike—not in the leg, as U.S. officials claimed for two years, but in the chest, when the ceiling of the building in which he was operating collapsed on him. Neither did he join Osama bin Laden in the eastern mountains of Tora Bora, as U.S. officials have also said. Bin Laden took only his most trusted fighters to Tora Bora, and al-Zarqawi was not one of them.

In December 2001, accompanied by some 300 fighters from Jund al-Sham, al-Zarqawi left Afghanistan once again, and entered Iran.During the next fourteen months, al-Zarqawi based himself primarily in Iran and in the autonomous area of Kurdistan, in northern Iraq, traveling from time to time to Syria and to the Ayn al-Hilwah Palestinian refugee camp in the south of Lebanon—a camp that became his main recruiting ground. More often, however, al-Zarqawi traveled to the Sunni Triangle of Iraq. He expanded his network, recruited and trained new fighters, and set up bases, safe houses, and military training camps.

In Iran, he was reunited with Saif al-Adel—who encouraged him to go to Iraq and provided contacts there—and for a time, al-Zarqawi stayed at a farm belonging to the fiercely anti-American Afghan jihad leader Gulbaddin Hekmatyar. In Kurdistan he lived and worked with the separatist militant Islamist group Ansar al-Islam, ironically in an area protected as part of the "no-fly" zone imposed on Saddam Hussein by Washington.

One can only imagine how astonished al-Zarqawi must have been when Colin Powell named him as the crucial link between al-Qaeda and Saddam Hussein's regime. He was not even officially a part of al-Qaeda, and ever since he had left Afghanistan, his links had been not to Iraq but to Iran.

In the beginning the Iranians gave him automatic weapons, uniforms, military equipment, when he was with the army of Ansar al-Islam. Now they essentially just turn a blind eye to his activities, and to those of al-Qaeda generally. The Iranians see Iraq as a fight against the Americans, and overall, they'll get ric of Zarqawi and all of his people once the Americans are out.

In the summer of 2003, three months after the American invasion, al-Zarqawi moved to the Sunni areas of Iraq. He became infamous almost at once. On August 7, he allegedly carried out a car-bomb attack at the Jordanian embassy in Baghdad. Twelve days later, he was linked to the bombing of the United Nations headquarters, in which twenty-two people died. And on August 29, in what was then the deadliest attack of the war, he engineered the killing of over a hundred people, including a revered cleric, the Ayatollah Muhammad Baqr al-Hakim, in a car bombing outside Shia Islam's holy shrine in Najaf. The suicide bomber in that attack was Yassin Jarad, from Zarqa. He was al-Zarqawi's father-in-law.

Even then—and even more so now—Zarqawi was not the main force in the insurgency. To establish himself, he carried out the Muhammad Hakim operation, and the attack against the UN. Both of them gained a lot of support for him—with the tribes, with Saddam's army and other remnants of his regime. They made Zarqawi the symbol of the resistance in Iraq, but not the leader. And he never has been."

The Americans have been patently stupid in all of this. They've blown Zarqawi so out of proportion that, of course, his prestige has grown. And as a result, sleeper cells from all over Europe are coming to join him now.

Of course, no one did more to cultivate that image than al-Zarqawi himself. He committed some of the deadliest attacks in Iraq, though they still represent only some 10 percent of the country's total number of attacks. In May 2004, he inaugurated his notorious wave of hostage beheadings; he also specialized in suicide and truck bombings of Shiite shrines and mosques, largely in Shiite neighborhoods. His primary aim was to provoke a civil war. "If we succeed in dragging [the Shia] into a sectarian war," he purportedly wrote in a letter intercepted by U.S. forces and released in February 2004, "this will awaken the sleepy Sunnis who are fearful of destruction and death at the hands of the Shia."

Al-Zarqawi courted chaos so that Iraq would provide him another failed state to operate in after the overthrow of the Taliban in Afghanistan. He became best known for his videotaped beheadings. One after the other they appeared on jihadist Web sites, always the same. In the background was the trademark black banner of al-Zarqawi's newest group: al-Tawhid wa al-Jihad, or Monotheism and Jihad. In the foreground, a blindfolded hostage, kneeling and pleading for his life, was dressed in an orange jumpsuit resembling those worn by the detainees at Guantánamo Bay.

Al-Zarqawi's first victim was a Pennsylvania engineer named Nicholas Berg. In the video, five hooded men, dressed in black, stand behind Berg. After a recitation, one of the men pulls a long knife from his shirt, steps forward, and slices off Berg's head. The U.S. military quickly announced that the executioner was al-Zarqawi himself, and although no one doubts that he planned the operation, questions soon arose: the figure seems taller than al-Zarqawi, and he uses his right hand to wield the knife. Al-Zarqawi was said to be left-handed.

Regardless of his growing notoriety in Iraq, al-Zarqawi never lost sight of his ultimate goal: the overthrow of the Jordanian monarchy. His efforts to foment unrest in Jordan included the 2002 assassination of the U.S. diplomat Lawrence Foley, and, on a far larger scale, a disrupted plot in 2004 to bomb the headquarters of the Jordanian intelligence services—a scheme that, according to Jordanian officials, would have entailed the use of trucks packed with enough chemicals and explosives to kill some 80,000 people. Once it was uncovered, al-Zarqawi immediately accepted responsibility for the plot, although he denied that chemical weapons would have been involved.

Later that year, in October 2004, after resisting for nearly five years, al-Zarqawi finally paid bayat to Osama bin Laden—but only after eight months of often stormy negotiations. After doing so he proclaimed himself to be the "Emir of al-Qaeda's Operations in the Land of Mesopotamia," a title that subordinated him to bin Laden but at the same time placed him firmly on the global stage.

One explanation for this coming together of these two former antagonists was simple: al-Zarqawi profited from the al-Qaeda franchise, and bin Laden needed a presence in Iraq. Another explanation is more complex: bin Laden laid claim to al-Zarqawi in the hopes of forestalling his emergence as the single most important terrorist figure in the world, and al-Zarqawi accepted bin Laden's endorsement to augment his credibility and to strengthen his grip on the Iraqi tribes. Both explanations are true. It was a pragmatic alliance, but tenuous from the start.

The attacks, which represented an expansion of al-Zarqawi's sophistication and reach, also showed his growing independence from the al-Qaeda chief. They came only thirteen months after he had sworn bayat. The alliance had already begun to fray.

The signs were visible as early as the summer of 2005. In a letter purportedly sent to al-Zarqawi in July from Ayman al-Zawahiri, the Egyptian surgeon who is bin Laden's designated heir, al-Zarqawi was chided about his tactics in Iraq. And although some experts have cast doubt on the letter's authenticity (it was released by the office of the U.S. Director of National Intelligence), few would dispute its message: namely, that al-Zarqawi's hostage beheadings, his mass slaughter of Shiites, and his assaults on their mosques were all having a negative effect on Muslim opinion—both of him and, by extension, of al-Qaeda—around the world. In one admonition, al-Zawahiri allegedly advised al-Zarqawi that a captive can be killed as easily by a bullet as by a knife.

Then, in early April, Huthaifa Azzam announced that the "Iraqi resistance's high command" had stripped al-Zarqawi of his political role and relegated him to military operations. It was the second time that al-Zarqawi's profile had seemingly been lowered—or that he had lowered it—this year. The first had come in January, when it was announced that al-Qaeda in Iraq had joined five other Sunni insurgent groups to form a coalition called the Mujahideen Shura Council. By early May, U.S. counterterrorism analysts were still puzzling over what the two events meant and what changes they could portend.

As they debated, al-Zarqawi sprang to life again, in a video posted on the Internet on April 24. It was the first time he had appeared in a jihadist videotape, and the first time he had shown his face. Dressed in black fatigues and a black cap, he had ammunition pouches strapped across his chest. He appeared fit, if overweight, as he posed in the desert firing an automatic weapon and as he sat with a group of masked aides, apparently plotting strategy. It seemed an extremely risky thing for him to do, and yet it also appeared to be very deliberate. It was a useful tool for recruitment, intending to show al-Zarqawi as both a flamboyant fighter and a pensive strat¬egist. More important than anything else, however, it was meant to show the world that Abu Musab al-Zarqawi—the brash young man who had come of age in the rough-and-tumble of Zarqa—remained relevant.

Back to the Future

Military action is necessary to halt the spread of the ISIS "cancer," said President Obama. In his much anticipated address, he called for expanded airstrikes across Iraq and Syria, and new measures to arm and train Iraqi and Kurdish ground forces.

Missing from the chorus of outrage, however, has been any acknowledgement of the integral role of covert US and British regional military intelligence strategy in empowering and even directly sponsoring the very same virulent Islamist militants in Iraq, Syria and beyond, that went on to break away from al-Qaeda and form 'ISIS', the Islamic State of Iraq and Syria, or now simply, the Islamic State (IS).

Since 2003, Anglo-American power has secretly and openly coordinated direct and indirect support for Islamist terrorist groups linked to al-Qaeda across the Middle East and North Africa. This ill-conceived patchwork geo-strategy is a legacy of the persistent influence of neoconservative ideology, motivated by longstanding but often contradictory ambitions to dominate regional oil resources, defend an expansionist Israel, and in pursuit of these, re-draw the map of the Middle East.

Now despite Pentagon denials that there will be boots on the ground – and Obama's insistence that this would not be another "Iraq war" – local Kurdish military and intelligence sources confirm that US and German special operations forces are already "on the ground" here. US airstrikes on ISIS positions and arms supplies to the Kurds have also been accompanied by British RAF reconnaissance flights over the region and UK weapons shipments to Kurdish peshmerga forces.

Early during the 2003 invasion and occupation of Iraq, the US covertly supplied arms to al-Qaeda affiliated insurgents even while ostensibly supporting an emerging Shi'a-dominated administration.

Pakistani defense sources interviewed by Asia Times in February 2005 confirmed that insurgents described as "former Ba'ath party" loyalists – who were being recruited and trained by "al-Qaeda in Iraq" under the leadership of the late Abu Musab Zarqawi – were being supplied Pakistan-manufactured weapons by the US. The arms shipments included rifles, rocket-propelled grenade launchers, ammunition, rockets and other light weaponry.

These arms "could not be destined for the Iraqi security forces because US arms would be given to them", a source told Syed Saleem Shahzad – the Times' Pakistan bureau chief who, "known for his exposes of the Pakistani military" according to the New Yorker, was murdered in 2011. Rather, the US is playing a double-game to "head off" the threat of a "Shi'ite clergy-driven religious movement," said the Pakistani defense source. This was not the only way US strategy aided the rise of Zarqawi, a bin Laden mentee and brainchild of the extremist ideology that would later spawn 'ISIS.'

Dividing Enemies

According to a little-known report "Dividing Our Enemies", made by US Joint Special Operations University (JSOU), post-invasion Iraq was an interesting case study of fanning discontent among enemies, leading to 'red-against-red' [enemy-against-enemy] firefights. While counter-insurgency on the one hand requires US forces to ameliorate harsh or deprived living conditions of the indigenous populations to publicly win local hearts and minds.

In other words, US forces would pursue public legitimacy through conventional social welfare while simultaneously de-legitimizing local enemies by escalating intra-insurgent violence, knowing full-well that doing so will in turn escalate the number of innocent civilians "caught in the crossfire." The idea is that violence covertly calibrated by US special operations will not only weaken enemies through in-fighting but turn the population against them.

In this case, the 'enemy' consisted of jihadists, Ba'athists, and peaceful Sufis, who were in a majority but, like the militants, also opposed the US military presence and therefore needed to be influenced. The JSOU report referred to events in late 2004 in Fallujah where "US psychological warfare (PSYOP) specialists" undertook to "set insurgents battling insurgents."

This involved actually promoting Zarqawi's ideology, ironically, to defeat it: "The PSYOP warriors crafted programs to exploit Zarqawi's murderous activities – and to disseminate them through meetings, radio and television broadcasts, handouts, newspaper stories, political cartoons, and posters – thereby diminishing his folk-hero image," and encouraging the different factions to pick each other off. "By tapping into the Fallujans' revulsion and antagonism to the Zarqawi jihadis the Joint PSYOP Task Force did its 'best to foster a rift between Sunni groups.'"

Yet as noted by Dahr Jamail, one of the few unembedded investigative reporters in Iraq after the war, the proliferation of propaganda linking the acceleration of suicide bombings to the persona of Zarqawi was not matched by meaningful evidence. His own search to substantiate the myriad claims attributing the insurgency to Zarqawi beyond anonymous US intelligence sources encountered only an "eerie blankness".

The US military operation in Fallujah, largely justified on the claim that Zarqawi's militant forces had occupied the city, used white phosphorous, cluster bombs, and indiscriminate air strikes to pulverize 36,000 of Fallujah's 50,000 homes, killing nearly a thousand civilians, terrorizing 300,000 inhabitants to flee, and culminating in a disproportionate increase in birth defects, cancer and infant mortality due to the devastating environmental consequences of the war.

To this day, Fallujah has suffered from being largely cut-off from wider Iraq, its infrastructure largely unworkable with water and sewage systems still in disrepair, and its citizens subject to sectarian discrimination and persecution by Iraqi government backed Shi'a militia and police. "Thousands of bereaved and homeless Falluja families have a new reason to hate the US and its allies," observed The Guardian in 2005. Thus, did the US occupation plant the seeds from which Zarqawi's legacy would coalesce into the Frankenstein monster that calls itself "the Islamic State."

Camp Bucca

Beyond conspiracy theories – which are often justified in an era where everything appears as though it is part of a plan or a scheme – we have the right to ask why the majority of the leaders of the Islamic State (IS), formerly the Islamic State in Iraq and Syria (ISIS), had all been incarcerated in the same prison at Camp Bucca, which was run by the US occupation forces near Omm Qasr in southeastern Iraq.

In the context of conspiracy theories, there are a lot of rumors about links between IS and the US intelligence or affiliated organizations. But to what extent are these theories credible? Is there evidence that corroborate them?

These questions seem legitimate, provided that ready-made answers are not accepted without convincing evidence. However, it is difficult to get this kind of evidence, and we might need another Edward Snowden or WikiLeaks to learn the real truth about the relationship between IS and US intelligence.

Yet not having this evidence should not prevent us from trying to gather some clues that may not amount to definitive evidence, but which will no doubt question the narrative that fully exonerates US intelligence from involvement with the jihadis.First of all, most IS leaders had passed through the former U.S. detention facility at Camp Bucca in Iraq. So who were the most prominent of these detainees?

Abu Ayman al-Iraqi... also "graduated" from Camp Bucca, and currently serves as a member on IS' military council. The leader of IS, Abu Bakr al-Baghdadi, tops the list. He was detained from 2004 until mid-2006. After he was released, he formed the Army of Sunnis, which later merged with the so-called Mujahideen Shura Council.

What happened during Baghdadi's detention in Bucca remains a mystery. Some press reports said he had been detained as a "civilian" in prison for 10 months in 2004, while other reports stated he was captured by the US forces in 2005 and held for four years at Camp Bucca. This latter possibility is unlikely, given that Baghdadi had formed the Army of Sunnis and joined the Mujahideen Shura Council shortly before the assassination of Abu Musab al-Zarqawi in June 2006. This is while bearing in mind that this council was established in January 2006, which makes it more likely that Baghdadi had been released either in late 2005 or early 2006.

It should be noted that after the Army of the Sunnis merged with the Mujahideen Shura Council, the Americans were able to successfully hunt down the leaders of al-Qaeda in Iraq, starting with Zarqawi in 2006, and not ending with Abu Omar al-Baghdadi and Abu Hamza al-Muhajir in 2010, the death of the former being the event that paved the way for Abu Bakr al-Baghdadi to become the organization's leader.

Another prominent IS leader today is Abu Ayman al-Iraqi, who was a former officer in the Iraqi army under Saddam Hussein. This man also "graduated" from Camp Bucca, and currently serves as a member on IS' military council.

Another member of the military council who was in Bucca is Adnan Ismail Najm. He was known a(Abu Abdul_Rahman al-Bilawi). IS named the operation for the "invasion of Mosul" after him. He was detained on January 2005 in Bucca, and was also a former officer in Saddam's army. He was the head of a shura council in IS, before he was killed by the Iraqi army near Mosul on June 4, 2014.

Camp Bucca was also home to Haji Samir, aka Haji Bakr, whose real name is Samir Abed Hamad al-Obeidi al-Dulaimi. He was a colonel in the army of the former Iraqi regime. He was detained in Bucca, and after his release, he joined al-Qaeda. He was the top man in ISIS in Syria, but was killed in Aleppo in the first week of January 2014.

According to the testimonies of US officers who worked in the prison, the administration of Camp Bucca had taken measures including the segregation of prisoners on the basis of their ideology. This, according to experts, made it possible to recruit people directly and indirectly. Former detainees had said in documented television interviews that Bucca, which was closed down in September 2009, was akin to an "al-Qaeda school» where senior extremist gave lessons on explosives and suicide attacks to younger prisoners. A former prisoner named Adel Jassem Mohammed said that one of the extremists remained in the prison for two weeks only, but even so was able to recruit 25 out of 34 inmates who were there. Mohammed also said that U.S. military officials did nothing to stop the extremists from mentoring the other detainees.

While Camp Bucca is the common denominator among most IS leaders, another one is the fact that a majority of them were officers in the Baathist army, which explains the ease with which the radical group has been able to infiltrate the clans and coax some of their leaders into joining its ranks.

Another noteworthy point is that none of the leaders who had emerged out of Bucca and who were subsequently killed, were killed in U.S. airstrikes, but rather at the hands of the Iraqi army, the Syrian army, or in fighting with other armed groups.

What had happened in Bucca then? What were the circumstances that made all those former detainees subsequent leaders in the extremist group? These questions require answers and serious investigations. No doubt, we will one day discover that many more leaders in the group had been detained in Bucca as well, which seems to have been more of a "terrorist academy" than a prison.

Fitna

In the years after the U.S. invasion of Afghanistan but before the invasion of Iraq, Zarqawi had not yet achieved infamy. He bounced around between Iran, Iraqi Kurdistan, Syria, and the Sunni Triangle in Iraq, gaining new jihadist contacts. Within a half year after the invasion of Iraq, however, Zarqawi became a household name for his brutal personal beheadings and fast-paced suicide bombing campaign against Shiite religious targets and Sunni civilians, among others.

As a result of these successes, many foreign fighters wanted to join, and the group needed more resources to continue and expand its operations. Further, not to be outdone by Zarqawi, bin Laden himself wanted to "own" the Iraq jihad as well as remain relevant while hiding from the United States. Given these dynamics, in the October 2004 issue of Muaskar al-Batar (The Sword

Training Camp),12 Zarqawi relented to bin Laden, pledging baya to him and renaming his group al-Qaeda in the Land of Two Rivers after eight months of negotiations.

In Iraq, and now part of the al-Qaeda network, Zarqawi's group controlled resources and the flow of foreign fighters, helping it gain loyalty from individual fighters. This is important because AQI thus controlled many of the informal networks and the future generation of the jihadist movement. One of the key factors now separating ISIS from al-Qaeda relates to this generational difference.

In April 2013, overt enmity between ISIS and al-Qaeda broke out in full when ISIS leader Abu Bakr al-Baghdadi announced that he was extending the Islamic State of Iraq into Syria and changing the group's name to the Islamic State of Iraq and al-Sham. He also noted an open secret that ISIS and JN were one and the same. This did not sit well with JN leader Abu Muhammadal-Jawlani, who rebuºed the move into Syria and reaffirmed his allegiance to Zawahiri. In turn, Zawahiri later tried, but failed, to nullify Baghdadi's power play by telling ISIS to return to the Iraq front and leave the Syrian front to JN.

Neither Jawlani nor Zawahiri was allegedly consulted in advance about the expansion of the Islamic state. Baghdadi released an audio message stating ISIS would remain in Syria and would not adhere to a division based on the Sykes-Picot deal dating to World War I.

Moreover Baghdadi also gave Zawahiri al-Qaeda's most "brazen" rebuke from an affiliate ever, stating in the same audio message that Baghdadi had "chosen the command of my Lord over the command in the letter that contradicts it." Therefore, contrary to the original media narrative that JN had merged with ISIS, the two groups actually separated.

The context for the recent split can be found in late summer 2011, when ISI began the first stages of its comeback because of the Syrian uprising. Baghdadi dispatched operatives to Syria to set up a new jihadist organization, which Zawahiri was involved in planning, too. Among the operatives was Jawlani, whose group, JN, publicly announced itself in late January 2012.

By November 2012, Jawlani had built JN into one of the opposition's best fighting forces and locals viewed its members as fair arbiters when addressing corruption and providing social services. Such success helped inspire Baghdadi to extend his group's writ into Syria. Syrians, he felt, got to know JN members on their own terms rather than being falsely guided by media "misrepresentations" and therefore felt it opportune to announce the expansion.

At first, it appeared the JN-ISIS feud would be settled behind the scenes. Publicly, both ISIS and JN tried to put a good face on the matter, suggesting that a battle - field competition against a common foe, the Assad regime, would benefit everyone. Al-Qaeda also enlisted emissaries as mediators, among them Abu Khalid al-Suri, a now deceased senior leader in Ahrar al-Sham—a more locally focused Salafi rebel group in Syria—and Sheikh Abu Sulayman al-Muhajir, an Australian who serves as one of JN's top sharia officials.

None of these negotiations yielded success. Al-Qaeda's ultimate disaffiliation with ISIS occurred as a result of various factors, including the January 2014 uprising against ISIS by main-stream Syrian rebels over the group's excesses; the group's general predatory way of taking territory and resources from other rebel groups; and a failed public reconciliation effort by the independent Saudi cleric Abd Allah bin Muhammad al-Muhaysini—along-side the failed private attempts mentioned earlier.

On February 2, 2014, al-Qaeda's general command (AQGC) released a statement that said: ISIS is not a branch of the Qaidat al-Jihad group, we have no organizational relationship with it, and the group is not responsible for its actions.

Afterward, Adnani went after Zawahiri by responding, If God decrees to you [Zawahiri] to set foot in the and of the Islamic state, he should pledge allegiance to it and be a soldier of its amir [Baghdadi]. AQGC's statement began what both ISIS and al-Qaeda/JN describe as a fitna (state of discord), which has led to open warfare in Syria that continues to this day.

In addition to killing one another on the battle-field, including Abu Khalid al-Suri, both groups have used media to lure fence-sitters and possible defectors among the global jihadist community. It is likely that social media, especially Twitter, has amplified mutual hatred, with supporters of each camp refusing to back down rhetorically, likely signaling their steadfastness to their respective leaders. One wonders whether the situation would have become so hostile a decade ago, when al-Qaeda could control the message on its password-protected forums. Each group also released official testimonies from defectors from the other side. A JN video series from ISIS defectors is called "Muhajirinunder Siege."

A nine-part ISIS video series, "Series of the Life from the Words of the Ulama [religious scholars] on the Project of the Islamic State," high-lights positive comments about the creation of its Islamic state from its own past leaders (Zarqawi, Abu Hamza al-Muhajir, and Abu Omar al-Baghdadi), al-Qaeda leaders (bin Laden and Abu Yahya al-Libi), and a leader of al-Qaeda in the Arabian Peninsula, or AQAP (Anwar al-Awlaqi). The main argument between ISIS and al-Qaeda/JN is over authority and methodology (manhaj) as well as revisionist history. ISIS views Zawahiri's authority as illegitimate, even if prior sentiments noted earlier would suggest otherwise, and his organization as having deviated from the path of bin Laden. ISIS considers itself the true heir of bin Laden's al-Qaeda,but under the new banner of the Islamic state.

For example, in early April 2014, Adnani claimed that the leaders of al-Qaeda deviated from the right manhaj, we say this as sadness overwhelms us and bit-terness fills our hearts...Verily al-Qaeda today has ceased to be the base of jihad, rather its leadership has become an axe supporting the destruction of the project of the Islamic State and the coming khilafa (caliphate)...al-Qaeda now runs after the bandwagon of the majority and calls them as 'the Umma,' and softens in their stance at the expense of the religion, and the taghut (tyrants) of the Ikhwan (Muslim Brotherhood).

For their part, al-Qaeda and Zawahiri claim that Baghdadi did, in fact, pledge baya to Zawahiri, though privately. Therefore, according to this rea-soning, Baghdadi and ISIS broke a religious oath and have become a deviant group that disobeyed the emir's orders, specifically relating to its failure to carry out jihad in its designated location, Iraq.

Beyond the more technical arguments between leaders in these organizations, ISIS and JN have also acted differently on the ground in Syria. For ISIS, which believes it truly is an Islamic state, all residents of territory it takes over fall under the group's sovereign will and must abide by its interpretations of God's law. In this model, no competition or power sharing can be acceptable. It is true that ISIS has added a "hearts and minds" component to its governing strategy, but it has kept its narrower interpretations of sharia pertaining to social or criminal issues.

In contrast, JN views itself as one among many groups (primarily other Islamist allies) that must work together not only to fight against the Assad regime, but also to govern liberated spaces.

JN takes the long view that it cannot force its ideas on individuals and therefore must pursue a more gradualist approach, based on the lessons of past failed attempts at jihadist governance in Iraq last decade, as well as Somalia, Yemen, and Mali. The key is to socialize and normalize its ideas over time so that eventually the group can legitimately implement its more narrow interpretations of sharia. While this approach may have greater appeal for locals, ISIS's "forcing it down people's throats" style is more popular with its foreign fighter contingent, which makes up about 50 percent of its fighting force and provides support for its out-of-theater power projection.

While the fight between ISIS and al-Qaeda/JN has mainly played out within the Syrian zone of conflict, it has affected jihadist organizations and factions in other locales. For instance, while both AQAP and al-Qaeda in the Islamic Maghreb (AQIM) have kept a neutral position and called for reconciliation between the two groups, AQIM's central region came out in support of ISIS in late March 2014.5 The central region's legitimacy, however, has been questioned considering that the signers of its statement were previously unknown.

Additionally, in late January 2014, some AQAP fighters in Syria have in their own capacity backed ISIS, including as expressed by the AQAP leader Hatim al-Mamun. Closer to home, a breakaway faction of nine individuals in al-Qaeda in Afghanistan, including Maqdisi's brother and some other relevant leaders, pledged baya to Baghdadi in early April 2014.

This forced one of al-Qaeda's ideologues, Abu Amir al-Naji, to respond in late May 2014 that the nine-person letter made false claims against al-Qaeda. Such a response to the defection of just nine people illustrates al-Qaeda's worries about its ability to win the war of ideas with the future generation of global jihadists. In addition, other regional groups like Ansar al-Sharia in both Tunisia and Libya as well as jihadists in Gaza/Sinai and Indonesia have posted pro-ISIS propaganda.

All has not been lost for al-Qaeda, however. In late April 2014 Mokhtar Belmokhtar, the emir of the group al-Murabitun—an al-Qaeda branch in the greater Sahara—backed Zawahiri and al-Qaeda: It is incumbent upon us to confirm our confidence and commitment to the manhaj and guidance of our emir, Shaykh Ayman al-Zawahiri, out of our faith in the correctness of this manhaj, which is built upon perception and correct jurisprudence, and steady, successful, and blessed steps.

Additionally, in mid-May 2014, the emir of Harakat Shabab al-Mujahedin in Somalia, Sheikh Mukhtar Abu al-Zubair, confirmed support for Zawahiri's efforts in dealing with ISIS. Zubair also specifically endorsed Zawahiri's November 2012 release, "The Treatise of Supporting Islam," which highlights the importance of implementing sharia and liberating occupied Muslim lands.

Even more recently, Ali Abu Muhammad, the leader of the Caucasus Emirate (CE), a jihadist group that is not a branch of al-Qaeda, expressed sympathy for JN's side. This is likely because the CE's branch in Syria, Jaish al-Muhajireen wal Ansar, is close with JN. These three overt endorsements are unlikely to tip the scales toward al-Qaeda, but it does provide reassurances in addition to the support from JN, AQAP, and AQIM. It also highlights that al-Qaeda is not defeated.

Al-Qaeda is having a difficult time, given ISIS battlefield gains in both Syria and Iraq. Continued success for ISIS, of course, is by no means guaranteed, especially given the group's tendency to overplay its hand with locals. But unlike in Iraq a decade ago, there is no force like the United States on the ground to consolidate insurgent gains against ISIS. As seen in Syria since January, many nationalists, mainstream Islamists, and even JN have been unable to strategically defeat ISIS. And now that ISIS has gained new resources in the recent Iraq battles, it is pouring them into new offenses and regaining lost territory. Further, the reality of a proto-state and ISIS's willingness to try to govern—this khilafa project, as many within the group call it—is quite appealing to jihadists. ISIS is not only talking the talk about establishing an Islamic state, it is walking the walk. This has attracted many foreign fighters to its side.

In becoming the beacon for foreign fighters over the past year, ISIS now controls many recruitment and facilitation/logistics networks. Further, those who have fought with ISIS have made connections with one another and will likely keep in touch when they return to their places of origin. The solidarity and brotherhood established through fighting on the front lines and enduring the same hardships cements these relationships, which will be important for the future of the jihadist movement. Additionally, individuals like winners and, unlike al-Qaeda, which has not had a clear victory in a decade, ISIS continues to build its prestige and legitimacy within the overall movement.

The composition of foreign fighter sent to Syria (and now to Iraq again) indicates that the movement's future is being decided by Saucis, Libyans, Tunisians, and Jordanians. In terms of the Saudis, one question to be answered is whether returnees to AQAP can execute a coup against AQAP's leacership. AQAP remains loyal to Zawahiri given its emir Nasir al-Wihayshi's relations with bin Laden, which go back to Afghanistan. That said, if Wihayshi is killed in an American drone strike, anything could happen. AQAP, still viewed as al-Qaeda's strongest branch, is a bellwether and if it leans toward ISIS in the near to medium future, ISIS will have won the war against al-Qaeda. Similarly, with ISIS's victories next door in Iraq, members of JN may have more cause to defect back to ISIS, which could be a fatal blow to al-Qaeda as well. There are already small signs of such movement, especially in Deir al-Zour and Damascus.

Looking to North Africa, where a third safe haven exists outside the Syria/Iraq and Yemen arenas, many of the Tunisians and Libyans who fought in IS S were originally members of Ansar al-Sharia in Tunisia (AST) and Ansar al-Sharia in Libya (ASL), which could help make both groups kingpins in the Maghrebi landscape, especially since they continue to grow closer organizationally themselves.65 Addition-ally, the Darnah-based jihadist group Majlis Shura Shabab al-Islam publicly voiced support for ISIS earlier this week.

Unlike the Saudis, Libyans, and Tunisians, the Jordanians are still more sympathetic to JN than to ISIS, which could hurt the latter's ability to project further into the Levant. Lastly, in terms of Westerners, most of whom come from European Union countries (three thousand–plus), most are now with ISIS. Any plots or attacks in the West will thus more likely emanate from ISIS than from al-Qaeda. Various possibilities could either help or hinder the prospects of ISIS or al-Qaeda.

For ISIS, major local backlash or deaths in the leadership could do harm. For al-Qaeda, drone strikes against the leadership in Pakistan or AQAP's leaders in Yemen could potentially accelerate ISIS's claim over the global jihacist movement. There are even rumors that there could be a Ramadan reconciliation between the two in the coming weeks, which would likely beet ISIS, since it has more of the leverage over al-Qaeda in light of the recent Iraq offensives. It is impossible to of course predict the future since for example many in 2006 viewed Zarqawi and AQI as permanently eclipsing al-Qaeda, yet this did not end up happening.

If al-Qaeda wants to reclaim some semblance of legitimacy, it will desperately pursue a major strike along the lines of the Madrid train bombings, the July 7, 2005, London attacks, or actualizing the failed AQAP plots in 2009 and 2010. At this point, though, momentum toward ISIS may be too great for both the short and the longer term. Will the U.S. withdrawal from Afghanistan help resuscitate an organization that has taken many leadership hits in the past few years? It is too early to know, but if current trends hold, ISIS has opened up a lead on al-Qaeda, which has a steep hill to climb just to stave off its own relative decline...

Syrian Jihad

In an unexpected and unprecedented turn of events, al-Qaeda members and jihadists from all over the world who embrace the ideology of global jihad are now doubting the group's leader, Ayman al-Zawahiri, and calling for his removal.

While the Syrian Jihad has been of paramount concern to world governments, with hundreds of foreign fighters pouring in to participate in the fighting, the country has also been an arena for internal strife and bloody battles between the al-Qaeda-affiliated al-Nusra Front and al-Qaeda's former branch, the Islamic State in Iraq and the Levant (ISIL). Members of al-Qaeda and jihadists together blame Zawahiri for mismanaging the conflict in Syria and enflaming sedition, and advocate new leadership.

Under Zawahiri's command, al-Qaeda assigned the al-Nusra Front to be its arm in Syria, and disavowed the ISIL, telling jihadists that it does not acknowledge its founding and rejects its activities. Shortly after al-Qaeda clearly delineated its position, on February 23, 2014, Zawahiri's representative in Syria, Abu Khalid al-Suri, was killed in a suicide bombing in Aleppo. This was the watershed moment for the conflict. The al-Nusra Front and their supporters accused the ISIL of perpetrating the act and demanded they submit to arbitration by an independent Shariah body, while the ISIL denied having any connection.

Representing al-Qaeda's core leadership, Adam Gadahn (AKA Azzam the American) spoke first on the issue, noting that jihadi factions in Syria blamed a "group that is known for its extreme nature and radical behavior," which infuriated pro-ISIL supporters, believing that Gadahn was referring to the ISIL.

After Zawahiri made a similar accusation in a speech released on April 4, 2014, those same jihadists quickly attacked him, questioning his wisdom and demanding his removal. While the entire situation is unprecedented in the contemporary jihad, it is unfathomable that jihadists not only express such vitriol towards the leader of al-Qaeda, but on an al-Qaeda-affiliated password-protected forums, the house for al-Qaeda for a decade, to brand him a disbeliever and seek a replacement. The assault on Zawahiri became so fierce, that administrators of the top-tier jihadi forum Shumukh al-Islam deleted all the posts in the discussion thread for the speech, "Eulogy for the Martyr of Sedition Abu Khalid al-Suri," and locked it. A few hours later, the forum went down for "maintenance".

As some jihadists cursed Zawahiri and others questioned his authority, in a separate discussion, a Shumukh al-Islam user, "Ta'ir al-Nawras," representing the views of the many members who were angered by Zawahiri's message, demanded that Zawahiri be stripped of his leadership position and that it be given to al-Qaeda in the Arabian Peninsula (AQAP) chief Abu Baseer Nasser al-Wuhayshi.

Sheikh Abu Baseer is closer to the course of events in the Islamic world, and he is wiser, more cunning, and more capable to deal with it. He was one of the assistants of Sheikh Usama, may Allah have mercy on him, he was enabled to restructure the al-Qaeda branch in the Arabian Peninsula. He strengthened it, and made it a difficult number, and one of the most powerful branches of the organization in the world, superior even to the Central Command. The branch of the organization was enabled under his leadership to reach the United States of America with several operations, among which was the invasion of Umar al-Farouk, may Allah release him.

Also, the command of al-Qaeda in the Arabian Peninsula is stronger and has better capabilities, and the experiences of its leaders are better, and the efficiency of its personnel is higher.Still, there are some jihadists who hope to calm the situation and restore order. One forum user, "Nasa'im al-Kheir," illustrates the views from the other side, explained that while Zawahiri made "mistakes" in his handling of the Syrian conflict, it does not allow Muslims to attack him and brand him a "disbeliever".

He wrote: Although we disagree with the Sheikh, may Allah the Almighty preserve him, on the issue of al-Sham [Syria] and what happened in it, and it is a huge dispute, it does not contest the religion of the Sheikh and the authenticity of his method. Who are we to question the religion of the Sheikh, let alone speak of his mistakes and imperfections?

Similar to "Ta'ir al-Nawras" in his post, "Nasa'im al-Kheir" also pointed out Zawahiri's isolation in the Afghanistan-Pakistan area, far away from Syria, as a reason for his faulty judgment:

The mistakes of the Sheikh are mistakes that happen with any commander, and we still excuse him (if we excuse he who fell into the disbelief by ignorance). So it is the foremost excuse for the Sheikh that he is away from the reality in al-Sham and the truth is absent from him.

As the conflict rages and jihadists further entrench themselves in separate camps, al-Qaeda will remain marginalized in Syria until it is able to broker a solution. The sedition has impacted the jihadists and al-Qaeda on many fronts: from the disputes on the jihadi forums and social media to as far as the battlefield, with the ongoing bloody fights between the two sides.

The jihadi generation raised on the unquestionable leadership of Usama bin Laden, the fiery speeches of Abu Musab al-Zarqawi, and the brazen actions of al-Qaeda's branch in Iraq for nearly a decade is finding it difficult to accept a leader who is far from the battlefield in question and unable to exercise authority or connect with his followers. Pro-ISIL jihadists view the group as holding the birthright of al-Qaeda in Iraq, and not the al-Nusra Front, and accept its positions as truth and those who oppose them as the enemy, including Ayman al-Zawahiri and Adam Gadahn.

Back in 2003

Military action is necessary to halt the spread of the ISIS "cancer," said President Obama. In his much anticipated address, he called for expanded airstrikes across Iraq and Syria, and new measures to arm and train Iraqi and Kurdish ground forces.

Missing from the chorus of outrage, however, has been any acknowledgement of the integral role of covert US and British regional military intelligence strategy in empowering and even directly sponsoring the very same virulent Islamist militants in Iraq, Syria and beyond, that went on to break away from al-Qaeda and form 'ISIS', the Islamic State of Iraq and Syria, or now simply, the Islamic State (IS).

Since 2003, Anglo-American power has secretly and openly coordinated direct and indirect support for Islamist terrorist groups linked to al-Qaeda across the Middle East and North Africa. This ill-conceived patchwork geo-strategy is a legacy of the persistent influence of neoconservative ideology, motivated by longstanding but often contradictory ambitions to dominate regional oil resources, defend an expansionist Israel, and in pursuit of these, re-draw the map of the Middle East.

Now despite Pentagon denials that there will be boots on the ground – and Obama's insistence that this would not be another "Iraq war" – local Kurdish military and intelligence sources confirm that US and German special operations forces are already "on the ground" here. US airstrikes on ISIS positions and arms supplies to the Kurds have also been accompanied by British RAF reconnaissance flights over the region and UK weapons shipments to Kurdish peshmerga forces.

Early during the 2003 invasion and occupation of Iraq, the US covertly supplied arms to al-Qaeda affiliated insurgents even while ostensibly supporting an emerging Shi'a-dominated administration.

Pakistani defense sources interviewed by Asia Times in February 2005 confirmed that insurgents described as "former Ba'ath party" loyalists – who were being recruited and trained by "al-Qaeda in Iraq" under the leadership of the late Abu Musab Zarqawi – were being supplied Pakistan-manufactured weapons by the US. The arms shipments included rifles, rocket-propelled grenade launchers, ammunition, rockets and other light weaponry.

These arms "could not be destined for the Iraqi security forces because US arms would be given to them", a source told Syed Saleem Shahzad – the Times' Pakistan bureau chief who, "known for his exposes of the Pakistani military" according to the New Yorker, was murdered in 2011. Rather, the US is playing a double-game to "head off" the threat of a "Shi'ite clergy-driven religious movement," said the Pakistani defense source. This was not the only way US strategy aided the rise of Zarqawi, a bin Laden mentee and brainchild of the extremist ideology that would later spawn 'ISIS.'

UK's covert action in Syria

According to former French foreign minister Roland Dumas, Britain had planned covert action in Syria as early as 2009: "I was in England two years before the violence in Syria on other business," he told French television. "I met with top British officials, who confessed to me that they were preparing something in Syria. This was in Britain not in America. Britain was preparing gunmen to invade Syria."

Leaked emails from the private intelligence firm Stratfor, including notes from a meeting with Pentagon officials, confirmed that as of 2011, US and UK special forces training of Syrian opposition forces was well underway. The goal was to elicit the "collapse" of Assad's regime "from within."

Since then, the role of the Gulf states – namely Saudi Arabia, Qatar, Kuwait, the United Arab Emirates, and Jordan (as well as NATO member Turkey) – in officially and unofficially financing and coordinating the most virulent elements amongst Syria's rebels under the tutelage of US military intelligence is no secret. Yet the conventional wisdom is that the funneling of support to Islamist extremists in the rebel movement affiliated to al-Qaeda has been a colossal and regrettable error.The reality is very different. The empowerment of the Islamist factions within the 'Free Syrian Army' (FSA) was a foregone conclusion of the strategy.

West training rebels

With their command and control center based in Istanbul, Turkey, military supplies from Saudi Arabia and Qatar in particular were transported by Turkish intelligence to the border for rebel acquisition. CIA operatives along with Israeli and Jordanian commandos were also training FSA rebels on the Jordanian-Syrian border with anti-tank and anti-aircraft weapons.

In addition, other reports show that British and French military were also involved in these secret training programs. It appears that the same FSA rebels receiving this elite training went straight into ISIS – one ISIS commander, Abu Yusaf, said, "Many of the FSA people who the west has trained are actually joining us."

The National thus confirmed the existence of another Command and Control Center in Amman, Jordan, "staffed by western and Arab military officials," which "channels vehicles, sniper rifles, mortars, heavy machine guns, small arms and ammunition to Free Syrian Army units." Rebel and opposition sources described the weapons bridge as "a well-run operation staffed by high-ranking military officials from 14 countries, including the US, European nations and Arabian Gulf states, the latter providing the bulk of materiel and financial support to rebel factions."

The FSA sources interviewed by The National went to pains to deny that any al-Qaeda affiliated factions were involved in the control center, or would receive any weapons support. But this is difficult to believe given that "Saudi and Qatari-supplied weapons" were being funneled through to the rebels via Amman, to their favored factions.

Classified assessments of the military assistance supplied by US allies Saudi Arabia and Qatar obtained by the New York Times showed that "most of the arms shipped at the behest of Saudi Arabia and Qatar to supply Syrian rebel groups... are going to hardline Islamic jihadists, and not the more secular opposition groups that the West wants to bolster."

Lest there be any doubt as to the extent to which all this covert military assistance coordinated by the US has gone to support al-Qaeda affiliated factions in the FSA, it is worth noting that earlier this year, the Israeli military intelligence website Debkafile – run by two veteran correspondents who covered the Middle East for 23 years for The Economist – reported that: "Turkey is giving Syrian rebel forces, including the al-Qaeda-affiliated Nusra Front, passage through its territory to attack the northwestern Syrian coastal area around Latakia."

In August, Debkafile reported that "The US, Jordan and Israel are quietly backing the mixed bag of some 30 Syrian rebel factions", some of which had just "seized control of the Syrian side of the Quneitra crossing, the only transit point between Israeli and Syrian Golan." However, Debkafile noted, "al-Qaeda elements have permeated all those factions." Israel has provided limited support to these rebels in the form of "medical care," as well as "arms, intelligence and food".

ISIS sponsors

The Islamic State of Iraq and Syria (ISIS), now threatening Baghdad, was funded for years by wealthy donors in Kuwait, Qatar, and Saudi Arabia, three U.S. allies that have dual agendas in the war on terror.

It's an ironic twist, especially for donors in Kuwait (who, to be fair, back a wide variety of militias). ISIS has aligned itself with remnants of the Baathist regime once led by Saddam Hussein. Back in 1990, the U.S. attacked Iraq in order to liberate Kuwait from Hussein's clutches. Now Kuwait is helping the rise of his successors.

As ISIS takes over town after town in Iraq, they are acquiring money and supplies including American made vehicles, arms, and ammunition. The group reportedly scored $430 million when they looted the main bank in Mosul. They reportedly now have a stream of steady income sources, including from selling oil in the Northern Syrian regions they control, sometimes directly to the Assad regime.

But in the years they were getting started, a key component of ISIS's support came from wealthy individuals in the Arab Gulf States of Kuwait, Qatar and Saudi Arabia. Sometimes the support came with the tacit nod of approval from those regimes; often, it took advantage of poor money laundering protections in those states, according to officials, experts, and leaders of the Syrian opposition, which is fighting ISIS as well as the regime.

"Everybody knows the money is going through Kuwait and that it's coming from the Arab Gulf," said Andrew Tabler, senior fellow at the Washington Institute for Near East Policy. "Kuwait's banking system and its money changers have long been a huge problem because they are a major conduit for money to extremist groups in Syria and now Iraq."

Iraqi Prime Minister Nouri al-Maliki has been publicly accusing Saudi Arabia and Qatar of funding ISIS for months. Several reports have detailed how private Gulf funding to various Syrian rebel groups has splintered the Syrian opposition and paved the way for the rise of groups like ISIS and others

Gulf donors support ISIS, the Syrian branch of al Qaeda called al Nusrah Front, and other Islamic groups fighting on the ground in Syria because they feel an obligation to protect Sunnis suffering under the atrocities of the Assad regime.

Many of these backers don't trust or like the American backed moderate opposition, which the West has refused to provide significant arms to.

Under significant U.S. pressure, the Arab Gulf governments have belatedly been cracking down on funding to Sunni extremist groups, but Gulf regimes are also under domestic pressure to fight in what many Sunnis see as an unavoidable Shiite-Sunni regional war that is only getting worse by the day.

"ISIS is part of the Sunni forces that are fighting Shia forces in this regional sectarian conflict. They are in an existential battle with both the (Iranian aligned) Maliki government and the Assad regime," said Tabler. "The U.S. has made the case as strongly as they can to regional countries, including Kuwait. But ultimately when you take hands off, leading from behind approach to things, people don't take you seriously and they take matters into their own hands."

Donors in Kuwait, the Sunni majority Kingdom on Iraq's border, have taken advantage of Kuwait's weak financial rules to channel hundreds of millions of dollars to a host of Syrian rebel brigades, according to a December 2013 report by The Brookings Institution, a Washington think tank that receives some funding from the Qatari government.

"Over the last two and a half years, Kuwait has emerged as a financing and organizational hub for charities and individuals supporting Syria's myriad rebel groups," the report said. "Today, there is evidence that Kuwaiti donors have backed rebels who have committed atrocities and who are either directly linked to al-Qa'ida or cooperate with its affiliated brigades on the ground."

Kuwaiti donors collect funds from donors in other Arab Gulf countries and the money often travels through Turkey or Jordan before reaching its Syrian destination, the report said. The governments of Kuwait, Qatar, and Saudi Arabia have passed laws to curb the flow of illicit funds, but many donors still operate out in the open. The Brookings paper argues the U.S. government needs to do more.

"The U.S. Treasury is aware of this activity and has expressed concern about this flow of private financing. But Western diplomats' and officials' general response has been a collective shrug," the report states.

When confronted with the problem, Gulf leaders often justify allowing their Salafi constituents to fund Syrian extremist groups by pointing back to what they see as a failed U.S. policy in Syria and a loss of credibility after President Obama reneged on his pledge to strike Assad after the regime used chemical weapons.

That's what Prince Bandar bin Sultan, head of Saudi intelligence since 2012 and former Saudi ambassador in Washington, reportedly told Secretary of State John Kerry when Kerry pressed him on Saudi financing of extremist groups earlier this year. Saudi Arabia has retaken a leadership role in past months guiding help to the Syrian armed rebels, displacing Qatar, which was seen as supporting some of the worst organizations on the ground.

The rise of ISIS, a group that officially broke with al Qaeda core, is devastating for the moderate Syrian opposition, which is now fighting a war on two fronts, severely outmanned and outgunned by both extremist groups and the regime. There is increasing evidence that Assad is working with ISIS to squash the Free Syrian Army.

But the Syrian moderate opposition is also wary of confronting the Arab Gulf states about their support for extremist groups. The rebels are still competing for those governments' favor and they are dependent on other types of support from Arab Gulf countries. So instead, they blame others—the regimes in Tehran and Damascus, for examples—for ISIS' rise.

"The Iraqi State of Iraq and the [Sham] received support from Iran and the Syrian intelligence," said Hassan Hachimi, Head of Political Affairs for the United States and Canada for Syrian National Coalition, at the Brookings U.S.-Islamic World Forum in Doha this week.

"There are private individuals in the Gulf that do support extremist groups there," along with other funding sources, countered Mouaz Moustafa, executive director of the Syrian Emergency Task Force, a Syrian-American organization that supports the opposition "[The extremist groups] are the most well-resourced on the ground... If the United States and the international community better resourced [moderate] battalions... then many of the people will take that option instead of the other one."

US aid

Officially, the US government's financial support for the FSA goes through the Washington DC entity, the Syrian Support Group (SSG), which was incorporated in April 2012. The SSG is licensed via the US Treasury Department to "export, re-export, sell, or supply to the Free Syrian Army ('FSA') financial, communications, logistical, and other services otherwise prohibited by Executive Order 13582 in order to support the FSA."

In mid-2013, the Obama administration intensified its support to the rebels with a new classified executive order reversing its previous policy limiting US direct support to only nonlethal equipment. As before, the order would aim to supply weapons strictly to "moderate" forces in the FSA.

US government had "little oversight over whether US supplies are falling prey to corruption – or into the hands of extremists," and relies "on too much good faith." The US government kept track of rebels receiving assistance purely through "handwritten receipts provided by rebel commanders in the field," and the judgement of its allies. Countries supporting the rebels – the very same which have empowered al-Qaeda affiliated Islamists – "are doing audits of the delivery of lethal and nonlethal supplies."

Thus, with the Gulf states still calling the shots on the ground, it is no surprise that by September last year, eleven prominent rebel groups distanced themselves from the 'moderate' opposition leadership and allied themselves with al-Qaeda.

By the SSG's own conservative estimate, as much as 15% of rebel fighters are Islamists affiliated to al-Qaeda, either through the Jabhut al-Nusra faction, or its breakaway group ISIS. But privately, Pentagon officials estimate that "more than 50%" of the FSA is comprised of Islamist extremists, and according to rebel sources neither FSA chief Gen Salim Idris nor his senior aides engage in much vetting, decisions about which are made typically by local commanders.

Follow the money

Media reports following ISIS' conquest of much of northern and central Iraq have painted the group as the world's most super-efficient, self-financed, terrorist organization that has been able to consolidate itself exclusively through extensive looting of Iraq's banks and funds from black market oil sales.

Much of this narrative, however, has derived from dubious sources, and overlooked disturbing details.

One senior anonymous intelligence source told Guardian, for instance, that over 160 computer flash sticks obtained from an ISIS hideout revealed information on ISIS' finances that was completely new to the intelligence community. "Before Mosul, their total cash and assets were $875m [£515m]," said the official on the funds obtained largely via "massive cash flows from the oil fields of eastern Syria, which it had commandeered in late 2012."

Afterwards, "with the money they robbed from banks and the value of the military supplies they looted, they could add another $1.5bn to that." The thrust of the narrative coming from intelligence sources was simple: "They had done this all themselves. There was no state actor at all behind them, which we had long known. They don't need one."

Follow the oil

But while ISIS has clearly obtained funding from donors in the Gulf states, many of its fighters having broken away from the more traditional al-Qaeda affiliated groups like Jabhut al-Nusra, it has also successfully leveraged its control over Syrian and Iraqi oil fields.

New York Times reported that "Islamist rebels and extremist groups have seized control of most of Syria's oil and gas resources", bolstering "the fortunes of the Islamic State of Iraq and Syria, or ISIS, and the Nusra Front, both of which are offshoots of al-Qaeda." Al-Qaeda affiliated rebels had "seized control of the oil and gas fields scattered across the country's north and east," while more moderate "Western-backed rebel groups do not appear to be involved in the oil trade, in large part because they have not taken over any oil fields."

In April 2013, for instance, the Times noted that al-Qaeda rebels had taken over key regions of Syria: "Nusra's hand is felt most strongly in Aleppo", where the al-Qaeda affiliate had established in coordination with other rebel groups including ISIS "a Shariah Commission" running "a police force and an Islamic court that hands down sentences that have included lashings." A -Qaeda fighters also "control the power plant and distribute flour to keep the city's bakeries running."

Additionally, they "have seized government oil fields" in provinces of Deir al-Zour and Hasaka, and now make a "profit from the crude they produce."

Lost in the fog of media hype was the disconcerting fact that these al-Qaeda rebel bread and oil operations in Aleppo, Deir al-Zour and Hasaka were directly and indirectly supported by the US and the European Union (EU). One account by the Washington Post for instance refers to a stealth mission in Aleppo "to deliver food and other aid to needy Syrians — all of it paid for by the US government," including the supply of flour. "The bakery is fully supplied with flour paid for by the United States," the Post continues, noting that local consumers, however, "credited Jabhat al-Nusra — a rebel group the United States has designated a terrorist organisation because of its ties to al-Qaeda — with providing flour to the region, though he admitted he wasn't sure where it comes from."

And in the same month that al-Qaeda's control of Syria's main oil regions in Deir al-Zour and Hasaka was confirmed, the EU voted to ease an oil embargo on Syria to allow oil to be sold on international markets from these very al-Qaeda controlled oil fields. European companies would be permitted to buy crude oil and petroleum products from these areas, although transactions would be approved by the Syrian National Coalition. Due to damaged infrastructure, oil would be trucked by road to Turkey where the nearest refineries are located.

Turkey's dirty game

Even as al-Qaeda fighters increasingly decide to join up with IS, the ad hoc black market oil production and export infrastructure established by the Islamist groups in Syria has continued to function with, it seems, the tacit support of regional and western powers.

According to Ali Ediboglu, a Turkish MP for the border province of Hatay, IS is selling the bulk of its oil from regions in Syria and Mosul in Iraq through Turkey, with the tacit consent of Turkish authorities: "They have laid pipes from villages near the Turkish border at Hatay. Similar pipes exist also at [the Turkish border regions of] Kilis, Urfa and Gaziantep. They transfer the oil to Turkey and parlay it into cash. They take the oil from the refineries at zero cost.

Using primitive means, they refine the oil in areas close to the Turkish border and then sell it via Turkey. This is worth $800 million." He also noted that the extent of this and related operations indicates official Turkish complicity. "Fighters from Europe, Russia, Asian countries and Chechnya are going in large numbers both to Syria and Iraq, crossing from Turkish territory. There is information that at least 1,000 Turkish nationals are helping those foreign fighters sneak into Syria and Iraq to join ISIS. The National Intelligence Organization (MIT) is allegedly involved. None of this can be happening without MIT's knowledge."

Similarly, there is evidence that authorities in the Kurdish region of Iraq are also turning a blind eye to IS oil smuggling. In July, Iraqi officials said that IS had begun selling oil extracted from in the northern province of Salahuddin. One official pointed out that "the Kurdish peshmerga forces stopped the sale of oil at first, but later allowed tankers to transfer and sell oil."

State of Law coalition MP Alia Nasseef also accused the Kurdistan Regional Government (KRG) of secretly trading oil with IS: "What is happening shows the extent of the massive conspiracy against Iraq by Kurdish politicians... The [illegal] sale of Iraqi oil to ISIS or anyone else is something that would not surprise us." Although Kurdish officials have roundly rejected these accusations, informed sources told the Arabic daily Asharq Al-Awsat that Iraqi crude captured by ISIS was "being sold to Kurdish traders in the border regions straddling Iraq, Iran and Syria, and was being shipped to Pakistan where it was being sold 'for less than half its original price.'"

"Countries like Turkey have turned a blind eye to the practice" of IS oil smuggling, said Luay al-Khateeb, a fellow at the Brookings Doha Center, "and international pressure should be mounted to close down black markets in its southern region." So far there has been no such pressure. Meanwhile, IS oil smuggling continues, with observers inside and outside Turkey noting that the Turkish government is tacitly allowing IS to flourish as it prefers the rebels to the Assad regime.

According to former Iraqi oil minister Isam al-Jalabi, "Turkey is the biggest winner from the Islamic State's oil smuggling trade." Both traders and oil firms are involved, he said, with the low prices allowing for "massive" profits for the countries facilitating the smuggling.

Buying ISIS oil?

Early last year, a tanker carrying over a million barrels in crude oil from northern Iraq's Kurdish region arrived at the Texas Gulf of Mexico. The oil had been refined in the Iraqi Kurdish region before being pumped through a new pipeline from the KRG area ending up at Ceyhan, Turkey, where it was then loaded onto the tanker for shipping to the US. Baghdad's efforts to stop the oil sale on the basis of its having national jurisdiction were rebuffed by American courts.

In early September, the European Union's ambassador to Iraq, Jana Hybášková, told the EU Foreign Affairs Committee that "several EU member states have bought oil from the Islamic State (IS, formerly ISIS) terrorist organisation that has been brutally conquering large portions of Iraq and Syria," according to Israel National News. She however "refused to divulge the names of the countries despite being asked numerous times."

A third end-point for the KRG's crude, once again shipped via Turkey's port of Ceyhan, was Israel's southwestern port of Ashkelon. This is hardly news though. In May, Reuters revealed that Israeli and US oil refineries had been regularly purchasing and importing KRG's disputed oil.

Meanwhile, as this triangle of covert oil shipments in which ISIS crude appears to be hopelessly entangled becomes more established, Turkey has increasingly demanded that the US pursue formal measures to lift obstacles to Kurdish oil sales to global markets. The KRG plans to export as much as 1 million barrels of oil a day by next year through its pipeline to Turkey.

Among the many oil and gas firms active in the KRG capital, Erbil, are ExxonMobil and Chevron. They are drilling in the region for oil under KRG contracts, though operations have been halted due to the crisis. No wonder Steve Coll writes in the New Yorker that Obama's air strikes and arms supplies to the Kurds – notably not to Baghdad – effectively amount to "the defense of an undeclared Kurdish oil state whose sources of geopolitical appeal – as a long-term, non-Russian supplier of oil and gas to Europe, for example – are best not spoken of in polite or naïve company." The Kurds are now busy working to "quadruple" their export capacity, while US policy has increasingly shifted toward permitting Kurdish exports – a development that would have major ramifications for Iraq's national territorial integrity.

To be sure, as the offensive against IS ramps up, the Kurds are now selectively cracking down on IS smuggling efforts – but the measures are too little, too late.

Saudis' dubble game

As ISIS went public with its expansion into Iraq followed by a succession of reports about its takeover of Iraqi cities and towns, in parallel with mass executions against civilians, the Western media was stunned. Several editorials raised questions about ISIS' funding and support. On June 13, officials at the US Treasury Department said Saudi Arabia was "on the same wavelength" as the United States, with both sides agreeing on the need to put an end to the radical group's operations.

In June as well, Lori Plotkin Boghardt of the Washington Institute for Near East Policy, wrote, "At present, there is no credible evidence that the Saudi government is financially supporting ISIS. Riyadh views the group as a terrorist organization that poses a direct threat to the kingdom's security." She continued, "Many governments in the region and beyond sometimes fund inimical parties to help achieve particular policy objectives. Riyadh has taken pleasure in recent ISIS-led Sunni advances against Iraq's Shia government, and in jihadist gains in Syria at Bashar al-Assad's expense."

Boghardt added, "Today, Saudi citizens continue to represent a significant funding source for Sunni groups operating in Syria. Arab Gulf donors as a whole – of which Saudis are believed to be the most charitable – have funneled hundreds of millions of dollars to Syria in recent years, including to ISIS and other groups."

At around the same time, Boghardt's colleague at the Washington Institute Andrew Tabler said candidly, "Everybody knows the money is going through Kuwait and that it's coming from the Arab Gulf. Kuwait's banking system and its money changers have long been a huge problem because they are a major conduit for money to extremist groups in Syria and now Iraq."

In addition to the issue of funding, the tone of some articles as concerns Saudi Arabia specifically changed over the recent period. Some analysts went back to the US ties to Osama bin Laden's al-Qaeda in the 1980s in Afghanistan, while others called on Saudi Arabia, Qatar, Gulf nations, and Turkey to put an end to their involvement immediately.

Some journalists and writers in the mainstream Western media finally broke their silence. Headlines were saying it more candidly now: Saudis must stop exporting extremism. Some journalists and writers in the mainstream Western media finally broke their silence. Headlines were saying it more candidly now: Saudis must stop exporting extremism, as an editorial by Ed Husain declared in NYT a few weeks ago. Husain wrote, "ISIS atrocities started with Saudi support for Salafi hate." Husain said that it was not enough for Saudi to give $100 million to the UN fund for counterterrorism, but that it must stop supporting a l extremist Salafi groups around the world, and stop promoting extremist Salafi ideas and teachings among Saudis and Muslims elsewhere.

The writer, who had declared himself to be a Sunni Muslim at a meeting organized by the U.S. Council on Foreign Relations, explained at length the danger the Wahhabi ideology poses to the region and the world, saying, "I'd say the Iranians haven't been as vociferous. Yes, they've funded Hezbollah and, yes, they've funded the Assad government, but neither have the level of dislike and hatred of Sunnis that the Saudis have pumped into their institutions, the r syllabi in various mosques and madrassas that they control that has led to real hatred of Shia Muslims from Pakistan to the Caucasus to parts of Africa to Afghanistan to mostly in the Middle East."

For its part, The Washington Post recently decided to re-highlight the issue of human rights violations in the kingdom, in a front-page editorial rather than in the international section.

Meanwhile, WP contributor David Ignatius, who is close to Saudi's allies in the region, recalled in a recent article Bandar's "unpredictable" policies in Syria. Ignatius conveyed timidly accusations against the Saudi prince of having supported al-Qaeda-affiliated groups in Syria "unintentionally." He wrote, "U.S. officials were relieved when Bandar was removed as steward of the Syrian opposition." Ignatius also described Bandar as an "untrustworthy operator," as per the view held by some US officials, and as "flamboyant" and a Saudi "wild card."

Last month, The Atlantic quoted a senior Qatari official as saying that ISIS was a Saudi project. The magazine also said that the radical jihadi group was an essential part of Bandar's covert strategy in Syria.

Patrick Cockburn in the British newspaper The Independent quoted the former head of the British Secret Intelligence Service, MI6, Sir Richard Dearlove, who in turn was quoting what Bandar told him personally shortly before 9/11, as saying, "The time is not far off in the Middle East, Richard, when it will be literally 'God help the Shia'." Dearlove pointed out that the Saudi and Qatari regimes had turned a blind eye to the funds being sent to ISIS, and explained that ISIS's takeover of areas in Iraq and the extent at which the group had grown could not have happened "spontaneously." Dearlove said what Bandar had told him and subsequent events in the region were "chilling."

The Coalition of hypocrisy

The Islamic State (ISIS) did not become the monster it is today by accident. The Western media and governments bore witness to the inception, growth, and expansion of this radical jihadi group, with funding from the Arab Gulf, sectarian agitation, and political blessing, until ISIS became a monster.

When the Saudi king charged Bandar bin Sultan with handling the Syrian file, as the latter was appointed chief of Saudi intelligence in 2012, Western analysts saw the move as an indication that Saudi Arabia was stepping up its involvement in Syria and of its intention to play a greater role there. But what role could that have been? No one identified the nature or type of this escalation.

"Thank God for the Saudis and Prince Bandar, we're starting to see a little bit of reversal there [in Syria]," said Republican Senator John McCain to CNN. The senator restated his gratitude at a security conference in Munich later, with a new twist. He said, "Thank God for the Saudis, Prince Bandar, and our Qatari friends."

Between 2013 and February 2014 – that is, throughout Prince Bandar's handling of the Syrian file – press reports covered extensively the rise of al-Nusra Front and ISIS in Syria, and how they became the dominant opposition forces along the battlefronts in the country. But where did the two groups get their cash and weapons? According to investigative reports, wealthy people from Saudi, Qatar, and Kuwait have been financing the radical groups, though these reports did not name the regimes of those countries as being involved because "there was no clear evidence" to this effect.

In November 2013, The New York Times ran a report that said huge amounts of money were being transferred from banks in Kuwait to support opposition fighters in Syria. Ghanim al-Mteiri, a Kuwaiti in charge of one the campaigns raising funds for the armed groups in Syria, told the NYT, "Once upon a time we cooperated with the Americans in Iraq (in 1991). Now we want to get Bashar out of Syria, so why not cooperate with al-Qaeda?"

"Qatari support for Syrian fighters"; "Wealthy Saudi and Kuwaiti sponsors"; "through banks in Kuwait": These revelations and more were mentioned repeatedly in most Western articles investigating the source of al-Nusra and ISIS funding, in addition to enumerating other sources such as seizure of weapons caches, robbing banks, and looting of other assets in Syria.

Recruitment for the "jihad" began in earnest, overtly and through the Internet, using religious and material inducements, with logistical facilities on the border. The radical jihad monster thus grew in plain sight of everyone. In the meantime, Bandar was lobbying U.S. representatives and senators to support a US military strike on Syria. Bandar's self-confidence reached such an extent that he started criticizing Barack Obama's Syria policy publically.

Syria was drowning in weapons but the American military strike never came. Bandar was removed from his post at the helm of Saudi intelligence and the Syrian file in February 2014. US officials and analysts came out to say that a new less extreme Saudi phase would begin in Syria, and that Bandar had "gone too far" in supporting Syrian fighters. What does "too far" mean in this context? No one has yet explained it. Bandar's involvement in Syria and the region was stopped. But the ISIS monster had already become bigger, stronger, and richer. In June 2014, ISIS formalized this by declaring itself a state, not only in Syria, but also in Iraq.

Bandar Bin Sultan

Prince Bandar bin Sultan, one-time long-serving ambassador to the United States, later head of Saudi intelligence, now adviser and special envoy to the king as well as secretary-general of the Saudi National Security Council (NSC).

Bandar fell out with the Obama Administration in 2012-2014 over the question of support for opposition fighters in Syria whom he wanted to back enthusiastically despite U.S. objections. Because of this, the White House came to view him as out of control and refused to work with him. Eventually, in April 2014, clearly responding to U.S. pressure, the king sacked him as intelligence chief but allowed him to keep his nebulous Saudi NSC role. Three months later, Bandar was back in favor in Riyadh, taking a special envoy role and has been seen at several top-level meetings since.

Saudi Arabia regards itself as the leader of the Muslim world, and as such sees itself as existing in an existential struggle with Iran for dominance of this world. The centuries old Sunni/Shiite divide, which has opened up dangerously since the 1979 Iranian revolution, is compounded by the political Islam of the Brotherhood, which views Arab monarchies such as the House of Saud as anachronisms at best but, more dangerously, un-Islamic.

For its part, Washington's principal interest in Saudi Arabia is safeguarding its role as the world's largest exporter of oil, with subsidiary interests of allowing Saudi Arabia to use market leverage to keep prices stable and not too high. This policy approach—which prompted U.S. military involvement after Saddam Hussein's 1990 invasion of Kuwait and explains the continuing naval and air force commitments in the Gulf area, though Saudi Arabia does not host any U.S. bases—tolerates (for the most part) often extraordinary behavior by the Saudis in their attempts to preserve what they regard as their Islamic pre-eminence.

Certainly in the past this has included support for terrorism. A particularly outrageous example of this: From about 1996 to around 2003, Defense Minister Prince Sultan and Interior Minister Prince Nayef paid off Osama bin Laden so al Qaeda would not target the kingdom.

Today, the Saudis deny any support for terrorists and, indeed, have made it a criminal offense for its citizens to fight in Syria or to provide support for opposition fighters. But this is at odds with decades of Saudi practice, sending religious youth to fight in Afghanistan, Chechnya, Bosnia, and elsewhere. It is also not the way Bandar spoke of his instructions from King Abdullah when he was appointed intelligence chief: he stated that he was charged with getting rid of Bashar al Assad, containing Hezbollah in Lebanon, and cutting off the head of the snake (Iran). For emphasis of Saudi sincerity of purpose in Syria, he said that he would follow his monarch's instructions, even if it meant hiring "every SOB jihadist" he could find.

In policy circles in Washington, there is a common wisdom that Saudi support for fighters in Syria has not included al Qaeda types—though it's pretty obvious that Qatar, the kingdom's small neighbor but big diplomatic competitor has been supporting fighters of an al Qaeda affiliate (Jabhat al-Nusra).

In reality, the spectrum of opposition fighters—from President Obama's "teachers and pharmacists" through to IS, ISIS, ISIL (call it what you will)—is full of muddy distinctions. This could explain why Jordan, sandwiched between Saudi Arabia and Syria, declined to allow Bandar to set up training camps for hundreds, perhaps thousands, of opposition fighters. Jihadi types might influence disaffected Jordanian youth and would certainly annoy Assad, who could orchestrate a refugee crisis that might overwhelm Jordan. King Abdullah of Saudi Arabia was evidently so annoyed at the veto that he cut off all aid to cash-strapped Jordan this year, which had been running at $1 billion annually.

Despite the diplomacy which suggests an emerging coalition that includes Saudi Arabia and will take on the fighters of the Islamic State in Iraq and perhaps Syria, the House of Saud will likely continue to try to balance the threat of the head-chopping jihadists, while also trying to deliver a strategic setback to Iran by overthrowing the regime in Damascus.

From a Saudi point of view, the move of IS forces into Iraq contributed the removal of Nouri al-Maliki in Baghdad, who they regarded as a stooge of Tehran. Despite official support by Riyadh for the new Baghdad government, many Saudis who despise Shiites probably regard IS as doing God's work.

Saudi Arabia has denied giving any support to the Islamic State of Iraq and the Levant (Isis), the jihadi group that has captured swaths of territory across northern and central Iraq, as well as controlling large parts of northern Syria.

Stung by accusations from the Iraqi prime minister, Nouri al-Maliki, the normally reticent Saudi government issued a statement rejecting what it called "false allegations" and a "malicious falsehood".

Maliki claimed in a statement on Tuesday that the Saudis were facilitating genocide. Riyadh hit back by blaming Maliki's "exclusionary policies" for fomenting the crisis – a reference to the Shia politician's widely criticised sectarianism vis-a-vis Iraq's Sunni minority.

The Saudi monarchy has been a vocal supporter of the overthrow of the Syrian president, Bashar al-Assad, and sent money and weapons to rebel groups fighting against him from early on in the Syrian uprising. It has also called repeatedly for western arms – including anti-tank and anti-aircraft weapons – to be given to Syrian rebels "to level the playing-field" in the war.

Wealthy individuals and religious foundations in Saudi Arabia, Kuwait, Qatar and elsewhere in the Gulf have channelled millions of dollars to the anti-Assad opposition, though it is not clear with what degree of official connivance.

But since last autumn the Saudi government has diverted its support to a broad Islamic Front which has been fighting against jihadi formations such as Isis and the Syrian group Jabhat al-Nusra. There is other evidence of a rethink in the replacement of the Saudi intelligence chief, Prince Bandar bin Sultan, with Prince Mohamed bin Nayef, the interior minister and architect of a successful campaign against al-Qaida. The Saudis are also co-ordinating more closely with the US than previously. "There is Saudi money flowing into Isis but it is not from the Saudi state," said Lina Khatib of the Carnegie Foundation.

The fear in Saudi Arabia is of an Afghan-style "blowback" of returning jihadis. It is similar to the concern of the UK and other western governments which are increasingly pre-occupied by a counter-terrorist agenda as they struggle to contain the effect of wars in Syria and Iraq that have merged into one and allowed Isis to claim that it is on the way to creating an Islamic emirate.

"The Saudis have made many mistakes but I don't think support for Isis has been one of them," said Shashank Joshi, of the Royal United Services Institution. "The kingdom recognizes the severity of the threat that Isis poses, particularly in the last few months. Private donations from Saudi and other Gulf states have probably been directed to Isis and those nations have generally been lax about monitoring those flows. Groups that Saudi Arabia has knowingly supported may have bled equipment, arms and funding to Isis but I don't think Riyadh had any real intention to support Isis as a counterweight to Assad or to Iran. They have been burned by Isis's jihadi forerunners. This is not to exculpate them for their carelessness. Maliki is trying to shift blame from himself and is echoing Iranian propaganda."

The Saudi statement said:"The Kingdom of Saudi Arabia wishes to see the defeat and destruction of all al-Qaida networks and the Islamic State of Iraq and al-Sham (Isis) operating in Iraq. Saudi Arabia does not provide either moral or financial support to Isis or any terrorist networks."

Israel's strategy

Longstanding neocon dreams to partition Iraq into three along ethnic and religious lines have been resurrected. White House officials now estimate that the fight against the region's 'Islamic State' will last years, and may outlive the Obama administration.

But this 'long war' vision goes back to nebulous ideas formally presented by late RAND Corp analyst Laurent Muraweic before the Pentagon's Defense Policy Board at the invitation of then chairman Richard Perle. That presentation described Iraq as a "tactical pivot" by which to transform the wider Middle East.

Brian Whitaker, former Guardian Middle East editor, rightly noted that the Perle-RAND strategy drew inspiration from a 1996 paper published by the Israeli Institute for Advanced Strategic and Political Studies, co-authored by Perle and other neocons who held top positions in the post-9/11 Bush administration.

The policy paper advocated a strategy that bears startling resemblance to the chaos unfolding in the wake of the expansion of the 'Islamic State' – Israel would "shape its strategic environment" by first securing the removal of Saddam Hussein. "Jordan and Turkey would form an axis along with Israel to weaken and 'roll back' Syria." This axis would attempt to weaken the influence of Lebanon, Syria and Iran by "weaning" off their Shi'ite populations. To succeed, Israel would need to engender US support, which would be obtained by Benjamin Netanyahu formulating the strategy "in language familiar to the Americans by tapping into themes of American administrations during the cold war."

The 2002 Perle-RAND plan was active in the Bush administration's strategic thinking on Iraq shortly before the 2003 war. According to US private intelligence firm Stratfor, in late 2002, then vice-president Dick Cheney and deputy defense secretary Paul Wolfowitz had co-authored a scheme under which central Sunni-majority Iraq would join with Jordan; the northern Kurdish regions would become an autonomous state; all becoming separate from the southern Shi'ite region.

The strategic advantages of an Iraq partition, Stratfor argued, focused on US control of oil: The expansion of the 'Islamic State' has provided a pretext for the fundamental contours of this scenario to unfold, with the US and British looking to re-establish a long-term military presence in Iraq in the name of the "defense of a young new state."

In 2006, Cheney's successor, Joe Biden, also indicated his support for the 'soft partition' of Iraq along ethno-religious lines – a position which the co-author of the Biden-Iraq plan, Leslie Gelb of the Council on Foreign Relations, now argues is "the only solution" to the current crisis.

Also in 2006, the Armed Forces Journal published a map of the Middle East with its borders thoroughly re-drawn, courtesy of Lt. Col. (ret.) Ralph Peters, who had previously been assigned to the Office of the Deputy Chief of Staff for Intelligence where he was responsible for future warfare. As for the goals of this plan, apart from "security from terrorism" and "the prospect of democracy", Peters also mentioned "access to oil supplies in a region that is destined to fight itself."

In 2008, the strategy re-surfaced – once again via RAND Corp – through a report funded by the US Army Training and Doctrine Command on how to prosecute the 'long war.' Among its strategies, one scenario advocated by the report was 'Divide and Rule' which would involve:

The Sionist strategy

Almost thirty years ago, a prominent group of neoconservative hawks found an effective vehicle for advocating their views via the Committee on the Present Danger, a group that fervently believed the United States was a hair away from being militarily surpassed by the Soviet Union, and whose raison d'être was strident advocacy of bigger military budgets, near-fanatical opposition to any form of arms control and zealous championing of a Likudnik Israel. Considered a marginal group in its nascent days during the Carter Administration, with the election of Ronald Reagan in 1980 CPD went from the margins to the center of power.

Just as the right-wing defense intellectuals made CPD a cornerstone of a shadow defense establishment during the Carter Administration, so, too, did the right during the Clinton years, in part through two organizations: the Jewish Institute for National Security Affairs (JINSA) and the Center for Security Policy

(CSP). And just as was the case two decades ago, dozens of their members have ascended to powerful government posts, where their advocacy in support of the same agenda continues, abetted by the out-of-government adjuncts from which they came.

Industrious and persistent, they've managed to weave a number of issues—support for national missile defense, opposition to arms control treaties, championing of wasteful weapons systems, arms aid to Turkey and American unilateralism in general--into a hard line, with support for the Israeli right at its core.

On no issue is the JINSA/CSP hard line more evident than in its relentless campaign for war--not just with Iraq, but "total war," as Michael Ledeen, one of the most influential JINSAns in Washington, put it last year. For this crew, "regime change" by any means necessary in Iraq, Iran, Syria, Saudi Arab a and the Palestinian Authority is an urgent imperative. Anyone who dissents--be it Colin Powell's State Department, the CIA or career military officers--is committing heresy against articles of faith that effectively hold there is no difference between US and Israeli national security interests, and that the only way to assure continued safety and prosperity for both countries is through hegemony in the Middle East--a hegemony achieved with the traditional cold war recipe of feints, force, clientism and covert action.

For example, the Pentagon's Defense Policy Board--chaired by JINSA/CSP adviser and former Reagan Administration Defense Department official Richard Perle, and stacked with advisers from both groups--recently made news by listening to a briefing that cast Saudi Arabia as an enemy to be brought to heel through a number of potential mechanisms, many of which mirror JINSA's recommendations, and which reflect the JINSA/CSP crowd's preoccupation with Egypt. (The final slide of the Defense Policy Board presentation proposed that "Grand Strategy for the Middle East" should concentrate on "Iraq as the tactical pivot, Saudi Arabia as the strategic pivot [and] Egypt as the prize.")

Ledeen has been leading the charge for regime change in Iran, while old comrades like Andrew Marshall and Harold Rhode in the Pentagon's Office of Net Assessment actively tinker with ways to re-engineer both the Iranian and Saudi governments. JINSA is also cheering the US military on as it tries to secure basing rights in the strategic Red Sea country of Eritrea, happily failing to mention that the once-promising secular regime of President Isaias

Afewerki continues to slide into the kind of repressive authoritarianism practiced by the "axis of evil" and its adjuncts.

Indeed, there are some in military and intelligence circles who have taken to using "axis of evil" in reference to JINSA and CSP, along with venerable repositories of hawkish thinking like the American Enterprise Institute and the Hudson Institute, as well as defense contractors, conservative foundations and public relations entities underwritten by far-right American Zionists (all of which help to underwrite JINSA and CSP).

It's a milieu where ideology and money seamlessly blend: "Whenever you see someone identified in print or on TV as being with the Center for Security Policy or JINSA championing a position on the grounds of ideology or principle--which they are unquestionably doing with conviction--you are, nonetheless, not informed that they're also providing a sort of cover for other ideologues who just happen to stand to profit from hewing to the Likudnik and Pax Americana lines," says a veteran intelligence officer.

JINSA / CSP

Founded in 1976 by neoconservatives concerned that the United States might not be able to provide Israel with adequate military supplies in the event of another Arab-Israeli war, over the past twenty-five years JINSA has gone from a loose-knit proto-group to a $1.4-million-a-year operation with a formidable array of Washington power players on its rolls.

Until the beginning of the previous Bush Administration, JINSA's board of advisers included such heavy hitters as Dick Cheney, John Bolton and Douglas Feith, the third-highest-ranking executive in the Pentagon during W. Bush administration. Both Perle and former Director of Central Intelligence James Woolsey, two of the loudest voices in the attack-Iraq chorus, are still on the board, as are such Reagan-era relics as Jeane Kirkpatrick, Eugene Rostow and Ledeen--Oliver North's Iran/contra liaison with the Israelis.

According to its website, JINSA exists to "educate the American public about the importance of an effective US defense capability so that our vital interests as Americans can be safeguarded" and to "inform the American defense and foreign affairs community about the important role Israel can and does play in bolstering democratic interests in the Mediterranean and the Middle East." In practice, this translates into its members producing a steady stream of op-eds and reports that have been good indicators of what the Pentagon's civilian leadership is thinking.

JINSA relishes denouncing virtually any type of contact between the US government and Syria and finding new ways to demonize the Palestinians. To give but one example (and one that kills two birds with one stone): According to JINSA, not only is Yasir Arafat in control of all violence in the occupied territories, but he orchestrates the violence solely "to protect Saddam.... Saddam is at the moment Arafat's only real financial supporter.... [Arafat] has no incentive to stop the violence against Israel and allow the West to turn its attention to his mentor and paymaster."

And if there's a way to advance other aspects of the far-right agenda by intertwining them with Israeli interests, JINSA doesn't hesitate there, either. A recent report contends that the Arctic National Wildlife Refuge must be tapped because "the Arab oil-producing states" are countries "with interests inimical to ours," but Israel "stand[s] with us when we need [Israel]," and a US policy of tapping oil under ANWR will "limit [the Arabs'] ability to do damage to either of us."

The bulk of JINSA's modest annual budget is spent on taking a bevy of retired US generals and admirals to Israel, where JINSA facilitates meetings between Israeli officials and the still-influential US flag officers, who, upon their return to the States, happily write op-eds and sign letters and advertisements championing the Likudnik line. (Sowing seeds for the future, JINSA also takes US service academy cadets to Israel each summer and sponsors a lecture series at the Army, Navy and Air Force academies.)

In one such statement, issued soon after the outbreak of the latest intifada, twenty-six JINSAns of retired flag rank, including many from the advisory board, struck a moralizing tone, characterizing Palestinian violence as a "perversion of military ethics" and holding that "America's role as facilitator in this process should never yield to America's responsibility as a friend to Israel," as "friends don't leave friends on the battlefield."

However high-minded this might sound, the post service associations of the letter's signatories--which are almost always left off the organization's website and communiqués--ought to require that the phrase be amended to say "friends don't leave friends on the battlefield, especially when there's business to be done and bucks to be made." Almost every retired officer who sits on

JINSA's board of advisers or has participated in its Israel trips or signed a JINSA letter works or has worked with military contractors who do business with the Pentagon and Israel.

While some keep a low profile as self-employed "consultants" and avoid mention of their clients, others are less shy about their associations, including with the private mercenary firm Military Professional Resources International, weapons broker and military consultancy Cypress International and SY Technology, whose main clients include the Pentagon's Missile Defense Agency, which oversees several ongoing joint projects with Israel.

Military-Industrial Complex

The behemoths of military contracting are also well represented in JINSA's ranks. For example, JINSA advisory board members Adm. Leon Edney, Adm. David Jeremiah and Lieut. Gen. Charles May, all retired, have served Northrop Grumman or its subsidiaries as either consultants or board members. Northrop Grumman has built ships for the Israeli Navy and sold F-16 avionics and E-2C Hawkeye planes to the Israeli Air Force (as well as the Longbow radar system to the Israeli army for use in its attack helicopters).

It also works with Tamam, a subsidiary of Israeli Aircraft Industries, to produce an unmanned aerial vehicle. Lockheed Martin has sold more than $2 billion worth of F-16s to Israel since 1999, as well as flight simulators, multiple-launch rocket systems and Seahawk heavyweight torpedoes. At one time or another, General May, retired Lieut. Gen. Paul Cerjan and retired Adm. Carlisle Trost have labored in LockMart's vineyards. Trost has also sat on the board of General Dynamics, whose Gulfstream subsidiary has a $206 million contract to supply planes to Israel to be used for "special electronics missions."

By far the most profitably diversified of the JINSAns is retired Adm. David Jeremiah. President and partner of Technology Strategies & Alliances Corporation (described as a "strategic advisory firm and investment banking firm engaged primarily in the aerospace, defense, telecommunications and electronics industries"), Jeremiah also sits on the boards of Northrop Grumman's Litton subsidiary and of defense giant Alliant Techsystems, which--in partnership with Israel's TAAS--does a brisk business in rubber bullets. And he had a seat on the Pentagon's Defense Policy Board, chaired by Perle.

About the only major defense contractor without a presence on JINSA's advisory board is Boeing, which has had a relationship with Israeli Aircraft Industries for thirty years. (Boeing also sells F-15s to Israel and, in partnership with Lockheed Martin, Apache attack helicopters, a ubiquitous weapon in the occupied territories.)

But take a look at JINSA's kindred spirit in things pro-Likud and pro-Star Wars, the Center for Security Policy, and there on its national security advisory council are Stanley Ebner, a former Boeing executive; Andrew Ellis, vice president for government relations; and Carl Smith, a former staff director of the Senate Armed Services Committee who, as a lawyer in private practice, has counted Boeing among his clients. "JINSA and CSP," says a veteran Pentagon analyst, "may as well be one and the same."

Not a hard sell: There's always been considerable overlap beween the JINSA and CSP rosters--JINSA advisers Jeane Kirkpatrick, Richard Perle and Phyllis Kaminsky also served on CSP's advisory council; current JINSA advisory board chairman David Steinmann sits on CSP's board of directors; and before returning to the Pentagon Douglas Feith served as the board's chair. At th s writing, twenty-two CSP advisers--including additional Reagan-era remnants like Elliott Abrams, Ken deGraffenreid, Paula Dobriansky, Sven Kraemer, Robert Joseph, Robert Andrews and J.D. Crouch--have reoccupied key positions in the national security establishment, as have other true believers of more recent vintage.

While CSP boasts an impressive advisory list of hawkish luminaries, its star is Frank Gaffney, its founder, president and CEO. A protégé of Perle going back to their days as staffers for the late Senator Henry "Scoop" Jackson (a k a the Senator from Boeing, and the Senate's most zealous champion of Israe in his day), Gaffney later joined Perle at the Pentagon, only to be shown the door by Defense Secretary Frank Carlucci in 1987, not long after Perle left.

Gaffney then reconstituted the latest incarnation of the Committee on the Present Danger. Beyond compiling an A-list of influential conservative hawks, Gaffney has been prolific over the past fifteen years, churning out a constant stream of reports (as well as regular columns for the Washington Times) making the case that the gravest threats to US national security are China, Iraq, still-undeveloped ballistic missiles launched by rogue states, and the passage of or adherence to virtually any form of arms control treaty.

Gaffney and CSP's prescriptions for national security have been fairly simple: Gut all arms control treaties, push ahead with weapons systems virtually everyone agrees should be killed (such as the V-22 Osprey), give no quarter to the Palestinians and, most important, go full steam ahead on just about every national missile defense program. (CSP was heavily represented on the late-1990s Commission to Assess the Ballistic Missile Threat to the United States, which was instrumental in keeping the program alive during the Clinton years.)

Looking at the center's affiliates, it's not hard to see why: Not only are makers of the Osprey (Boeing) well represented on the CSP's board of advisers but so too is Lockheed Martin (by vice president for space and strategic missiles Charles Kupperman and director of defense systems Douglas Graham). Former TRW executive Amoretta Hoeber is also a CSP adviser, as is former Congressman and Raytheon lobbyist Robert Livingston. Ball Aerospace & Technologies--a major manufacturer of NASA and Pentagon satellites--is represented by former Navy Secretary John Lehman, while missile-defense computer systems maker Hewlett-Packard is represented by George Keyworth, who is on its board of directors. And the Congressional Missile Defense Caucus and Osprey (or "tilt rotor") caucus are represented by Representative Curt Weldon and Senator Jon Kyl.

CSP was instrumental in developing the arguments against the Anti-Ballistic Missile Treaty. Largely ignored or derided at the time, a 1995 CSP memo co-written by Douglas Feith holding that the United States should withdraw from the ABM treaty has essentially become policy, as have other CSP reports opposing the Comprehensive Test Ban Treaty, the Chemical Weapons Convention and the International Criminal Court.

A Clean Break

But perhaps the most insightful window on the JINSA/CSP policy worldview comes in the form of a paper Perle and Feith collaborated on in 1996 with six others under the auspices of the Institute for Advanced Strategic and Political Studies. Essentially an advice letter to ascendant Israeli politician Benjamin Netanyahu, "A Clean Break: A New Strategy for Securing the Realm" makes for insightful reading as a kind of US-Israeli neoconservative manifesto.

The paper's first prescription was for an Israeli rightward economic shift, with tax cuts and a selloff of public lands and enterprises--moves that would also engender support from a "broad bipartisan spectrum of key pro-Israeli

Congressional leaders." But beyond economics, the paper essentially reads like a blueprint for a mini-cold war in the Middle East, advocating the use of proxy armies for regime changes, destabilization and containment.

Indeed, it even goes so far as to articulate a way to advance right-wing Zionism by melding it with missile-defense advocacy. "Mr. Netanyahu can highlight his desire to cooperate more closely with the United States on anti-missile defense in order to remove the threat of blackmail which even a weak and distant army can pose to either state," it reads. "Not only would such cooperation on missile defense counter a tangible physical threat to Israel's survival, but it would broaden Israel's base of support among many in the United States Congress who may know little about Israel, but care very much about missile defense"-- something that has the added benefit of being "helpful in the effort to move the US embassy in Israel to Jerusalem."

Though the general agenda put forth by JINSA and CSP continues to be reflected in councils of war, even some of the hawks (including Rumsfeld deputy Paul Wolfowitz) are growing increasingly leery of Israel's settlements policy and Gaffney's relentless support for it. Indeed, his personal stock in Bush Administration circles is low. "Gaffney has worn out his welcome by being an overbearing gadfly rather than a serious contributor to policy," says a senior Pentagon political official. Since earlier this year, White House political adviser Karl Rove has been casting about for someone to start a new, more mainstream defense group that would counter the influence of CSP.

According to those who have communicated with Rove on the matter, his quiet efforts are in response to complaints from many conservative activists who feel let down by Gaffney, or feel he's too hard on President Bush. "A lot of us have taken [Gaffney] at face value over the years," one influential conservative says. "Yet we now know he's pushed for some of the most flawed missile defense and conventional systems. He considered Cuba a 'classic asymmetric threat' but not Al Qaeda. And since 9/11, he's been less concerned with the threat to America than to Israel."

ISIS and Israel

Why is IS – formerly known as the Islamic State in Iraq and Syria (ISIS) – not fighting Israel? Would anything change if its fighters were to gain access to the borders with occupied Palestine?

While the Israeli military machine was massacring people in Gaza – and amid the euphoria among some jihadis over the news of the announcement of an "Islamic caliphate" – video footage of masked individuals firing rockets into Israel was posted online, and attributed to IS. Many cheered for what they saw as the "Muslim caliph's" response to calls for succor from the people of Gaza, even believing the "caliphate" was very close to liberating Jerusalem. But the euphoria did not last very long.

The video turned out to be from an old footage dating back to 2012, recorded by the militant group known as the Mujahideen Shura Council, and was repurposed to be attributed to IS. IS-affiliated social media activists such as Turujman al-Asawirti were also quick to question the authenticity of the video attributed to their group.

Al-Akhbar had a number of questions for IS supporters from Lebanon, Syria, and Iraq, including the following: Why has IS maintained its distance from the events in Palestine? Are the people of Gaza not Muslims after all? Does this posture not reinforce the premise that there is a hidden link between Zionism and Salafi-Jihadism that appeases Israel, or is geography alone to blame for their inaction?

In a speech by IS leader Abu Bakr al-Baghdadi, after he installed himself as caliph of the Muslims, he spoke about the terror inflicted on Palestine, but he did so only in passing, in the wider context of the terror Muslims face around the world.

In substance, they believe that liberating Palestine is irrelevant without the establishment of the caliphate in the countries surrounding Palestine first. Before him, in the time of the late leader of al-Qaeda Osama bin Laden, the jihadi attitude on Palestine was also controversial. Why have the jihadis never declared Palestine an arena for their jihad?

In effect, the leader of global jihadism Sheikh Ayman al-Zawahiri had an interesting position, approaching the issue from the angle of priorities on the basis of "Dar al-Kufr and Dar al-Islam," or the abode of disbelief and the abode of belief in jihadi lore. Zawahiri argues that fighting in Palestine should be on the basis that it is an abode of Islam, and that therefore, liberating it is a duty for every Muslim, as stated in his speech "truths about the conflict between Islam and infidelity" in 2007. But despite this, Palestine remains at the bottom of the list of priorities for most jihadis.

In form, most adherents of Salafi-Jihadism believe that "Shias are more dangerous than Jews." In substance, they believe that liberating Palestine is irrelevant without the establishment of the caliphate in the countries surrounding Palestine first.

Sources linked to IS told Al-Akhbar, "The final war that will liberate Palestine will be led by the caliphate, preceded by the establishment of this state in the Levant and Iraq," on the basis of sayings they attribute to Prophet Mohammad. The sources add, "Allah alone knows just how much the soldiers of the caliphate yearn for skipping the necessary stages and battle the Jews in Palestine, but he who rushes something before its time comes shall be punished by being denied it."

The sources, who are based in the Raqqa province of Syria, enumerate these necessary stages, saying, "The priority is to liberate Baghdad, then head to Damascus and liberate all of the Levant, before liberating Palestine."

This is the principle that IS soldiers follow: "Fighting nearby apostates is more important than fighting faraway infidels." To justify this, they rely on the Wars of Apostasy initiated by the Caliph Abu Bakr (against Muslims who renounced their religion following the death of the Prophet), who made it a priority over fighting infidels and Muslim conquests.

According to IS fighters, the adherents of all Islamic sects who do not submit to their "caliph" are either "apostates or misguided folk, who should be fought and killed, forced to repent and let themselves be guided, or be liberated from apostate rule." A jihadi adds here, "We the followers of this path follow sharia not the whims of men," adding that the Prophet had fought Quraysh first before moving on to fight the Jews of Banu Qurayza.

These sharia-based arguments are "reinforced" by the reality on the ground. A jihadi argues, "No one can initiate a battle against Israel except through the [direct] borders." The jihadi then adds sarcastically, "Certainly, the mujahideen will not be able to bomb Israel by air," before he said, "IS is still far from Israel. If it reaches Jordan and southern Syria (the Golan and Quneitra), then things would be different."

The jihadis base their vision on their perception that "Syria, Lebanon, Egypt, and Jordan all collaborate with Israel," and argue that any attack they initiate would be stopped by what they call the "idolatry" regimes in the name of security. A jihadi opines, "Since the countries adjacent to Israel do not fire a single bullet at it, this means they do not want a confrontation with Israel. Any attempt to use their territories to target Israel means automatically a confrontation with these regimes. Therefore, we must first purge these countries to get to Israel."

The IS-affiliated jihadis conclude that "the enmity the Arab countries and Arab groups have with Israel are in words not deeds, that is, only in politics and slogans. As long as this is the case, any group that wants to operate will confront these regimes." As proof of their point, the jihadis give the example of the Abdullah Azzam Brigades' operations out of South Lebanon, and the subsequent crackdown on the group's members after they fired rockets into Israel. For this reason, these jihadis believe that the priority is for their "state" to expand gradually, and that everything else is meaningless and illogical.

With regards to suicide operations, the jihadis said, "This is on the table, but the time for it has not yet come."

ISIS Propaganda

A common misconception about Islamic State propaganda is that it starts and finishes with brutality. However, whether it is a video depicting the execution of a group of men by firing squad in the desert, a mass beheading, or both, ultraviolence is merely part of the bigger picture.

Brutality is just one of six broad themes that Islamic Sate uses to bolster its presence and further its strategic goals; the other five are mercy, victimhood, war, belonging and utopianism. Similar to the mechanisms by which they are conveyed, these themes are not discrete. Indeed, they are regularly employed together.

One cannot deny the pride of place that brutality enjoys in Islamic State's messaging; all of IS committed ideological supporters derive satisfaction from it. After all, it supports a key aspect of its propaganda, triumphalism. Every time an execution is carried out, documented and publicized, it serves as a reminder of the group's self-proclaimed supremacy and its ability to exact revenge on behalf of Sunni Muslims against the Crusader-Shi'ite-Zionist conspiracy allegedly mounted against them. Islamic State's most brutal propaganda serves as a vehicle by which to convey both vengeance and supremacy.

As touched upon above, this content is not just aimed at declared supporters. In fact, they are not even the primary target audience. Rather, this material is intended for Islamic State's active or potential opponents. Exactly which usually depends on the unit responsible for its production and on who is being executed.

For instance, the November 2014 video that documented the execution of three members of Bashar al-Assad's Syrian Arab Army had a very different audience to the one in which Japanese journalist Kenji Goto was killed. Both videos were brutal and shocking, but for obvious reasons, only one – the latter – had international traction. When Islamic State depicts the gruesome execution of men that it alleges are 'spies', it is seeking to warn potential local dissenters of the unwavering ruthlessness with which they will be dealt.

Whatever the case, weaving brutality into the fabric of Islamic State's messaging has four motivations. Beyond the simple gratification of supporters, it seeks to intimidate enemies, warn local populations of the punishments associated with espionage or dissent, provoke outrage from the international media and cause knee-jerk responses from hostile policymakers. Often, all four Motivations are sought – and achieved – in the same release.

The mercy narrative is regularly featured in tandem with brutality. It is closely connected to the idea of repentance, before God and the Islamic State itself. A particularly striking example of this may be found in an April 2015 video entitled "From the Darkness to the Light", in which fighters from Jabhat al-Nuṣra, the Free Syrian Army and the Syrian Arab Army – all of whom are said to be former sworn enemies of Islamic State and each other – are shown reneging on their former beliefs and joining Islamic State together. Islamic State regularly circulates content like this, where people are seen responding to its istitāba (appeals for repentance). Upon repenting, footage like this invariably shows individuals being received into the embraces of the jihadists.

The message is clear: Islamic State will forgive one's past affiliation, provided it is wholly rejected and obedience to the 'caliphate' is guaranteed. If these conditions are met, an individual may become 'one of the gang'.

This 'mercy' does not just extend to fighters, but also to civilians and former government employees. For example, in the run up to the first caliphate 'school year', primary and secondary school teachers in Syria were reportedly shown to be repenting en masse, after which they were re-inserted into the education system. There has even been a thirty minute documentary-style video on the topic. In aggregate, the mercy narrative has an almost symbiotic relationship with that of brutality. The two ideas are regularly entwined, presenting as they do the populations under attack from Islamic State with a stark choice: resist, and be killed, or willingly submit, recant past beliefs and be rewarded with mercy.

Victimhood

The next narrative, a recurrent theme shared in the propaganda of all jihadist groups, is that of Sunni Muslims' victimization at the hands of a perceived global war on Islam. Like that of mercy, the idea of victimhood is regularly used in tandem with brutality. One of the clearest examples of this came in the al-Furqān Foundation's "Healing of the Believers' Chests", in which

Jordanian pilot Muadh al-Kasasbeh is burned alive before rubble is bulldozed over his body. Here, the binary opposites of victimhood and retributive violence are strikingly manipulated.

Seconds before the sequence that depicted Mr. al-Kasasbeh's final moments, footage of the aftermath of coalition airstrikes was cut in, showing images of dead or dying children. This was done for two reasons: firstly, to remind the observer of the justification for the "resistance" narrative in the Islamic State war and, secondly, to drive home the theological basis from which this means of execution was derived, namely mumāthila, or retaliation in kind. A similar juxtaposition of violence and victimhood was also used in a November 2014 video in which twenty-two members of the SAA were simultaneously beheaded in Syria.

A June 2015 video from Islamic State's Nineveh Province provides another good example of this. It opens with the depiction of a fighter handling a child's disembodied arm at an unnamed bombsite. Shortly after, three groups of alleged 'spies' are burned alive in a car hit by a rocket propelled grenade, drowned in a steel cage and beheaded with explosives.

The depiction of the child's corpse at the beginning of the video is intended to drive home the victimization of Iraq's Sunnis as well as justify what followed. Evidently, the brutality narrative was also tapped into here and exploited most successfully. Locally, the video sought to intimidate Sunnis considering leaving or fighting against Islamic State; internationally, it was intended to be transmitted by Western media outlets and conveyed to disengaged, hostile publics. To be sure, the propagandists achieved their objectives – some media outlets published still images of the 'spies' in the process of being executed, which were shared tens of thousands of times in a matter of hours.

It is worth noting that Islamic State's propagandists regularly eschew this juxtaposition altogether, choosing to focus solely on the aftermath, for example, of coalition air-raids on what they claim are civilian targets. Whatever the case, collateral damage is the Islamic State propagandist's friend; dead babies and maimed children are instrumentalised, routinely integrated into a catalogue of crimes that have been perpetrated by the 'enemy'.

This is no surprise. Since President Obama's decision to engage in military airstrikes against Islamic State in August 2014, its decision to manipulate the victimhood narrative to play on the hearts of its audience was inevitable.

War

Islamic State's war machine is a fourth, very prominent, part of the brand. Its propagandists routinely zoom in on the IS military gains, with regular depictions of training camps, parades featuring artillery guns, tanks and armored vehicles, as well as martyrdom operations through photographs and videos. They also circulate footage of frontline fighting, delivered almost in real time by the roving "war reporters" of IS' A'māq News Agency.

Besides this, there is a particular preoccupation with "booty" – the looting of enemies' weapons and munitions – something that plays well into the propagandists' intention to portray both its momentum and supremacy. All of the above, combined with the uniforms, the discipline and the choreography, are intended to feed into the idea that Islamic State is a real 'state' with a real army, hence contributing to its utopia-building narrative.

Although ostensibly aimed at instilling fear in hostile forces and raising fighters' morale, this content also serves a tactical purpose. As well as presenting supporters and sympathizers with a skewed understanding of its successes, its proliferation enables IS to obfuscate on-ground realities by disseminating disinformation to its enemies. After all, though it likes to give the impression of doing so, Islamic State does not publicize the whole of its war. On occasion, its propagandists intensively document fighting on one front while a media blackout is imposed on another.

In a conflict where human intelligence is scarce, intelligence that can be gathered online from open sources has never been more tempting as a resource. Taking this into account, it seeks to curate the information available by cultivating a monopoly on battlefield reporting. Its Ramadi offensive in the spring of 2015 was a paradigmatic example of this.

In the early weeks of the offensive, visual evidence that it was taking place was almost totally non-existent. Concurrently, Islamic State propagandists saturated the airwaves with photographs and videos from a separate assault on Bayji oil refinery, which drew observers' attention in the wrong direction. Hence, when it came in May 2015, the final assault on the Anbar capital was, in their own words, a surprise to many of those directly involved.

Belonging

Closely connected to, but distinct from, the above four themes is that of belonging. This idea is one of Islamic State's most powerful draws to new recruits, particularly those from Western states. Through their regular publication of, for example, videos and photographic reports depicting istirāḥat al-mujāhidīn – fighters relaxing with tea and singing with each other – the propagandists emphasize the idea of brotherhood in the 'caliphate'.

The carefully branded camaraderie that one is absorbed into upon arrival in Islamic State-held territories is, as the propagandists would have their audiences believe, almost overwhelming. In most of the foreign-language videos to emerge from the al-Ḥayāt Media Centre, for example, 'brothers' from around the world are filmed with each other in parks having a good time, their faces a picture of serenity.

It is not difficult to recognize why this narrative is exploited; if Islamic State is to continue replenishing its ranks, it needs to target foreign recruits. Understanding radicalization better than most, its propagandists recognize that offers of friendship, security and a sense of belonging are powerful draws for its supporters abroad. The same ideas are also manipulated to draw in recruits from closer to home. For example, in "On the Prophetic Methodology", the al-Furqān Foundation's propagandists insert clips of fresh recruits rapturously embracing their new brethren shortly after pledging allegiance to al-Baghdadi.

Islamic State turbo-charges the concept of the Umma and takes it beyond al-Qaeda's elite vanguard narrative. In so doing, it democratizes the ability to engage with the struggle, makes it a 'do-it-yourself' jihad. Along with the aforementioned thematic elements, this powerful idea of belonging is incorporated into the final component of the Islamic State brand, discussed below.

Utopianism

The final narrative that Islamic State propagandists exploit is that of apocalyptic utopianism, which is arguably the broadest and most important theme. Indeed, all of the above narratives support it cumulatively. Fertilized by new content several times a day, the idea of the utopia-'caliphate' runs strongly throughout all the IS messaging.

Its constant presence makes sense: Islamic State's establishment and implementation of the 'caliphate' is the IS unique selling point. Constantly reminding the world – particularly rival jihadist groups and potential recruits – of this is imperative. The more 'evidence' that is made available, the more resilient Islamic State becomes to assertions that it is illegitimate.

The desire to promote its 'state'-hood is something that has led to the appearance of the bizarre: from fishing trips and da'wa caravans to sheep cleaning and road-building. While this content may seem, at first sight, benign, its presence is critical. It is IS way of keeping up appearances. Along with its labelling of its 'Ministries', 'Departments' and 'Offices',

Islamic State is forever seeking to provide evidence that it is not just talking about the 'caliphate', but that it is enacting it, too: teaching children to recite the Quran by rote, establishing sharī'a courts, implementing ḥudūd punishments and collecting and dispensing zakāt. Its corner of the Internet is replete with such material, all motivated by the need to reinforce the implementation narrative.

Of course, much of this content is multipurpose. Taking its daily circulations of images depicting ḥudūd punishments as a case in point, it is clear that each target audience is affected very differently. To locals, it aims to demonstrate that, despite the fact that it is being attacked from all sides, Islamic State can provide security and stability.

The ruthlessness and efficiency with which crime is punished can be an appealing idea in the context of rampant warlordism and lawlessness. For potential opponents, this imagery serves as a warning. For ideological supporters and active members, such images provide legitimization and gratification on a most basic level.

For potential recruits, it is simply part of the 'evidence' that is used to convince them that Islamic State is legitimate. Finally, for non-jihadists – potential enemies, involved opponents and international publics – these punishments are worked into the brutality narrative outlined above, evincing as they do a rejection of international norms and the resolute defiance with which Islamic State is pursuing its 'caliphate' project.

By declaring the re-establishment of the 'caliphate' when it did, Islamic State seized the extremist Islamist initiative. It asserted itself above all other jihadist groups as the utopia that they all aspired to create. As such, its propagandists need to keep the idea afloat and, seeking to amplify it, further capitalize upon the strand of Islamic eschatology that is central to so much of the IS official rhetoric.

Routinely, the nearing apocalypse is emphasized to increase the sense of urgency. The idea is that, with the rise of Islamic State, the Day of Judgment looms ever nearer; the 'caliphate' has been established and, as of August 8 2014, the 'Crusaders' are being confronted head on. The message is simple: join now or face an eternity in Hell.

Eschatological allusions are not a novel introduction to jihadist propaganda. However, the amount that Islamic State media emphasizes this idea is new. In every high-profile address from the leadership, the looming nature of the end of the world is emphasized, and every time a new issue of Dabiq surfaces, its pages are replete with references to Armageddon. The emphasis on eschatology lends urgency to the IS narrative and incentivizes other jihadists – individuals or groups – to join IS.

In the year that followed the Caliphate declaration, some responded to this call, incorporating themselves as new 'provinces', at least in terms of their messaging, into the 'caliphate'.

At every opportunity, these assimilations are celebrated; whenever a new bay'a (oath of allegiance) to Abu Bakr al-Baghdadi is announced on Islamic State social media, it is projected far and wide as evidence of IS divinely ordained success. Then, in the weeks that follow, countless provincial videos emerge showing the happy reactions of the civilian population. This is geared towards maintaining a sense of momentum. After all, the perception of continually growing power is not just symbolically important, it spawns real authority.

Islamic State has eschewed many of the traditional resistance-based aspects of its rivals' narratives, opting instead for "the propaganda of winners" and, through the synthesis of the above six themes, it is able to incite with unparalleled efficacy. It leverages urgency and religio-political legitimacy with one another such that the imperative to act – whether the 'act' in question is joining, disseminating propaganda, or carrying out an attack – is as pressing as possible.

Combined with the easy accessibility it has cultivated between its fighters and curious onlookers, this cocktail of reimagined, reinvigorated jihadist narratives has been of untold assistance to it as it has worked to maintain the perception of momentum and legitimacy. The manner in which its supporters, committed and otherwise, interpret the group is critical to its success – a well-defined, carefully refined image allows Islamic State to differentiate its product from that of rival groups like al-Qaeda and cause a sort of jihadist 'brain-drain'. Competition for resources among jihadist groups is fierce; recruits and donors are scarce indeed. Hence, perception is central to longevity.

Abu Bakr Naji

In jihadist strategist Abu Bakr Naji's 2004 book, The Management of Savagery, a text said to be one of the "most prominent" influences upon Islamic State's ideology and practices, he speaks extensively about the superpower's manipulation of a "deceptive media halo", a carefully managed media image that creates a feeling of invincibility, a feeling that "it is an all-encompassing, overwhelming power and [that] people are subservient to it not only through fear, but also through love because it spreads freedom, justice, equality among humanity, and various other slogans".

In a sense, Islamic State has mimicked what Naji claims is one of the key sources of the 'Crusaders'' success. At an accelerating rate over the last year, it has systematically set about creating an absorbing, comprehensive and easily accessible image of itself, one that saturates the Internet and, by its very prevalence, is the lifeblood of its momentum narrative.

As has been shown above, it is only through a holistic assessment of IS media activities that one can begin to garner an understanding of just how important propaganda is to the success of IS. It is evident – and perhaps unsurprising – that Islamic State has drawn from the propaganda rulebook of totalitarianism; its strategists rightly deem that a good image not only brings symbolic influence, but tangible power too. By creating content intended for consumption by a wide range of mass audiences, all meticulously branded with caliphate motifs, IS is able to consolidate appeal and cement its menace.

To non-jihadist audiences, Islamic State's propaganda has extraordinary salience, something that comes as a direct result of its manipulation of the media. Terrorist groups have long recognized that the mainstream media can assist them in their political ambitions. Regardless of the ideological inclination of the group in question, this is not new; it has persistently presented a conundrum to journalists for decades.

In the wake of an interview with Palestine Liberation Front terrorist Abu Abbas during the hijacking of the Achille Lauro cruise ship, it was "stressed that since liberal governments agree that a new mode of terrorism has emerged which depends on media exposure, there may be times when the public good is best served by deliberate 'non-exposure' by the press". Despite the sense behind this statement, even at the time it was unrealistic.

In the age of the 24 hour news cycle and social media, 'non-exposure' is not just unrealistic, but wholly unachievable. Islamic State's propagandists have recognized this vulnerability and continually exploit it. In doing so, they are able to ensure the continual perpetuation of their organization's relevance and menace. As a result of this, it is now undeniable that – rightly or wrongly – Islamic State has supplanted al-Qaeda as the world's most feared jihadist group, even if its longevity may be more questionable.

To members, sympathizers and potential recruits, the organization's propaganda has enabled it to assemble a multi-layered, nuanced brand that not only promises military escapades, but utopian adventure as well. Through the audio, video and photographic content that is circulated constantly, its propagandists paint a picture of jihad that no other group has come close to.

Because of it, joining the 'caliphate' is not simply an exploit for those wanting to shoot a gun – recruitment to the Islamic State cause is sold as a means of participating in God's project on Earth. There is a frontier-like allure to it, as uncommitted supporters are convinced to migrate and engage by the promise of being a 'founding father or mother' of this utopia. To one who does not relate to the Islamist caliphate project, such an idea is alien.

However, to those few extremists who both believe in the 'caliphate' idea and see Islamic State's violent means as justified, the vast quantity of 'evidence' that it produces to back up its claims is intensely alluring.

Beyond opponents, engaged and otherwise, and active supporters, Islamic State's propagandists tirelessly work to keep their disseminator and proselytizer audiences interested. Without he commitment of this self-appointed tier of propaganda peddlers, IS would have a far smaller reach.

Although IS is not unique in this, the sheer volume and quality of content that it produces has augmented a situation in which its disseminator and proselytizer supporters are more numerous, more aggressive and more viral than those of other groups.

In particular, their viral nature is crucial. On the Internet, no content, let alone terrorist propaganda, is viral in a vacuum – it requires committed 'fans', a body of consumers who derive satisfaction from transmission and promotion. Building on this premise, Islamic State has facilitated and encouraged the emergence of a tier of supporters who are obsessive in their live archiving of everything caliphal. The persistence and commitment of these individuals inflates their numbers and projects their voices. It thus follows that an understanding of how they operate, something that is currently lacking, is key to determining how to respond to the Islamic State propaganda machine.

As has been discussed in this report, much of the recruitment process can now be conducted over the Internet, an arena that has emerged as the modern-day jihadists' 'radical mosque', the place for already-radicalized potential recruits to receive first-hand accounts of violent jihad and advice on how to join in.

Couched in anonymity, supporters, sympathizers and the curious can have direct, interactive access with the battlefield without running the risk of being identified by the security services on their way in or out of extremist meetings, as was so often the case in the 1990s and 2000s.

Recognizing this, Islamic State shifted its messaging efforts from password-protected fora to open source social media. The regularity and consistent quality of its propaganda's transmission, coupled with the challenges presented by governments' attempts to censor it, has spawned a new class of jihadist sympathizers who are keen to express their rejection of the status quo but are all too conscious of the risks attached to doing so physically and so find solace and satisfaction in consumption and dissemination.

By no means is Islamic State the first jihadist group to produce high quality and widely disseminated propaganda. That its propagandists expend a great amount of energy catering to a range of audiences by manipulating varied narratives is not new either.

However, the complexity and efficiency of its media strategy, something that could only be a product of its time, is totally unprecedented. In any analysis of

IS, it is imperative that this is understood. It is a mistaken approach to try to interpret the group through the same lens used to comprehend al-Qaeda and its affiliates; likewise, countering it cannot be done using the same mind-set and tools developed to counter past jihadist threats. This extends to its messaging strategy, too.

Islamic State, capitalizing upon this in a wholly unprecedented manner, has succeeded in formulating and fortifying a branding exercise of almost epic proportions. Moving forward, it might be worth taking a leaf out of Islamic State's own strategy book. Of course, that does not mean boasting about executions and misogyny but, for example, it would help if the coalition were to recognize, as Islamic State does, that it is always broadcasting to different audiences – among them, members, sympathizers, enemies and publics. Different narratives appeal to different people, so it follows that some scaling up is required.

Al Maqdisi

It is news to few observers that thousands, even millions, of young Muslims are influenced—to some extent—by jihadi literature circulating on various Islamist websites and discussion forums. The mujahideen's use of the internet for communication, indoctrination, recruitment and public relations has been well demonstrated. Through this medium, a field of preachers and ideologues compete for the vast audience of young Muslims, attempting to sway their opinion and bring them to the "correct" practice and understanding of Islam. Those backing the global jihadi movement have succeeded in capturing this audience—perhaps more so than other contenders—and have gained a wide following of careful but loyal readers.

The literature is critical because it provides deeper motivation to the believer, who seeks ideological backing before taking action. A group of Muslim scholars—Abu Muhammad al-Maqdisi, Abu Basir al-Tartusi, Abu Qatada al-Filistini, 'Abd al-Qadir bin 'Abd al-'Aziz and a few other Saudi clerics—are the primary Salafi opinion-makers guiding the jihadi movement. These scholars are relied upon for their credibility since they have either been imprisoned or exiled by their home countries. They are also perceived as being true to Islam and putting the interests of Muslims before themselves, making them sincere, legitimate and incorruptible. For the mujahideen, they are portrayed as scholarly authorities and the source for doctrinal legitimacy.

Surprisingly, al-Qaeda leaders Osama bin Laden and Ayman al-Zawahiri are not highly cited in jihadi literature. They are not considered authorities in Islamic law or looked to as the ideological force behind the jihadi movement. Indeed, in the world of Salafi-Jihadi ideology, they are relatively minor players. One possible reason for this is that the two are figureheads, pioneers in carrying out successful attacks against one of the enemies of Muslims. This suggests that there is a role for charismatic leaders to bring Muslims to jihad, as soldiers to the battlefield, but there is a separate role for these Salafi scholars in setting the broader goals for the movement, the limits and terms of engagement and selecting valid and legal targets. They are, in essence, creating the Islamic legal framework for this struggle so that the basis upon which it is waged will be sound. It is then left to strategists and mujahid leaders to conduct successful campaigns within this framework.

There is no single governing body for determining Islamic law in the Muslim world. Movements tend to center around persuasive and influential scholars that can grant them legitimacy in the eyes of other Muslims. This has been the case for the Salafi movement, including militant Salafis who form the global jihadi movement. Although the mujahideen are not held accountable to their constituency, they understand the need for their fellow Muslims to support their actions, provide them with funding and safe haven and ultimately be able to mobilize them when needed. Accordingly, the advice and writings of Salafi scholars carry much weight with the mujahideen and Muslim readers— regardless of their affiliation.

For the most influential scholars of the Salafi movement, such as Abu Muhammad al-Maqdisi, Abu Qatada and Abu Basir, the end goal is never jihad itself. The objective is to bring Muslims to a Salafi reading of Islam and then to deliver salvation to the global Muslim community. As such, the primary element of the literature is the meaning and implementation of the Sharia. The scholars first bring their interpretation of Islamic law on various political and social issues and present their advice on the appropriate action. The common ground among the scholars behind the jihadi movement is their rejection of Muslims living under apostate laws and political systems governing outside what God has decreed. The required response—for all, but to differing degrees and with differing tactics—is resistance.

This drive to instill Islamic law into Muslim society, and ultimately recreate that society under their interpretation of the law, often translates into an endorsement for violent jihad as practiced by bin Laden and others. While there are many Muslim scholars who call for these sources of law to be the primary factors in how Muslims live, the important distinction lies in how one should confront political systems that rule by law other than Sharia. The debate over law and society is critical in jihadi literature. It establishes the framework through which young Muslims should struggle; for these scholars, it is clear their aim is not jihad, but the creation of such a society through jihad, an obligatory struggle for the believer.

Biography

Asim Tahir al-Barqawi, better known as Abu Muhammad al-Maqdisi, is one of the most prolific contemporary jihadi ideologues and a classically trained scholar. He was born in Nablus in 1959, but has been imprisoned intermittently since the 1990s by the Jordanian authorities for his criticism of the government and calls for jihad. Al-Maqdisi is regarded as one of the highest living authorities in Islam for Salafis, jihadis and other conservative Sunni Muslims who share elements of his program. His imprisonment, however, seems to have had little effect on his scholarly output. He was the most frequently cited living Salafi scholar, indicating the wide range of jihadis (from strategists to mujahideen to fellow scholars) that cite his writings.

Al-Maqdisi is well traveled; he moved to Kuwait as a child and later undertook studies in the University of Mosul in Iraq. After that al-Maqdisi traveled through Saudi Arabia, Pakistan and Afghanistan, where he met various jihadi groups and wrote some of his most famous books, such as Millat 'Ibrahim wa da'awet al-anbiya wa'l murseleen (The Creed of Abraham and the Preaching of the Prophets and the Deliverers) and Al-kawashif al-jaliyya fi kufr al-dawla al-Sa`udiyya (The Shameful Actions Manifest in the Saudi State's Disbelief).

In 1992 al-Maqdisi returned to Jordan and started to preach his ideology, which quickly spread among some youngsters. The shaykh criticized Jordanian officials, denouncing their rule as illegitimate and opposed to the Shari`a. A combination of direct rhetoric and well-circulated stories of how he confronted the judges and his interrogators by calling them tyrants and disbelievers, soon established al-Maqdisi as a charismatic ideologue and leader of Salafi-Jiahdism.

Al-Maqdisi's texts are frequently aimed at the youth in Jordanian prisons and similar Muslims around the world that are encouraged to hold steadfast to the path of jihad in accordance with the principles of Islamic law detailed in his texts. To be sure, the legal arguments are lost on many of his students who lack formal Islamic legal training, but he provides contemporary examples to buttress his points.

Many of his texts are in response to criticisms of jihad by other Salafi clerics, typically from the Gulf states or Saudi Arabia. Other writings include the education of the next generation of leaders, numerous issues relating to resistance to tyrannical regimes and the need to uphold the Sharia and one of his most-widely read works, the Creed of Abraham, on monotheistic faiths (which is highly critical of contemporary Christians and Jews).

Through his writings, al-Maqdisi sets out the "correct" agenda for the various mujahideen groups to follow, what their intentions and objectives should be as they enter jihad, what preparation is required and what they should avoid (such as hasty actions that make the mujahideen look inept, inexperienced, or indifferent to killing innocent Muslims). There are more nuanced discussions of espionage, defining apostasy, takfir (labeling another Muslim an unbeliever), different examples of interaction with tyrannical rule and explanations of when resistance is obligatory for the believer. Yet, in the end, a clear direction is set out for the mujahideen and those who support their cause on how best to proceed.

Al-Maqdisi's calls for unity are respected because of the scholarly weight behind his name and reputation. This also exposes one of the movement's weaknesses, and the shortcomings of governments confronting jihadi ideologues: a blow to his standing or a publicly lost debate would likely do much more to damage the unity of the jihadi movement than would his imprisonment.

On March 12, 2008 Abu Muhammad al-Maqdisi—born Isam Muhammad Tahir al-Barqawi in 1959—was released from a Jordanian prison after almost three years imprisonment without trial. Maqdisi has long played a pivotal role in defining jihadist ideology. After taking part in the Afghan jihad of the 1980s, he refined the ideology of declaring takfir against other Muslims—i.e. defining them as apostates and thus deserving of death—leading to the creation of jihadist groups in Jordan and 1995 attacks in Saudi Arabia—whose government he had denounced as un-Islamic as early as 1989. Between 1995 and 1999, Maqdisi was imprisoned in Jordan, during which time he expanded his ideas and built new radical networks with the help of his right-hand man, Abu Musab al-Zarqawi.

From 1999, Maqdisi has spent most of his time in Jordanian prisons, reemerging briefly in 2005 before being re-imprisoned for giving an interview to al-Jazeera television in which he criticized Zarqawi's attacks on civilians while reiterating his support for a broader jihad against the West and "un-Islamic" governments. Despite his long prison terms, however, Maqdisi has written and distributed several accessible books addressing key issues such as democracy, takfir and jihadist tactics, giving him an almost unmatched influence over the evolution of jihadist theory.

Maqdisi's Influence

Maqdisi's latest release from prison—apparently on grounds of ill-health—was reported extensively on radical Islamic websites. Significantly, even Islamic extremists outside the Arab world reacted euphorically to the news of his release. For example, a senior member of the islamicawakening.com forum, a prominent English-language Salafi website, responded to news of his release by writing: "AllahuAkbar! AllahuAkbar! Nothing describes the happiness of the mu'mineen [faithful] all around the world this day. AllahuAkbar! Our beloved Shaykh is released!" Similarly, on islambase.co.uk, the online home of many British extremists, one member described his release as "the best news in ages." Their attitude suggests that despite the death of Zarqawi and his own long imprisonment, Maqdisi's teachings—a mixture of bigotry and pragmatism—are still seen as relevant. Indeed, Maqdisi's correct predictions in 2004 and 2005 that Zarqawi's attacks on Muslim civilians would undermine support for al-Qaeda both in Iraq and abroad may have further boosted his standing among Islamic extremists worldwide. In light of Maqdisi's influence and popularity it is worth examining his key ideas in detail.

Maqdisi on Takfir

Like many jihadis, Maqdisi's ideology depends on declaring takfir against his Muslim rivals in order to permit violence against them. However, he repeatedly says that declaring takfir should not be undertaken lightly; in his 1997 book This Is Our Aqeedah (creed), he frequently quotes Qadi Iyad, a 12th century judge from Grenada, as saying: "Declaring the blood of those who pray, who are upon tawhid [belief in the unity of God], to be permissible is a serious danger".

Maqdisi adds that takfir should only be pronounced against those who have abandoned tawhid. He says a Muslim abandons tawhid, and hence Islam, if their actions show allegiance to un-Islamic entities by aiding them or participating in their legislation. In other words, he says only those who actively support non-Islamic governments or oppose jihadis should be targeted. Unlike many al-Qaeda members, Maqdisi repeatedly warns on both moral and strategic grounds against pronouncing takfir—and hence carrying out attacks—against ordinary Muslims, saying that in the absence of an Islamic state, it is understandable that many Muslims are unable to perfectly practice Islam.

In his July 2004 book, An Appraisal of the Fruits of Jihad (Waqafat me'a themerat al-jihad), he writes contemptuously of jihadis who "start bombing cinemas or make plans to blow up recreation grounds, sports clubs and other such places frequented by sinful Muslims." Similarly, in This is Our Aqeedah, he criticizes extremists who kill for small infractions of Islamic principles: "The shaving of the beard and imitation of the kuffar (infidel) and other forms of disobedience like it is a general affliction that is spread far and wide. It is not suitable by itself for evidence of takfir."

On Democracy

A large proportion of Maqdisi's writings are devoted to the discussion of democracy, which he regards as one of the main threats to Islam. Maqdisi does not object to democracy as a form of representative government, however, but because legislators deliberately create man-made laws to replace or supplement the sharia (Islamic law).

Maqdisi's arguments stem from his belief that a Muslim's faith is not complete unless he lives under sharia law. As he wrote in his early 1990s book, Democracy is a Religion (Al-Deemoqratiyya Deen): "Obedience in legislation is also an act of worship". Maqdisi consequently argued that anyone seeking to create legislation to replace the sharia is effectively seeking to take the place of God. From this, he concludes that "anyone who seeks to implement legislation created by someone other than Allah, is in fact a polytheist." Yet his dislike for democracy is not absolute; he accepts that consultation (shura) between a Muslim ruler and his subjects is a valid Islamic principle—but says that this principle has been hijacked by secularists to legitimize the legislative aspect of democracies. Unlike many al-Qaeda fighters, however, Maqdisi says that the illegitimacy of legislative elections does not necessarily permit attacks against anyone who votes, since some people vote only "to choose representatives for worldly living" rather than to subvert the sharia.

On Jihadi Tactics

Maqdisi believes that violent jihad against non-Muslims is a core part of Islam which can be carried out by individuals at any time or place. In an interview with al-Nida magazine in 1999, he described jihad as an "act of worship that's permissible any time". He also says that jihad is not dependent on living in an Islamist state or having a Caliph, nor is it restricted to battlefields or places of open conflict. Despite this, however, Maqdisi criticizes would-be jihadis whose enthusiasm for glory blinds them to political and religious realities. In An Appraisal of the Fruits of Jihad, he mocks the "youths moved by their zeal." He continues:

"[They] have studied neither the sharia nor reality. They have newly begun practicing the religion and have not yet rid themselves of the arrogance, pride, and tribalism of their pre-Islamic days, such that some of them even consider it shameful, cowardly, and disgraceful to be secret and discrete. Others proclaim that they are carrying automatic weapons or bombs that they roam about with in their cars here and there, showing them to this person and that person; they think it is a trivial matter to blab to everyone about how they dream and hope to kill Americans and destroy the American military bases in their lands. They then become astonished at how the enemies of Allah ask him about these things when they interrogate him, and he wonders how they knew about it?!"

Maqdisi also complains that many jihadist attacks are not carried out for strategic benefit but because such attacks are easy: "There are other young enthusiasts who oppose us by attacking churches or killing elderly tourists, or relief agency delegates—and other such trivial targets—whereby they do not consider what will benefit the da'wah [call to religion], jihad or Islam, nor do they give preference to what will cause most injury to the enemies of Allah. Rather, their choice is only based on the easiest target."

Maqdisi describes the best mujahideen as those who are "looking for targets that will bring down the enemy combatants and defy them—such as nuclear weapons, or intelligence centers and political posts, or centers of legislation and economy in the land of the polytheists".

Maqdisi also criticizes those who attack Shiite Muslims, objecting to the attacks on both theological and practical grounds. In a 2005 interview with al-Jazeera, he said that ordinary Shiites could not be held responsible for their beliefs: "The laypeople of the Shiite are like the laypeople of the Sunna, I don't say 100 percent, but some of these laypeople only know how to pray and fast and do not know the details of the [Shiite] sect". This pragmatism does not contradict his intellectual hatred for Shiite teachings, saying in This Is Our Aqeedah: "We declare our hostility toward the path of the Rawafid [the Shiites] who hate the companions of the prophet and curse them."

Maqdisi frequently writes that hating non-Muslims is an Islamic duty. In his 1984 book, The Religion of Abraham (Millat Ibrahim), he says that this hatred "should be shown openly and declared from the outset." In An Appraisal of the Fruits of Jihad, he writes that any attacks on non-Muslims are theologically justified regardless of whether they result in any progress toward creating, or "consolidating," an Islamic state and regardless of changing political circumstances: "Any fighting done for the sake of inflicting injury upon the enemies of Allah is a righteous, legislated act, even if it brings about nothing more than inflicting this injury, angering the enemy [and] causing them harm." Simultaneously, however, he argues that for strategic reasons the mujahideen should at present concentrate their efforts on trying to establish a pure Islamic state in the Muslim world, saying that "one of the greatest tragedies of the Muslims today is that they do not have an Islamic state that establishes their religion on the earth." He also says that "the mammoth, accurately planned operations that were carried out in Washington and New York, despite their size, they do not amount to more than fighting for injury"—i.e. that they were justified only because they killed non-Muslims but had no strategic benefit. Importantly, however, he also says that if such attacks make it harder for the mujahideen to consolidate and build a true Islamic state, they should be avoided.

Through his writings which simultaneously justify both extreme violence and tactical pragmatism, Maqdisi has gained an iconic status in radical circles at a time when many jihadis—perhaps including even Osama bin Laden and Ayman al-Zawahiri—are becoming increasingly discredited. As a result, a public retraction of his more extreme views would send shockwaves through the jihadist community; on the other hand, a systematic recalibration of jihadist theory focusing attacks on Western military installations and secularists in the Arab world could reinvigorate the jihadi movement and perhaps win it new followers. Given that Jordan has reportedly forbidden Maqdisi from speaking publicly as part of the conditions of his release, it seems unlikely that his views have changed while in prison.

A poem allegedly written by Maqdisi in May 2007 tellingly describes a conversation between himself and the prison authorities in which they tell him: "Renounce [your views]; many shaykhs have... Renounce and you will be generously rewarded with material [benefits]. In return, you shall [have freedom to] speak". Maqdisi records his response as "Prison is sweeter to me ... My suffering for the sake of religion is sweet."

If Maqdisi has indeed remained loyal to his ideals, much will depend on how much freedom Jordan's government gives him to propagate his ideas; Maqdisi has consistently shown himself willing to continue promoting jihadist ideology regardless of the personal consequences.

Abu Basir & Abu Qatada

Abu Basir al-Tartusi is another prolific contemporary scholar of Syrian origin. He is a slightly more moderate Salafi ideologue who resides in London, more often criticizing past jihadi mistakes and urging caution and selective action. His tone is due in large part to the scrutiny he was put under following the 2005 London train bombings. He has provided scholarly arguments to back armed resistance to tyrannical rule (by employing jihadi tactics), also prefaced on the importance of Muslims living by the Sharia.

Abu Qatada al-Filistini, born in 1960 in the West Bank, is another example of a Palestinian-born cleric who encourages jihad against apostate rule in accordance with the Sharia and is among the most frequently cited authors in the study. His writings contend that, according to the Sharia, it is every Muslim's individual obligation to overthrow and expel any secular government from Muslim lands by bombing, sabotage, coup, or other means available to them that would advance the implementation of Sharia in that land.

These Salafi scholars play a critical but not widely observed role in the global jihadi movement. Ideology is often overlooked and is considered separate from the strategic and operational aspects of Islamist militancy. Yet, the scholars behind the jihadi movement set the framework for debates and provide direction that is by and large adhered to, or is at the least a determining factor in the planning of attacks. By better understanding their role in the movement, governments combating terrorism can attempt to intervene earlier in the radicalization process and ultimately work toward undermining their influence.

The "salafi" conflict

After the war in Iraq started, Zarqawi quickly became one of the most wanted terrorists in the world. As the leader of al-Qaʻida in Iraq, he was involved in the killing of hundreds of Iraqi civilians and the beheading of US citizen Nick Berg before being killed by an American air strike in 2006. These actions were also noticed by other radical Islamists, including Zarqawi's former mentor, Abu Muhammad al-Maqdisi. In 2004 and 2005, the latter criticized Zarqawi for his extreme use of violence. This criticism and the conflict between them that followed are the subject of several academic publicationsas is the claim that al-Maqdisi's critique was a sign of revisionism. The same is true for the arguments between the supporters of the two men and how this conflict led to the establishment of a fatwa council to "protect" jihad from faulty practices.

The division among Salafi-Jihadis in Jordan started in mid-2005 when al-Maqdisi directed an open letter entitled "Munasara wa Munasaha" (Advocating and Advising) to the leader of al-Qaeda in Iraq, Abu Musab al-Zarqawi, criticizing him for targeting Shiite and Christian civilians and accusing al-

Zarqawi's organization of being infiltrated by Jordanian security. The shaykh also emphasized the importance of mujahideen leadership being in Iraqi hands.

A few weeks later, al-Zarqawi responded to al-Maqdisi's letter, arguing that the latter's criticism did not have a negative impact on him but instead sabotaged the "jihad in Iraq." These accusations caused divisions to erupt between sympathizers of both parties, a situation intensified by the recent emergence of the so-called the "Neo-Zarqawists."

Similar posts have increased noticeably in jihadi forums, indicating that the division between the "neo-Zarqawists" and the "Maqdisists" is becoming deeper and suggesting that the radical faction of Salafi-Jihadis is growing in Zarqa. Although the mainstream Salafi-Jihadis (as represented by the Maqdisists) are fighting back, the neo-Zarqawists see themselves as inheriting the legacy of Abu Musab al-Zarqawi, which may play a major role in attracting young extremists to this new faction.

Several scholars briefly acknowledge that these discussions and the subsequent rifts between Jordanian radicals after 2004 are rooted in the 1990s, though there is a lack of literature on this period. It was in the 1990s that Zarqawi, Maqdisi, and several other like-minded Jordanians are said to have formed a group known as Bay'at al-Imam, or "Fealty to the Leader."

Bay'at Al Imam

The group known as Bay'at al-Imam formed during a time of regional and national turmoil in Jordan. In the early 1990s, the Middle East witnessed the first Palestinian intifada, the American-led invasion of Iraq after the latter's occupation of Kuwait in the 1990/91 Gulf War, and renewed efforts to start an Arab-Israeli peace process in Madrid in December 1991. Meanwhile in Jordan, economic problems forced the regime to raise taxes and cut subsidies, which caused prices to rise and led to protests throughout the country.

These tensions were exacerbated by the arrival of several hundred thousand Palestinians with Jordanian citizenship who were expelled from Kuwait due to the Palestine Liberation Organization's support for the Iraqi regime during the Gulf War.

One of these Palestinian returnees was 'Isam al-Barqawi, who had adopted the name Abu Muhammad al-Maqdisi, and would eventually help found the radical

Islamist group mentioned above.This turmoil caused great disillusionment among many Jordanians. Economic hardship, uncertainty about the large scale in migration of Palestinians, the ease with which the American-led coalition invaded Iraq with the help of several Arab regimes despite widespread popular opposition, and the start of a peace process with Israel caused some Jordanians to lose faith in their regime altogether.

As a result, some disillusioned men began to look for radical solutions to these problems. Consequently, a disparate number of Islamist groups with vague, but radical ideas emerged in the early 1990s and engaged in violent acts against Christians, liquor stores, nightclubs, and Jordanian officials.

This trend of radicalization was reinforced by the return of the so-called "Afghan Arabs," i.e., Arabs who had gone to Afghanistan to fight the Soviet occupation and the Afghan communist regime, but later returned to their home countries. These "Afghan Arabs" were not welcomed home by the Jordanian authorities upon their return and often ended up living in poverty, frustrated by their inability to find work. With the military experience they had gained in Afghanistan, these men made a crucial contribution to the violent groups that were set up in Jordan in the early 1990s.

One of these returning "Afghan Arabs" was Ahmad al-Khalayila, who would later be known as Abu Mus'ab al-Zarqawi. Zarqawi and Maqdisi, who had also spent time in Pakistan and Afghanistan but focused on teaching there, seem to have first met in the Pakistani city of Peshawar, in the home of fellow "Afghan Arab" Abu al-Walid al-Ansari.

It is not entirely clear what their relationship was like in Peshawar, but the two met again in Jordan after Zarqawi returned from Afghanistan and Maqdisi from Kuwait, where he had moved after leaving Peshawar. According to Maqdisi, Zarqawi was "yearning to help the unity of God and the call to God."

The two attracted a group of mostly poor, uneducated young men of both Palestinian-Jordanian and East Bank Jordanian origin, some of whom had fought in Afghanistan as well. These men seem to have followed Maqdisi because he had already written nu-merous books and articles, therefore offering precisely what they had lacked: a coherent ideology.

On the basis of al-Maqdisi's radical ideas of applying takfir (excommunication) to the regimes of the Muslim world because of their alleged unwillingness to apply shari'a in full, these men formed a group that later became known as Bay'at al-Imam. Although very little has been written about "Bay'at al-Imam," much of the existing literature that does pay attention to the group describes it in far more violent terms than is justified by the available evidence. Some simply refer to the group as a "terrorist organization."

Others label it one of many "radical jihadist groups . . . whose task was to ignite a revolutionary jihad" and that was willing to use "terrorist tactics or an "anti-monarchist jihadi underground." Some even go so far as to label it "a global Jihadist recruiting network," used by Maqdisi and Zarqawi to "coordinate the movement of Jordanian fighters in and out of Afghanistan," without offering any evidence for this argument. The members of "Bay'at al-Imam" were certainly radical, but the available evidence is far less conclusive than the idea of "Bay'at al-Imam" as a "jihadi"

The first reason "Bay'at al-Imam" cannot be described as a terrorist organization is that the group formed by Maqdisi and Zarqawi never used this name in identifying itself. Its members are said to have named their group only informally and to have referred to themselves mostly as Jama'at al-Tawhid (the Society of the Unity of God) or, especially, Jama'at al-Muwahhidin (the Society of the Upholders of the Unity of God).

As one of the group's leaders, Maqdisi was adamantly against the use of the name "Bay'at al-Imam," stating that it "is a fabricated name about us that the intelligence services have stuck on us"

The name "Bay'at al-Imam," which was later used by the Jordanian press and courts to describe the Jama'at al-Muwahiddin, was not entirely fabricated, but the name of a different group altogether. During the Gulf War, a Jordanian man called Nabil Abu Harithiyya (also known as Abu Mujahid) started a group called Harakat Bay'at al-Imam (the Movement of Fealty to the Leader) together with another Jordanian, Ghanim 'Abduh.

Abu Harithiyya is said to have been a friend and neighbor of Maqdisi's brother-in-law, and 'Abduh was a member of the Jordanian branch of Hizb ut-Tahrir, a radical but nonviolent pan-Islamic group with branches across the world. Together, Abu Harithiyya and 'Abduh issued several communiqués in the name of this group, which believed that the Jordanian regime was un-Islamic. 'Abduh allegedly wrote a treatise entitled Ba'yat al-Imam that argued for believers to pay allegiance to a religious leader, or imam

He showed the document to Maqdisi, who liked the idea in principle, but found it impractical. Because Abu Harithiyya was later arrested and sent to prison together with Maqdisi, Zarqawi, and other members of "Bay'at al-Imam" (i.e., Jama'at al-Muwahhidin), the intelligence services likely assumed that they all belonged to one and the same group called Bay'at al-Imam.

Given the plethora of radical groups in Jordan at the time, the lack of clarity around the name "Bay'at al-Imam," and the ideological closeness between the actual Bay'at al-Imam and Jama'at al-Muwahhidin, it is quite possible that the intelligence services themselves confused or con-flated the two groups, not being able to make heads or tails of all the different names. A second reason "Bay'at al-Imam" cannot be labeled a terrorist organization is that it was not an organization, in the sense of being a structured and organized group. In fact, "Bay'at al-Imam" seems to have been similar to the many other groups that came into existence in the early 1990s, in that it was quite informal and loosely organized.

Members of Bay'at al-Imam usually met in one another's houses, as some individual members, such as Sharif 'Abd al-Fattah (known as Abu Ashraf) and Abu al-Muntasir have confirmed. Meetings were also held in mosques in various towns throughout Jordan, such as the 'Abdullah bin 'Abbas Mosque in al-Zarqa'.

The group was so informally organized that Maqdisi did not even associate the name Jama'at al-Muwahhidin with the group's actual members in Jordan, but simply equated it with his personal religious advocacy in which he had been engaged for years, even before he came to Jordan.

A third reason to reject the labels "terrorist group" or "jihadi organization" for "Bay'at al-Imam" is that it suggests that the group was primarily or even entirely concerned with planning violent action against civilians or the Jordanian regime. While there are some indications to support this view, a closer look at the literature on the group reveals that the character of the group and the nature of its activities are not consistent or clear. Several authors mention some plans for violent attacks in which "Bay'at al-Imam" was supposedly involved, but none of the plans resulted in actual armed operations.

Moreover, their information is based on the confessions of Zarqawi and Khalid al-'Aruri, another member of "Bay'at al-Imam," to the Jordanian State Security Court (SSC) or appears to come from a former intelligence official.

Given the reputation of the Jordanian General Intelligence Department (GID) with regard to the use of torture of political prisoners to induce forced confessions that can subsequently be used in the SSC, this information is suspect. Furthermore, considering the large number of radical groups active in Jordan in the early 1990s, such plans may have been wrongly attributed to "Bay'at al-Imam."

Notwithstanding the above, "Bay'at al-Imam" was caught planning one armed attack. Many sources mention that Maqdisi, after returning from Kuwait, had brought some weapons with him that had been abandoned by the Iraqi army after it pulled out of the country, which Maqdisi himself confirmed.

In 1994, after an Israeli settler called Baruch Goldstein had murdered 29 Palestinians in the Ibrahimi Mosque in Hebron, some members of "Bay'at al-Imam" wanted to plan an attack on Israel to avenge them. It is said only two members were engaged in planning this attack, namely 'Abd al-Hadi Daghlas and Sulayman Damra (also known as Sulayman Hamza).

Maqdisi reluctantly issued a fatwa to permit this operation, stating that it was legitimate, but that he himself preferred to focus on spreading his message in Jordan.

However, the plans were discovered by the Jordanian security services before the attack took place, along with the weapons that Maqdisi had smuggled out of Kuwait. As a result, the whole group was arrested and tried as "Bay'at-Imam" in 1994.

In the end, 16 men were sentenced to 15 years imprisonment for involvement in this operation. "Bay'at al-Imam" was thus only involved in one attack that we can be certain of, and it is likely this was indeed the only one.

Moreover, this one attack never materialized due to intervention by the security services. If this "terrorist group" did not engage in terrorism, with what kind of activities did it keep itself busy? Their main activities were spreading their message through missionary outreach (da'wa), as well as organizing lessons and sermons that Maqdisi gave in people's houses throughout Jordan.

Members of "Bay'at al-Imam" also copied the writings of Maqdisi and distributed them among like-minded men. On called Millat Ibrahim(The Community of Abraham), which Maqdisi wrote in 1984. In this book, Maqdisi argues that contemporary Muslim rulers show loyalty to what he refers to as "man-made laws" (qawanin wad'iyya) instead of to the shari'a, which violates the unity of God (tawhid), which should be present in all spheres of life, especially legislation. He calls on Muslims to disavow (bara'a) these regimes by declaring them apostates (murtaddun).

Another book by Maqdisi that builds on this idea is Al-Dimuqratiyya Din (Democracy Is a Religion), in which he writes that democracy, because it is based on the idea that the people and their laws are the ones who decide things — not God and the shari'a, is actually a different religion. Consequently, Maqdisi asserts that those who are aware of this idea and still consciously support democracy through voting and parliamentary politics are unbelievers (kuffar).

Given the fact that the Jordanian regime had organized parliamentary elections in 1989 and 1993 — the first in decades — this was a highly topical issue, and Maqdisi's book on the subject played an important role in spreading his views among Jordanian Islamist radicals.

When the members of "Bay'at al-Imam" were put on trial, the group's message of rejecting "man-made laws" and regimes that made such laws spread to a wider audience. Members of the group consciously used the platform they were given to denounce the court, the judge, the "man-made laws" on which the justice system was based, democracy, and the Jordanian regime.

While "Bay'at al-Imam" may not have been the "jihadi" (i.e., using armed violence) or "terrorist" organization that it has been described as, the group was unapologetically radical. The way in which this radicalism should be expressed, however, was disputed among the group's members. Some, most prominently Maqdisi, argued in favor of da'wa (proselytizing), while others, including Daghlas, Damra, and possibly Zarqawi too at this point, favored a more violent approach. Moreover, they probably also disagreed over what target to attack: Israel or the Jordanian regime.

When the members of "Bay'at al-Imam" were imprisoned, they continued their da'wa activities as if nothing had changed. The aforementioned Abu al-Muntasir claims that he regularly preached on Fridays, and fellow "Bay'at al-Imam" member 'Abd al-Hadi Daghlas also gave numerous sermons in the mid-1990s that were later collected and printed.

While most of these missionary activities seem to have been directed towards the group's own members and the other prisoners, this was apparently not always the case. According to one source, for example, a prison warden once informed Zarqawi that the Jordanian interior minister was going to visit them and told him and another inmate to "try to have a nice chat (kalaman hi wani) with him to show that you have changed so that you can go home."

Zarqawi allegedly answered the warden, "We have come here to call to Islam (li-nad'u li-hadha al-din), not to go home." When a group of politicians eventually came, Zarqawi warned them "by God the Most High, to be in the ranks of Islam (fi saff al-Islam) and not to help anyone against your brothers, the upholders of the unity of God."

Being the scholar of the group, Maqdisi was greatly involved in these da'wa efforts, and went even further in his attempts to engage prison personnel. In several pieces he wrote in jail, for instance, Maqdisi describes how he tried to explain to guards why — despite their own protestations — they were not Muslims, but actually unbelievers because they worked to protect and uphold an unIslamic regime and its laws.

Maqdisi appears to portray his own position in these conversations as that of a scholar with superior knowledge. This is not just apparent from the fact that the guard in one of these debates speaks Jordanian Colloquial Arabic while Maqdisi speaks Classical Arabic, but also from his use of takfir against a warden of one of the prison's departments. The warden and Maqdisi both apparently considered each other to be unbelievers, but Maqdisi claims that his excommunication of the warden carries more authority because it is based on "much Islamic legal evidence (adilla shar'iyya kathira) that I have shown you several times," while the warden's is not.

Such nonviolent, yet confrontational behavior is bound to elicit a response from others, which is precisely what happened. Bitter debates occurred between fellow Islamist prisoners from the radical, but doctrinally different Hizb ut-Tahrir that sometimes ended with the parties accusing each other of unbelief.

One non-Islamist prisoner recalled how he came to know "Bay'at al-Imam" in prison and was shocked by their ideas, believing they would tear society apart with their willingness to brand some people who disagreed with them as infidels, and even wrote an article to warn others about them.

Prison personnel were cautious, if not hostile towards the radical members of "Bay'at al-Imam," frequently moving them from one prison to another in order to keep members apart and stop them from recruiting new followers. There were regular conflicts between the group's members and the personnel over violence against inmates and the wearing of prison uniforms. Members of "Bay'at al-Islam" are said to have protested such measures with the limited means at their disposal, which included blocking doors or refusing to follow daily routines.

While "Bay'at al-Islam"'s activities in prison were largely nonviolent, members' recollections of a particular incident perhaps illustrate the group's motivation behind their missionary activities. This incident suggests that some members of "Bay'at al-Imam" thought that they were part of a divine plan to resist the "infidel" regime inside prison. In this conflict, prison guards hurled tear gas canisters at the prisoners, leading 'Abd al-Hadi Daghlas to shout, "We have come to die!" The prisoners reportedly noticed, however, "that God honored them so that the gas thrown at them by force did not affect them."

When the inmates protesting their treatment later went to sleep, one of them had a dream about the Prophet Muhammad's army commander Khalid bin al-Walid and his companions coming to help the prisoners, telling the dreaming inmate not to worry because God would meet the requirements of the believers. When Zarqawi heard about this dream, he was delighted and considered it a sign.

Throughout its existence, "Bay'at al-Imam" had been an informally organized group, as shown above, and up until this point had not had a real leader. According to Abu al-Muntasir, however, Zarqawi and Khalid al-'Aruri argued from the time before their imprisonment that the group should have an official leader.

Abu al-Muntasir claims that they decided early on that Zarqawi would be the group's leader, while Maqdisi would be in charge of missionary activities, though it is unclear what this meant in practice. It seems obvious that a loosely organized group without a clear idea of what to do would naturally gravitate towards Maqdisi with regard to da'wa because of his seniority in knowledge and experience. When the group went to prison, its members organized, and Maqdisi is said to have then become its leader.

However, after prison guards beat a member of the group, leadership shifted from Maqdisi to Zarqawi, when the former was allegedly reluctant to take action after the incident Although Maqdisi himself claims that he and the rest of the group successfully protested the supposed insults to Islam by the prison personnel, it is clear that the admiration he enjoyed from the group was mostly due to his knowledge, not his leadership skills. As a result, Zarqawi was made the new leader of "Bay'at al-Imam."

Maqdisi himself would later claim that he gave up leadership of the group willingly in order to focus on writing and teaching, but he would also down-play the matter by stressing he was only resigning the leadership of a small group, and not a state or anything important.

Maqdisi's account may be a correct description of what happened, due to his inclination towards da'wa. Nevertheless, it seems that the two men's reputations began to diverge from this point onward. In the few pages dedicated to "Bay'at al-Imam" in the existing secondary litera-ure, perhaps no other issue features as prominently as Zarqawi's personality. He is described in various publications as a tough man of action when he was in prison, who used makeshift weights to keep himself fit and was aggressive towards those who got in his way.

 Given this toughness (ostensibly developed in Afghanistan and during his former career as a petty criminal) and loyalty to his fellow prisoners, Zarqawi seemed a natural leader in prison, where such characteristics are presumably seen as important qualities. This was also apparent in his treatment of other prisoners, whom he appears to have subjected to a strict regime, dictating what they should wear, what they should read, and when they could watch television.

Zarqawi's personality — characterized as it was by toughness, action, and discipline — contrasted sharply with that of Maqdisi. Not only was the latter a middle-class man of Palestinian origin — unlike the poor, East Bank Jordanian Zarqawi — but he was also friendly in his approach towards others, focused on reading and writing, and was perhaps more submissive in the face of violence.

Maqdisi is described as an easygoing man in prison who had normal relations with people, even those with whom he disagreed, and as someone who was very preoccupied "with knowledge", sometimes to the annoyance of others.

It is tempting to conclude from this that Maqdisi was a compromising and weak man, while Zarqawi was the exact opposite, as Abu Qudama Salih al-Hami — Zarqawi's brother-in-law and admiring biographer — has indeed concluded. Hami states that the other prisoners "considered [Maqdisi] to be opportunistic.

Although Hami's personal grudge against Maqdisi for criticizing Zarqawi means that his description of Zarqawi should be treated carefully, it seems that Maqdisi was indeed much friendlier and more tolerant than Zarqawi. Nevertheless, a Jordanian lawyer involved in the case of "Bay'at al-Imam" claims that members of the group were tortured by the General Intelligence Directorate, and several of their fellow prisoners claim that Maqdisi was one of them.

In fact, Hami himself writes that torture exacted a heavy toll from Maqdisi and that, apparently after one particularly brutal torture session, "some of his brothers did not [even] recognize him until he recognized them himself . . . and they cried over his condition."

This suggests that descriptions of Maqdisi as weak or feeble are exaggerated and that he probably could only be described as such in comparison with Zarqawi, who did seem to possess much more of the personal qualities a leader of radical Islamist inmates needs.

This became particularly clear when the members of "Bay'at al-Imam" were released as a result of the royal amnesty following King 'Abdullah II's succession to the throne in 1999. After his release, Maqdisi stayed in Jordan to continue his missionary activities, while Zarqawi, Daghlas, and several others went abroad to engage in jihad. Maqdisi has made it clear that their decision dismayed him, but also that he was not surprised, given Zarqawi's (and perhaps others') lack of patience to study and focus on da'wa

While the strict security situation in Jordan was a push factor in motivating members of "Bay'at al-Imam" to go abroad to relocate, the lure of al-Qa'ida's global jihad also acted as a pull factor for many radicals. This brings us to a final dimension of the differences between Maqdisi's and Zarqawi's leadership: jihadi authority.

While differences in personality and, to a lesser extent, ideological disagreements between Maqdisi and Zarqawi are mentioned in existing literature as a cause for their breakup, the issue of jihadi authority is entirely absent. Jihadi authority refers to the perceived status to speak authoritatively on armed jihad. One might expect Islamic scholars to have the most authority in this regard since they are experts on the religion from which jihad stems. This is true to a certain extent, and it is probably also the reason why some radical Jordanian Islamists flocked to Maqdisi in the early 1990s.

As time went by, however, it seems that the members of "Bay'at al-Imam," particularly when they were in prison, started favoring jihadi experience (i.e., having actually fought in a jihad) over religious knowledge on this subject, leading to a simultaneous devaluation of Maqdisi's status and a rise in Zarqawi's.

Though both Maqdisi and Zarqawi had gone to Afghanistan, only the latter had actually fought there, even if he came too late to fight the Soviets. The question of combat experience in a successful jihad against Afghanistan's Soviet occupiers and local communist regime became increasingly important to establishing jihadi authority among radical Islamists in general, and among members of "Bay'at al-Imam," in particular, during the group's imprisonment. Romanticizing of the Afghan jihad was not uncommon and could also be seen in Zarqawi's behavior in prison. Several authors state that he is said to have worn Afghan clothes in prison and that he took credit for his participation in battles in Afghanistan, but they only mention this in passing.

It seems, however, that such things were part of a development in which participation in the armed jihad in Afghanistan came to be seen as a quality that trumped all others in establishing jihadi authority.One former fellow inmate who was imprisoned with "Bay'at al-Imam" speaks highly of Zarqawi and several other members of the group, precisely because they fought in an actual jihad, as opposed to Maqdisi, whom he despises for not having done so, but nevertheless had the temerity to criticize Zarqawi.

Another former fellow prisoner states that, once in prison, the "Afghan Arabs" were increasingly divided into two groups: one consisting of men who had actually fought in Afghanistan and another comprised of people who had merely been there, but had not participated in combat. The former, he states, were seen as heroes, while the latter often joined them in admiration.

This is confirmed by Hami, who writes that there were "Afghan Jordanians [in prison] of whom none had [actually] gone to Afghanistan". He also stresses that the group had three leaders in prison prior to Maqdisi, at least two of whom had extensive experience in the Afghan jihad. This contrasts sharply with Maqdisi, about whom Hami keeps reminding his readers that "he was not a known fighter (muqatil) or jihad fighter (mujahid) who lived between the bullets, the missiles, and the tanks for [even] a day".

Given his lack of fighting credentials in Afghanistan, Hami claims Maqdisi knows little about jihad and does not have the authority to rule on issues in this regard. Hami states that the mujahideen perceive a reality that Maqdisi and others like him do not understand.

The mujahideen, he states, acquire "knowledge of Islam through a way that is higher (asma), purer (asfa) and deeper (a'maq) than [that of] those who read and study it while they are behind their desks."

Considering such high regard for combat experience at the expense of scholarly knowledge, as well as the presence of several prisoners who had actually fought in Afghanistan, it is not surprising that having participated in the Afghan jihad became a mark of distinction for the members of "Bay'at al-Imam" and others.

The Petro-Caliphate

Resolution 2170 (August 2014) calls upon all Member States "to take national measures to suppress the flow of foreign terrorist fighters to, and bring to justice, in accordance with applicable international law, foreign terrorist fighters of, ISIL, ANF and all other individuals, groups, undertakings and entities associated with Al Qaida," and reiterates Member States' obligation to prevent terrorist travel, limit supplies of weapons and financing, and exchange information on the groups.

Resolution 2178 (September 2014) requires Member States, consistent with international law, to prevent the "recruiting, organizing, transporting or equipping of individuals who travel to a State other than their States of residence or nationality for the purpose of the perpetration, planning of, or participation in terrorist acts."

On February 12, 2015, the Security Council unanimously adopted Resolution 2199, which reaffirmed and clarified the applicability of U.N. sanctions on IS-related individuals and entities that provide active and passive financial support to the Islamic State, ANF, and others associated with Al Qaeda.

Senior U.S. officials have described the Islamic State as one of the best-funded terrorist organizations, in spite of its relative reliance on resources in areas under its physical control. Its wealth has contributed to the group's ability to finance sophisticated military operations across parts of Iraq and Syria and may support operations by IS affiliates and terrorist operatives in other regions. The group also seeks to use locally-derived revenue to administratively control and govern the territory it has seized. In several respects, the Islamic State presents a unique policy challenge to combating terrorist financing.

Its financial strength lies in its ability to secure large amounts of funding from primarily internal sources, its correspondingly diminished vulnerability to efforts to target international sources of funds, and its exploitation of ungoverned spaces and porous borders to move funds with impunity. These characteristics often place the organization's finances beyond the reach of some of the most common counterterrorist financing policy tools.

The Islamic State controls a variety of public resources and infrastructure in parts of Iraq and Syria, enabling it to assemble multiple sources of revenue.

Some of these resources, such as oil and antiquities, can be smuggled and sold for considerable profit. Others—agriculture and energy and water utilities—generate limited revenue and require a significant investment in inputs or technical expertise, but help the group portray itself as exercising the functions of a legitimate government.

Activities such as kidnapping for ransom or the looting of banks and personal property may be profitable in the near-term but are not necessarily sustainable. In other cases, Islamic State control over a set of resources is notable not solely for the revenue the group derives from it, but also for the extent to which it limits the ability of the Iraqi and Syrian governments to conduct trade, provide utility services, or feed their citizens.

Targeting the Islamic State's finances is one of five core lines of effort to degrade and defeat the terrorist organization. General John Allen, the recently retired U.S. Special Presidential Envoy for the Global Coalition to Counter ISIL, stated in early 2015 that the United States cannot defeat the Islamic State through military efforts alone, and highlighted the need to deprive the group of access to financial resources.

At present, U.S. policy focuses on disrupting IS revenue streams, limiting the group's access to formal financial systems, and imposing sanctions on the group's senior leadership and financial facilitators. The United States also has sought to collaborate with international partners, including through cooperation on financial intelligence collection and analysis.

Although military airstrikes on Islamic State-linked oil infrastructure and supply networks have already altered the organization's financial profile, counterterrorist financing policy responses remain nascent. Policymakers continue to grapple with how to develop quick and effective responses to combat Islamic State financing. Some caution that counter-finance tactics may need to be balanced with consideration of the economic harm such actions may inflict on civilian particularly for key resources such as oil, utilities, and agriculture, efforts to counter Islamic State financing could damage local economies and services and contribute to expanding humanitarian crises.

The Islamic State's system of financing is likely shaped by the experiences of the group's predecessor organizations, the Islamic State of Iraq (ISI) and Al Qaeda in Iraq (AQI). Captured battlefield documents and media reports provide the basis for what researchers know about how precursors to the Islamic State were funded. For example, documents describing ISI operations in Sinjar reveal a group that was reliant on incoming foreign fighters for funds, internal transfers from other areas under ISI's control, local donations, and conflict loot.

This was due partly to the preponderance of locally sourced revenue streams, including the theft and resale of local high-value goods, such as construction equipment, generators, electrical cables, and cars, as well as extortion. Another battlefield document captured in 2008 appears to highlight the centrality of effective financial management for AQI's operations. In this document, ISI fighters compiled a list of lessons learned, based on what they perceived as Al Qaeda's failures in Iraq.

Among them was a critique of its use of financial resources, describing a failure to distribute funding among local cells effectively and the lack of a regular funding source, particularly a foreign state sponsor. U.S. and Iraqi forces to date have captured a limited number of internal Islamic State documents, which have not been publicly released. In June 2014, Iraqi special forces recovered a trove of documents on memory sticks and hard drives during a raid that killed Abdul Rahman al Bilawi, the Islamic State's military chief of staff for Iraqi territory. Some media outlets were permitted to review a selection of the material, which reportedly included details of the group's leadership structure as well as expenditure lists.

Sources of Revenue

Before protests against the Syrian government began in March of 2011, the oil sector played an important role in the national economy and government accounts. Although not a large oil producer or exporter in the world market, Syria produced approximately 400,000 barrels per day of crude oil from its oil fields in the eastern part of the country, near the Iraqi border, while exporting approximately 150,000 barrels per day of crude oil, virtually all to Europe, including Turkey. The oil sector provided 25% of Syrian government revenues, and about 45% of total Syrian exports.

The escalating combat in Syria since 2011 has damaged the oil sector on both the demand and supply sides of the market. Demand for Syrian exports has evaporated as sanctions imposed by the United States and others, including, critically, the European Union, took effect. Fighting in Syria has damaged oil facilities, causing oil production to fall to approximately 20,000 barrels per day, or less, only 5% of average production before 2011. As a result, official exports have fallen to zero, and Syria has become a net importer of petroleum products. Syrian oil export facilities remain largely under government control while oil producing areas remain under rebel control, so exports are unlikely to resume without a political settlement even if facilities were physically repaired. In addition, combat conditions have caused international oil companies to suspend operations in Syria, leading to a shortage of trained personnel and compounding the effects of a shortage of equipment and parts due to the international sanctions.

Syrian Oil and the Islamic State

Much of the physical and economic damage to the Syrian oil sector took place between March 2011 and June 2014, when IS forces expanded their control of oil producing regions in northeast Syria. The Islamic State organization needs and uses oil for a variety of purposes. Refined oil is needed to fuel ISIS vehicles as well as for civilian use within areas under IS control. Crude oil can be sold for cash to finance the group, or traded for refined products.

Selling IS oil is technically difficult because the group has no traditional export facilities or access to the open market. As a result, the group must ship its oil by truck to the Turkish border where oil brokers and traders buy the oil and make cash payments, or payments in kind of petroleum products. Because the Syrian government considers IS oil to be stolen contraband and because international sanctions limit the markets the oil can legally enter, IS oil trades at a steeply discounted price.

Reliable, documented oil quantity and price data for IS transactions are unavailable due to their illegal nature. It has been reported that IS oil might have been selling for as little as $18 per barrel at the Turkish border, when Brent, a world price reference crude oil was selling for about $107 per barrel. Recently, the price of Brent has declined to about $65 per barrel, a decrease of over 50% since June 2014. The fall in world oil prices has likely further reduced the net price received by IS leaders for the oil they sell.

Iraqi Oil and the Islamic State

The status of the oil fields in northern Iraq, and of the Baiji refinery further south, have been in a state of flux since the summer of 2014. The situation is complicated by the existence of three organized military forces in the region; the Iraqi army, the Islamic State, and the Kurdish peshmerga forces, as well as other groups fighting the Iraqi government.

The Islamic State has been in control of a number of relatively small oil fields in northern Iraq, selling volumes of oil through Turkey in essentially the same manner as their sales of Syrian oil. In June 2014 the group captured the Bayji refinery which, with its production capacity of 170,000 barrels per day, supplied petroleum products for northern Iraq. While in IS hands, the refinery produced only a fraction of its rated capacity due to lack of both personnel and a secure oil supply. Iraqi forces retook the refinery five months later, although control of the city remained contested.

The Turkish border region also is a conduit for the sale of illicit Iraqi oil, both by the Islamic State, which holds several small fields in Iraq, and by the Kurds. In theory, Turkey could close the border to these activities, reducing the volume of contraband oil entering the world market.

However, beyond the physical difficulty in closing the large and porous border, Turkey also faces the risk of retaliation by the Islamic State inside Turkish territory. While IS forces are not in control of a modern operating oil refinery, the group has refined oil in crude, small, mobile refineries with capacities of about 300 to 500 barrels per day of petroleum products. Refined products may be more useful to the group than crude oil because these products (gasoline and diesel fuel) can be directly used to fuel IS military movements. Petroleum products may also be easier to sell to Turkish brokers because they can enter retail markets directly, avoiding the documentation attendant with processing at a legitimate refinery.

Natural Gas and the Islamic State

While crude oil can be moved using a variety of transportation modes, natural gas (used largely to fuel electric power generation) has more limitations. In Syria and northern Iraq, the only way to move natural gas is in the existing pipeline system. Due to the difficulty in capturing and selling natural gas, as well as the Islamic State's interest in governing the areas it controls—most of Syria's natural gas is used for power generation—the natural gas system has suffered relatively little damage compared to the oil sector. It has been estimated that Syrian natural gas production has declined by about 32% from 2011 to 2013.

U.S. airstrikes in Syria have targeted oil facilities because of their importance to IS financing. It has been estimated that by early October 2014, U.S. airstrikes had destroyed about 50% of IS refining capacity. Oil production facilities are also very vulnerable to airstrikes. In addition, reports suggest that since

October 2014, Turkey might be acting to limit IS oil sales, and some claim that oil sales might have declined by 80%.14 However, others have noted that while the United States has targeted refineries, it has generally avoided strikes on oil wells because of the potential impact on civilians and because it seeks to preserve key oil infrastructure for the post-conflict period.

Under Secretary of the Treasury for Terrorism and Financial Intelligence David Cohen in a November 2014 hearing reported that the Islamic State's revenue from oil sales had dropped from $1 million a day to several million dollars a week. In January 2015, U.S. Secretary of State John Kerry stated that coalition strikes had destroyed nearly 200 oil and gas facilities used by the Islamic State.

The resulting loss of revenue, Kerry said, was restricting the group's operations and in some cases limiting its ability to pay salaries. In February 2015, a Pentagon spokesperson stated that money from illicit oil sales was no longer the Islamic State's primary source of revenue, but did not say what had replaced it. It is difficult to assess which of the Islamic State's revenue streams is the largest, in part because of the limited financial details that are publicly available, the group's adaptation to shifting circumstances and opportunities, and the different ways that observers combine or disaggregate individual revenue streams when calculating their share of the group's overall income.

The Islamic State of Iraq and Syria (ISIS) is preparing to seize one of the few remaining major oil production centers in Syria not under its control, according to Syrian opposition officials. "ISIS is already in control of more than 60 percent of Syria's oil, with a total production rate of 180,000 barrel per day" and now plans to seize facilities in the northern province of Hassakah, an official from the Ministry of Energy in the interim Syrian opposition government, Yamin Al-Shami, told Asharq Al-Awsat.

Having seized control of the majority of oil fields in Raqqa province, in central Syria, and Deir Ezzor province, along the Iraqi border, ISIS is preparing to mobilize fighters in a new push towards the town of Rmelan, home to the largest oil fields in Hassakah. Rmealn is under the control of Kurdish People's Protection Units, or YPG.

Shami warned that oil production constitutes a significant source of revenue for ISIS, adding that the Islamist militant group is able to sell a barrel of crude oil for around 18 US dollars.

Oil is transported from ISIS-held areas with the help of local and foreign brokers, Shami said. Despite its recent advances in Iraq, ISIS has been unable to take control of oil resources comparable to those it holds in Syria, and its recent attempt to capture the key Baiji refinery was successfully deterred by Iraqi forces. But Iraq's oil infrastructure is far from secure, and there are frequent reports that huge amounts of crude oil are being smuggled out of the country by militants.

"Militant groups, along with ISIS, are stealing crude oil from fields near the Hamrin mountains" in northeastern Iraq, a local administrative official, Shallal Abdool, told Asharq Al-Awsat. "Kurdish Peshmerga forces that control the area have seized more than 50 tankers loaded with stolen crude oil," he added.

When asked about the destination to which oil is being taken, Abdool said: "There are many sides inside and outside Iraq that buy crude oil . . . and there are smugglers and brokers in Iraq who buy it for a cheap price in order to sell it abroad." Valerie Marcel, of London-based Chatham House think tank, said: "Fighters from ISIS can sell oil on the black market to buyers from Turkey, the Kurdistan region and Iran." "ISIS's use of temporary refineries allows them to sell oil more easily."

But, pointing to the fact that oil smuggling has been a problem for decades, others played down worries about ISIS's oil activities. "Oil smuggling operations from these sites exist and have been taking place for a long time before ISIS took over Nineveh province," the governor of Salah Al-Din province, Ahmed Abdullah Al-Jubouri, told Asharq Al-Awsat.

The "know-how" of ISIS's predecessors

Analysis of the group's documents found that by 2008—well before Abu Bakr al-Baghdadi became the ISI's leader—ISI funded itself in Mosul by exploiting the same local revenue sources ISIL currently exploits there. The documents also revealed that the group was wary of strings attached to revenue from external sponsors and was unlikely to seek external support as a major component of its overall financing.

This might have changed under Abu Bakr al-Baghdadi's leadership. Senior U.S. government officials have recently claimed that some of ISIL's funding now comes from external donors, and some believe external funding could become increasingly key to ISIL's financing if its finances in Iraq and Syria are squeezed and the group must look outward for financial support.

Moreover, if ISIL mends its relationship with Jabhat al-Nusra (JaN), which splintered from ISI to become an independent affiliate in Syria of the central al-Qaeda organization (based in Pakistan), it is possible that ISIL could integrate JaN's external funding network into its broader financial scheme. However, because only a modest share of ISIL's funding comes from external donors, sanctioning donors and external facilitators should be a secondary effort.

The many-fold growth of ISIS's wealth in recent years has also enabled ISIS to generate a budget surplus. This is a new development that occurred sometime after spring 2010. The group's Mosul financial ledgers from 2008 and 2009 reveal that it maintained a meticulously balanced budget. They also reveal that the group spent nearly all of the money it made very rapidly on its operating expenses, such as members' salaries and legal costs incurred on behalf of its detained members, and to fund military operations and attacks.

If reports published in June 2014 based on similar documents that were captured from a senior ISIS leader in Mosul are true, ISIS's surplus is now approximately $2 billion. Unlike in the past, ISIL no longer struggles to maintain a balanced budget each month—it instead enjoys a significant amount of surplus capital.

The question about this surplus is, how will ISIS use it? First, ISIS could use surplus funding to continue to expand its territorial base in Iraq and the Levant—the area of Syria, Lebanon, Jordan, Israel, the West Bank, and Gaza. Second, it could use it to expand its influence in other strategic parts of the Muslim world, including Pakistan and Afghanistan, as it attempts to usurp primacy in the jihadist world from al-Qaeda. Third, it could use this money to fund plots for attacks in North America, Western Europe, or elsewhere in the world. Fourth, it will need to spend some of its money to fund its members and to provide services and maintain its sharia-based order in the territory it currently controls.

Of the four options, the first and the last appear to be the most likely. ISIS's top priority appears to be building an Islamic caliphate emanating from Iraq and the Levant. For now, ISIS is focused primarily on controlling territory and establishing a viable caliphate in the region. It likely will spend a large share of its revenue on "state building"—that is, implementing its strict Salafi-jihadist governance structures in the territory it controls.

The group's financial holdings do not allow for the same level of spending the Iraqi government had budgeted for the governorates ISIS controls. ISIS requires far fewer resources to implement its sharia-based governance structures within this territory because ISIS's operating expenses and provision of other services is limited in comparison to what the government of Iraq would spend on services.

ISIS's wealth no doubt could contribute to a capability to conduct external operations. Media reporting has suggested that ISIS operatives have traveled to Pakistan and Afghanistan, among other countries, to attempt to recruit jihadi militants to join ISIS. Several commanders of the Pakistani Taliban, the leaders of the Abu Sayyaf Group in the southern Philippines, the splinter group led by the former leader of Jemaah Islamiyah in Indonesia, and Ansar Beit al-Maqcis in Egypt's Sinai Peninsula have all sworn allegiance to ISIS. Although the extent of the links between ISIS and these groups is unclear, it is clear that ISIS's media operations and deployment of teams of agents to conduct operations in distant countries requires money.

And some jihadists, such as the Philippines' Abu Sayyaf Group, which has stepped up kidnappings of Westerners in recent months, may shift their support to ISIS in exchange for financial support.

The third option is the least likely but has the highest stakes for U.S. national security. Although ISIS appears more intent on consolidating control in Iraq and the greater Levant and spreading its brand throughout the Muslim world, an ISIS terrorist attack in the West could boost the group's standing among jihadist elements worldwide and attract another wave of foreign jihadis to fight with ISIS in Iraq and Syria.

Such an attack would be costly for ISIS to plan and execute, but probably not costly enough for it to be impossible, even if the U.S. and its allies do manage to significantly degrade the group's finances. However, a financially degraded ISIS would pose less of a threat of successfully conducting a major attack using expensive and deadly weapons than a financially strong ISIS, which would have the resources necessary for such an attack: research and development, long-term surveillance and reconnaissance operations, training, weapons, and other materiel.

Media reports following ISIS' conquest of much of northern and central Iraq have painted the group as the world's most super-efficient, self-financed, terrorist organization that has been able to consolidate itself exclusively through extensive looting of Iraq's banks and funds from black market oil sales. Much of this narrative, however, has derived from dubious sources, and overlooked disturbing details.

One senior anonymous intelligence source told Guardian, for instance, that over 160 computer flash sticks obtained from an ISIS hideout revealed information on ISIS' finances that was completely new to the intelligence community. "Before Mosul, their total cash and assets were $875m [£515m]," said the official on the funds obtained largely via "massive cash flows from the oil fields of eastern Syria, which it had commandeered in late 2012."

Afterwards, "with the money they robbed from banks and the value of the military supplies they looted, they could add another $1.5bn to that." The thrust of the narrative coming from intelligence sources was simple: "They had done this all themselves. There was no state actor at all behind them, which we had long known. They don't need one."

Turkey's Dirty Game

A semi-laden with mortar rounds bound for Syria was stopped at Adana in January 1, 2014 because of an anonymous tip-off that it was carrying narcotics. In it, however, were 935 mortar rounds and 10 mortar tubes. Then, the Greek Coast Guard discovered 20,000 Kalashnikov rifles in a ship near Kardak in the Aegean Sea. The ship's captain and its three-man crew were Turks. According to the captain they were heading to Iskenderun, but in the system it was recorded as Libya and Syria. Russian media claims the ship had spent five days in Istanbul, but Turkish sources say the ship did not stop over at Istanbul.

All these reports reinforce perceptions in world opinion that Turkey is sending weapons to al-Qaeda elements fighting in Syria. This has been so much so that Star, the closest newspaper to the government and MIT, reported it as a "seizure of al-Qaeda ammunition." This kind of news makes Turkey appear to be a country supporting al-Qaeda terror.

Regarding the ammunition discovery, Prime Minister Erdogan said, "Syrian groups brought the molds for the ammunition manufacturing to Adana and Konya. They paid for them. The seizure of the ammunition shows Turkey's sensitivity to the issue."

This declaration itself, however, is problematic. As reported by the pro-government newspaper, al-Qaeda manufactures mortar ammunition in Konya and Adana and ships them to Syria. That load was discovered because of a t p on narcotics. Who knows, perhaps they would not have been found if the tip had been about weapons. Western observers reading the prime minister's explanation are likely to think: "Al-Qaeda is manufacturing weapons in Turkey but Turkish intelligence is totally unaware. If there had been no tip-off about narcotics — which obviously came from another intelligence service — that truckload of ammunition would have gone to Syria. Who knows how many truckloads of ammunition have already passed to Syria via Turkey?"

Under these conditions, the identity of Haitam Topalca, detained in Adana as the man transferring the ammunition, is significant. Who is Haitam Topalca? Haitam Topalca is a Syrian national Turkmen. He is involved in smuggling between Yayladag and Syria. According to a study by the think tank Center for Middle Eastern Strategic Studies (ORSAM), Haitam Topalca is the leader of a Turkmen unit called Al-Huwwa Billa that operates in Syria's Kasab-Beit Milk area.

More interesting still is that Yusuf Nazik and Mehmet Gezer, who were being sought as suspects in Reyhanli car bomb attack, mentioned Topalca in a statement immediately after the Reyhanli bombing: "Topalca is a Syrian Turkmen who is supporting jihadists in Syria. He is the one who tricked us." They went on to say: "It could be Haitam Topalca who set us up. We used to cooperate with Topalca from time to time to move stuff from Reyhanli. He is a veteran smuggler. He can cross the border both at Reyhanli and at Yayladag. We can't even go near Reyhanli. Jihadists control those areas. They would cut us up alive if they were to see us. He is definitely involved in this affair."

According to these suspects, Topalca, whose name was in newspapers months before the seizure of ammunition in Adana, was not even called in as a witness to the Reyhanli car bomb. If a man like him can freely have mortar ammunition manufactured in Adana and Konya and then ship them to Syria — where he is identified as the leader of a Turkmen organization — we are justified in thinking there is an intelligence outfit behind him. Then the question is: Who is Topalca? Who is behind him? Was he shipping that mortar ammunition to al-Qaeda?

A more important question is: Why is the Turkish media not following up on the story of mortar ammunition? How come after first-page headline coverage on the first day, they are all suddenly quiet? In what can only be called a stunning piece of journalism, the Cumhuriyet daily newspaper provided readers with noteworthy images of National Intelligence Organization (MİT) trucks stopped near the Syrian border by prosecutors and gendarmerie some time ago.

The surprise was the medicine boxes in those trucks. First and foremost, the fact that the arms in these trucks were hidden under medicine boxes indicates illegal activity. Unlike what the government is insisting, it's clear that the organization is involved in illegal operations. It's also clear that the arms were hidden under medicine boxes in order to block possible surface inspections and X-rays. This dimension alone proves the unfairness of the treatment received by prosecutors and gendarmerie who were removed from their positions after they stopped the trucks for inspection. After all, if those arms were being transported for a legal reason, why were they hidden under medicine boxes?

The second point here is that the quality of those particular boxes of medicine was quite striking. It was clear that that medicine was headed for fighters in

Syria. We're talking about medicine meant to help treat war wounds, strong medicine that you'd need in the war arena.

While it's tricky trying to figure out which arms make it to which groups, identifying the origins of a medicine box is much easier. A simple comparison between a medicine box found in an Islamic State of Iraq and the Levant (ISIL) area and a medicine box from those trucks would reveal much about where assistance from Turkey is really headed.

So yes, connecting the dots between a medicine box found in ISIL's hands and the factory that once produced said medicine box is easy. Medicine is not shrouded in secrecy the way arms are. Serial numbers and other identifying traits can be scraped off the surface of a gun, but medicine labels contain so much information -- from where they were produced to where they were packaged, who transported them and so on. Which is why, if that investigation into the stopped MİT trucks would actually just start, it would be very easy to quickly identify all the responsible parties in this mysterious incident.

The third relevant point here is that, when the MİT trucks were stopped, government officials stepped forward to assert, "Those trucks were carrying humanitarian aid to Turkmens in Bayirbucak." But the truth is, everyone knows those trucks were not headed to help the Turkmens. After all, the route a truck headed with aid for the Turkmens would take would be through Yayladere. But those trucks were stopped near Reyhanlı. The region those trucks were headed for at the time was one controlled by Al Qaeda.

If what the Turkish government had really wanted was to get help to the Turkmens at that time, the trucks would have passed through Turkey at the Yayladagi border point, which has Turkmen villages right on the other side.

The fact that Justice and Development Party (AKP) government officials claimed the trucks contained "humanitarian aid, medicine and so on" shows us that in fact, they knew quite well what was in those trucks.

Under normal conditions, all the risks are placed on the shoulders of the intelligence agents carrying out such a dangerous operation. And f and when the intelligence agents are caught, it's expected that officials will stand up and claim they have no idea who they are, thus maintaining the secrecy shrouding the operation.

But in this incident, what we saw was President Recep Tayyip Erdoğan and the AKP showing that they knew what was in the trucks, thus shouldering responsibility for what had happened.

Finally, it should be noted that one can always find arms on the black market. And since arms bought on the black market are generally paid for with money circulating on the black market, investigations into the sales, purchases, and cross-border transportation of such arms is generally quite difficult. Evidence and the criminals involved are tricky to discern amidst all the confusing pieces of the puzzle.

Unless the Erdoğan regime has built a special factory to produce medicine for the fighters in Syria, it would actually be much easier to pursue the money trails by following the payments made for the medicine. While the Erdoğan regime certainly cannot explain away the arms in those trucks, it would be able to escape most of the elements noted above if any inspection or investigation were to occur. An investigation done into the medicine boxes contained in those infamous trucks might have quite a different outcome, however, there is the possibility that it could provide us with a trail all the way to the top.

The Hatay Accident

A few days ago, Hatay police received a tip about a truck, which was allegedly carrying weapons to Syria. A prosecutor in charge of terrorism issues sought to have the gendarmerie search the truck, but written instructions from the Hatay Governor's Office halted the process. The truck continued on its route after the prosecutor took note of the incident. T

he governor of Hatay, Celalettin Lekesiz, sent a written notice to local law enforcement officers. "An official document posted on the Radikal's website showed that the truck and its personnel were on a MİT [National Intelligence Organization] mission and that laws prevented other law enforcement bodies from taking any sort of action without first obtaining consent from the Prime Minister's Office. Therefore, that they should immediately be set free," the daily reported.

"According to the document, Lekesiz's written instruction warned law enforcement officials that legal action could be taken against them if they stopped MİT personnel in an irregular way." Turkish media reported that police officers who followed the truck and stopped it were punished and removed from their positions after the incident.

Interior Minister Efkan Ala claimed that the truck was carrying aid to Turkmen in Syria. Some media outlets and the opposition parties, however, claim that the truck was carrying weapons to al-Qaeda militants. It seems that no matter where the truck was going, whether it was to the Turkmen or al-Qaeda, we can assume that the truck was carrying weapons. If it was just regular aid, not weapons, why would an MİT agent risk himself and try to stop the gendarmerie from searching the truck? Why would the governor of Hatay risk breaking the law to prevent the truck from being subject to a legal search?

When we think of all possibilities, there is no doubt left that the truck was carrying weapons illegally which is why MİT and the governor tried everything to stop the prosecutor from searching the truck.

The interior minister should come out and gives a convincing explanation as to why MİT was carrying "aid" to Turkmen through the Cilvegözü gate, an al-Qaeda controlled region in Syria, and not through the Yayladağı gate, where the Turkmen are located. Worse, this is the first time a governor has written an official document to law enforcement officers admitting that MİT was operating a truck illegally carrying "aid" to Syria.

Having such documents could create big problems for Turkey if an international actor claims that Turkey is helping al-Qaeda. If there is a lawsuit against Turkey in an international court, there will be this document -- from a governor, a high-ranking official -- admitting that MİT is taking part in illegal activities in relation to Syria. With this document, the governor has left Turkey's fingerprint at the scene, which could easily be used by Russia, Iran or Syria.

Since Erdoğan has a governor who leaves evidence that could implicate Turkey in international criminal courts, and since he has such an amateurish intelligence agency that cannot transfer weapons from one point to another inside the country, Erdoğan needs no enemy.

Erdogan's revelations

President Recep Tayyip Erdoğan validated claims previously made by critics who alleged that the Turkish government was sending weapon-filled trucks to radical groups in Syria by sarcastically asking, "So what if the MİT [National Intelligence Organization] trucks were filled with weapons?"

Pro-government figures had previously claimed that trucks belonging to MİT that were intercepted en-route to Syria contained "humanitarian aid" for the Bayır-Bucak Turkmens who live just over the border from Turkey's southern Hatay province. Many claims were made by the opposition and Turkish media that the trucks were, in fact, transporting weapons to radical factions in Syria.

Early in 2014, an anonymous tip led to the interception of a number of trucks on the suspicion of weapons smuggling. The first operation took place in Hatay on Jan. 1, 2014. Another anonymous tip led to three more trucks being stopped and searched in Turkey's southern Adana province on Jan. 19, 2014.

Speaking to a room full of teachers gathered for Teachers' Day, Erdoğan said, "You know of the treason regarding the MİT trucks, don't you? So what if there were weapons in them? I believe that our people will not forgive those who sabotaged this support."

Erdoğan was speaking just hours after Turkey shot down a Russian Su-24 aircraft near the Syrian border after, Ankara has said, it violated Turkish airspace despite repeated warnings.

Erdoğan accused the prosecutors investigating the MİT trucks of denying Turkmens the power to defend themselves. "Those [MİT] trucks were taking aid to the Bayır-Bucak Turkmens. Some were saying, 'Prime Minister Erdoğan said, there were no weapons inside those trucks;' So what if there were?"

Justice and Development Party (AK Party) officials called the 2014 investigation of the MİT trucks "treason and espionage" on the part of the prosecutors because the trucks were claimed to be transporting humanitarian aid to the Bayır-Bucak Turkmens.

Erdoğan, who was prime minister at the time, said during a television program immediately after the interception of the trucks became public knowledge that the trucks were carrying aid supplies to Turkmens in Syria. Many high-level Turkish officials, including then-President Abdullah Gül, said the trucks' cargo was a "state secret," which led some to speculate that the trucks were carrying arms. However, Syrian-Turkmen Assembly Vice Chairman Hussein al-Abdullah said in January 2014 that no trucks carrying aid had arrived from Turkey.

Turkmens call for help

The recent military operation of the Syrian government, backed by Russian air strikes, in the rural area of Latakia, inhabited by Bayır-Bucak Turkmens has caused thousands of Turkmens to flee to the Turkish border. A Turkmen brigade commander called for Turkey's assistance and expressed his frustration that Turkey's helping hand had not been extended far enough.

Turkmen Commander Ömer Abdullah of the Sultan Abdülhamit Brigade, who is fighting against the forces of Syrian President Bashar al-Assad, recently called on Turkey to help the Turkmens being pounded with cluster bombs by the Syrian regime and Russian forces.

"We are trying to survive under unbearable brutality and we need Turkey's help," said Abdullah. Expressing criticism of the AK Party, Abdullah said: "Every day our Turkmen brothers are dying. We expect the government to support us. Why have they abandoned us? Our martyrs fall every day. Why are we being left alone? I don't understand."

Abdullah's claim pokes an important hole in the AK Party's claims, while also posing the question of to whom the MİT trucks, now widely accepted as transporting weapons, were sent.

Main opposition Republican People's Party (CHP) leader Kemal Kılıçdaroğlu said that Turkey had become a country importing terrorism from Syria. "We told them [the AK Party] not to. They said they were sending humanitarian aid. Later the documents were revealed [refuting these claims]."

Kılıçdaroğlu was referring to the Cumhuriyet daily's headline story in May which discredited AK Party and Erdoğan's earlier claims that the trucks were carrying humanitarian aid to Turkmens. The article showed photos from the search of the MİT trucks which were revealed to be carrying heavy munitions. Kılıçdaroğlu consequently asked to whom the trucks were going, if not to Turkmens.

After the publication of the stills as well as video, Erdoğan lashed out at Cumhuriyet and its editor-in-chief, Can Dündar, for publishing the evidence, publicly vowing that Dündar would "pay a heavy price" for his report. According to the report, there were six steel containers in the trucks which contained a total of 1,000 artillery shells, 50,000 machine gun rounds, 30,000 heavy machine gun rounds and 1,000 mortar shells. All of this is registered in the prosecutor's file on the MİT truck case, the report said.

Erdoğan personally sued Dündar and is requesting that he be given a life sentence, an aggravated life sentence and an additional 42-year term of imprisonment on charges related to a variety of crimes, ranging from espionage to attempting to topple the government and exposing secret information. Following the Cumhuriyet report, Prime Minister Ahmet Davutoğlu said that it is "none of anybody's business" what the trucks contained. Speaking in a live broadcast on the Habertürk news station, in May, Davutoğlu said, "This is a blatant act of espionage."

Tuğrul Türkeş, who made it into the AK Party cabinet after switching from the Nationalist Movement Party (MHP) in September, said in June that the trucks were not destined for Syrian Turkmens. Speaking on CNN Türk in June, Türkeş said: "I swear that those weapons were not sent to Turkmens as they [Erdoğan and other government officials] claim. We [the MHP] have connections with Turkmens [in Syria]."

A pro-government prosecutor who was appointed to the MİT trucks case inadvertently admitted in May that weapon-laden trucks made 2,000 trips to Syria, according to the lawyer of one of the defendants in the case. Hasan Tok, the lawyer for former Adana Provincial Gendarmerie Regiment Commander Col. Özkan Çokay, who was involved in the search of MİT trucks in January 2014, said that he learned that there had been at least 2,000 trips made by MİT trucks to Syria from the prosecutor, Ali Doğan.

Doğan, known as a government loyalist, filed for a verdict of non-prosecution regarding the investigation after he was appointed to the position of Adana chief public prosecutor. According to Tok, Doğan had asked the defendants in a previous hearing, "2,000 trucks have passed [into Syria], why was this one specially chosen?" "We didn't know 2,000 trucks had passed into Syria; may god bless Ali Doğan," said Tok.

Oil smuggling

According to Ali Ediboglu, a Turkish MP for the border province of Hatay, IS is selling the bulk of its oil from regions in Syria and Mosul in Iraq through Turkey, with the tacit consent of Turkish authorities: "They have laid pipes from villages near the Turkish border at Hatay. Similar pipes exist also at [the Turkish border regions of] Kilis, Urfa and Gaziantep. They transfer the oil to Turkey and parlay it into cash. They take the oil from the refineries at zero cost. Using primitive means, they refine the oil in areas close to the Turkish border and then sell it via Turkey. This is worth $800 million." He also noted that the extent of this and related operations indicates official Turkish complicity. "Fighters from Europe, Russia, Asian countries and Chechnya are going in large numbers both to Syria and Iraq, crossing from Turkish territory. There is information that at least 1,000 Turkish nationals are helping those foreign fighters sneak into Syria and Iraq to join ISIS. The National Intelligence Organization (MIT) is allegedly involved. None of this can be happening without MIT's knowledge."

Similarly, there is evidence that authorities in the Kurdish region of Iraq are also turning a blind eye to IS oil smuggling. In July, Iraqi officials said that IS had begun selling oil extracted from in the northern province of Salahuddin. One official pointed out that "the Kurdish peshmerga forces stopped the sale of oil at first, but later allowed tankers to transfer and sell oil."

State of Law coalition MP Alia Nasseef also accused the Kurdistan Regional Government (KRG) of secretly trading oil with IS: "What is happening shows the extent of the massive conspiracy against Iraq by Kurdish politicians... The [illegal] sale of Iraqi oil to ISIS or anyone else is something that would not surprise us." Although Kurdish officials have roundly rejected these accusations, informed sources told the Arabic daily Asharq Al-Awsat that Iraqi crude captured by ISIS was "being sold to Kurdish traders in the border regions straddling Iraq, Iran and Syria, and was being shipped to Pakistan where it was being sold 'for less than half its original price.'"

"Countries like Turkey have turned a blind eye to the practice" of IS oil smuggling, said Luay al-Khateeb, a fellow at the Brookings Doha Center, "and international pressure should be mounted to close down black markets in its southern region." So far there has been no such pressure. Meanwhile, IS oil smuggling continues, with observers inside and outside Turkey noting that the Turkish government is tacitly allowing IS to flourish as it prefers the rebels to the Assad regime. According to former Iraqi oil minister Isam al-Jalabi, "Turkey is the biggest winner from the Islamic State's oil smuggling trade." Both traders and oil firms are involved, he said, with the low prices allowing for "massive" profits for the countries facilitating the smuggling.

Oil exports

Early last month, a tanker carrying over a million barrels in crude oil from northern Iraq's Kurdish region arrived at the Texas Gulf of Mexico. The oil had been refined in the Iraqi Kurdish region before being pumped through a new pipeline from the KRG area ending up at Ceyhan, Turkey, where it was then loaded onto the tanker for shipping to the US. Baghdad's efforts to stop the oil sale on the basis of its having national jurisdiction were rebuffed by American courts.

In early September, the European Union's ambassador to Iraq, Jana Hybášková, told the EU Foreign Affairs Committee that "several EU member states have bought oil from the Islamic State (IS, formerly ISIS) terrorist organisation that has been brutally conquering large portions of Iraq and Syria," according to Israel National News. She however "refused to divulge the names of the countries despite being asked numerous times."

A third end-point for the KRG's crude, once again shipped via Turkey's port of Ceyhan, was Israel's southwestern port of Ashkelon. This is hardly news though. In May, Reuters revealed that Israeli and US oil refineries had been regularly purchasing and importing KRG's disputed oil.

Meanwhile, as this triangle of covert oil shipments in which ISIS crude appears to be hopelessly entangled becomes more established, Turkey has increasingly demanded that the US pursue formal measures to lift obstacles to Kurdish oil sales to global markets. The KRG plans to export as much as 1 million barrels of oil a day by next year through its pipeline to Turkey.

Among the many oil and gas firms active in the KRG capital, Erbil, are ExxonMobil and Chevron. They are drilling in the region for oil under KRG contracts, though operations have been halted due to the crisis. No wonder Steve Coll writes in the New Yorker that Obama's air strikes and arms supplies to the Kurds – notably not to Baghdad – effectively amount to "the defense of an undeclared Kurdish oil state whose sources of geopolitical appeal – as a long-term, non-Russian supplier of oil and gas to Europe, for example – are best not spoken of in polite or naïve company." The Kurds are now busy working to "quadruple" their export capacity, while US policy has increasingly shifted toward permitting Kurdish exports – a development that would have major ramifications for Iraq's national territorial integrity. To be sure, as the offensive against IS ramps up, the Kurds are now selectively cracking down on IS smuggling efforts – but the measures are too little, too late.

Arrest of journalists

Cumhuriyet Editor-in-Chief Can Dündar wrote on Twitter that he and the Ankara representative of the daily have been summoned by the prosecutor to testify as part of a terrorism investigation.

The investigation was launched after Cumhuriyet published the photos of arms in May, which it said were transferred to Syria in trucks operated by the National Intelligence Organization (MİT). In a tweet, Dündar announced that he and Cumhuriyet's Ankara representative Erdem Gül would go to the İstanbul Courthouse on Thursday to testify after a request from the public prosecutor.

The trucks in question were intercepted by the gendarmerie on two occasions in January 2014 after prosecutors received tip-offs that they were illegally carrying arms to Syria. There have been allegations that the arms were going to extremist groups fighting against the Syrian regime. Ankara, on the other hand, insisted that the trucks were carrying aid to Syrian Turkmens and branded their interception as an act of "treason" and "espionage."

The photos, published on the daily's front page in late May, show steel containers filled with mortar shells and ammunition underneath boxes of medicine. The daily also published a video showing the containers on trucks being opened and searched by gendarmerie.

Cumhuriyet said the trucks' cargo included 1,000 shells, 1,000 mortar shells, 50,000 machine gun bullets and 30,000 heavy artillery bullets. The editor-in-chief of the Cumhuriyet daily, Can Dündar, and the paper's Ankara representative Erdem Gül have been arrested on charges of being members of a terror organization, espionage and revealing confidential documents -- charges that could see them spend life in prison.

"We have been arrested!" Dündar tweeted after the 7th Penal Court of Peace ruled to arrest the two men pending trial, complying with prosecutor İrfan Fidan's request. Dündar and Gül were taken to the Silivri Prison after the court's decision. "Don't worry, these are medals of honor for us," Dündar was also quoted as saying by Cumhuriyet's website.

Dündar and Gül's supporters chanted: "Free press cannot be silenced" inside the courtroom after court announced its decision, Doğan news agency video footage showed. Main opposition Republican People's Party (CHP) leader

Kemal Kılıçdaroğlu said the decision marked a "black day" for democracy and freedoms.

CHP İstanbul deputy Mahmut Tanal said the arrests mark a "coup" staged against the press. "It is the massacre of the law to launch an investigation and now rule for the arrest of the two journalists with special orders," Tanal said, referring to the government's role in the prosecution of the journalists.

Opposition People's Democratic Party (HDP) also condemned the arrests in a joint statement by its co-leaders, who said the ruling once again revealed that judicial mechanisms are under the influence of President Recep Tayyip Erdoğan and the Justice and Development Party (AK Party) government.

If tried and found guilty on the charges, the sentence for being a member of a terrorist organization can reach a maximum of 10 years, while that for espionage can be up to 20 years. Revealing confidential government documents carries the highest punishment of all the charges -- life imprisonment. Both delivered their defense and a court decision is expected soon.

MIT and ISIS

Evidence has been growing that the twin suicide bombings in the Turkish capital of Ankara on Oct. 10, killing over 100 people and injuring hundreds more, primarily targeted the Kurds.

Several Turkish dailies have been running stories quoting the minutes of police interrogations which indicate that the suspected terrorists of the Islamic State in Iraq and the Levant (ISIL) who are allegedly responsible for the Ankara bombings reportedly confessed that the main pro-Kurdish Peoples' Democratic Party (HDP) was the target of the suicide bomb attack.

By the time the blast took place outside of Ankara's main train station, thousands of people from several trade unions, as well as the HDP, had gathered at the site to hold a peace rally against the resumed fighting between state security forces and the Kurdistan Workers' Party (PKK). In fact, Sırrı Süreyya Önder, a deputy from the HDP, told the media immediately after the incident that the suicide bombers blew themselves up deliberately among the crowd where mostly Kurdish groups had gathered.

Nevertheless, those who died during the attack included many Turkish Kurds and Turks. But revelations by the ISIL suspects of the Ankara bombing, as reported by some Turkish dailies, indicate that this radical terrorist group did not want to upset the Turkish government and therefore mainly targeted Kurds instead of directly carrying out an attack on Turkish state buildings, for instance. Similarly, ISIL was the prime suspect in the suicide bombing in Turkey's southeastern town of Suruç, where over 30 people -- mostly university students who represented pro-Kurdish socialist organizations -- were killed. The suicide bomber responsible for the Suruç attack was identified as a homegrown ISIL sympathizer.

In an interview with the Canadian CTV news channel soon after the Ankara twin suicide attacks, Dr. Chris Kilford, former defense attaché to the Canadian Embassy in Turkey, recalled that in Syria itself, Syrian Kurds supported by Kurds in Turkey were doing incredibly well in fighting ISIL. He indicated that Syrian Kurdish success in Syria against ISIL may be one of the ways to attack Kurds in Turkey out of vengeance. He went on to say that what ISIL would avoid is upsetting Ankara too much because there is a lot of evidence that Turkey is, perhaps, indirectly supporting ISIL and other groups such as Al Nusra. Hence, the Ankara attack can be seen as an attack on Kurds but not directly against Turks. It is a very fine line, he added.

It is no secret that there are factions within the Islam-sensitive Turkish government who are suspected of continuing their direct or indirect support of ISIL, even if the government denies such claims. Moreover, since the Suruç attack, families of the suicide bombers are telling the local media that despite the fact that they went to the police several times informing them about their sons' suspected linkage with ISIL, no measures were taken to stop such activities.

In fact, Sezgin Tanrıkulu, a deputy from the main opposition Republican People's Party (CHP), told the media on Oct. 18 that the number of Turks who have been arrested on charges of tweeting messages criticizing the government exceeds those who have been arrested on charges of being ISIL members. Thus, he said, the government is responsible for the Ankara massacre (for not taking adequate measures to stem ISIL growth in the country).

Though the AKP is largely believed to have been fomenting chaos in Turkey, paradoxically, the Ankara bomb attack may trigger more voters to cast their ballots for this party to bring it to power again, out of fear of further instability. This is not the first incident that has revealed the flaws in intelligence system.

This country has an intelligence agency whose false intelligence led to the Uludere tragedy, in which 34 civilians were mistaken for terrorists and killed by military airstrikes in Şırnak province's Uludere district. Despite its apparent failure, this agency has been unable to develop and eliminate its flaws since 2011. The Reyhanlı blasts, the Suruç bombings, the attacks on the Peoples' Democratic Party (HDP) rally in Diyarbakır, the attacks on the HDP's buildings in Adana and Mersin, the attack by Dina Ramazanov on a police station in İstanbul and the recent Ankara massacre are all related to the Syrian crisis and everyone believes that jihadist organizations in Syria are behind these attacks.

So we can conclude that the Turkish intelligence agency is considerably flawed regarding terror threats from Syria. This agency prides itself on its ability to conduct operations deep inside Syria. How can an intelligence agency that is capable of conducting comprehensive operations inside Syria and cooperating with the dissident groups there be so flawed in the face of terror threats from Syria? The answer the dissident groups in Syria give to this question is simple: The National Intelligence Organization (MİT) turned a blind eye to the jihadists in Syria and even supported them, and now they have gone out of control and this is MİT's main weakness.

This theory may be partially true. At least, it is certain that MİT has helped Syrian jihadists. MİT, too, does not deny this. There are ongoing judicial procedures about this matter. However, MİT extending a helping hand to Syrian jihadists does not entail a failure to see threats. If MİT is doing this on purpose, this is not intelligence but treason.

Moreover, this flaw does not belong only to MİT; the intelligence departments of the police and gendarmerie have that weakness as well. In this case, the flaw cannot be attributed solely to aiding the jihadists. There must be broader and greater sources of weakness.

The two main sources of this weakness are: First, all files and matters related to ISIL and jihadists are controlled exclusively by MİT. The intelligence activities concerning these groups are conducted by a top-secret team within MİT. Therefore, the gendarmerie and the police cannot perform intelligence activities targeting jihadist groups. With indoctrination from MİT, prosecutors and judges refrain from launching any domestic legal action against ISIL and jihadists.

Why hasn't a single operation been launched against the activities of ISIL and the al-Nusra Front inside Turkey, even though they have been declared terrorist organizations by the Cabinet? The reason for this is: The Justice and Development Party (AKP) government declared them terrorist organizations due to international pressure but treats them as such only on paper. In practice, only MİT is authorized to conduct operations regarding them. Thus, other state agencies are effectively prevented from monitoring and conducting surveillance on them. Only MİT employees keep tabs on these organizations and this certainly creates a major intelligence flaw. This is one of the sources of the weakness.

The second source is the politicization of the intelligence agency. MİT's head is a member of the AKP and his efforts to use the agency to promote the AKP's interests have met with resentment within the organization. Rumors have it that MİT's head does not trust anyone within the agency. It is even claimed that when he moves from one building to another, the buildings are evacuated for security considerations. If the MİT head does not trust his personnel, how can intelligence officers be expected to trust him? There are reportedly cliques within the organization due to increased politicization. This has turned intelligence into an internal fight.

One of the criticisms voiced internally about MİT's head is that he tries to conduct operations using unqualified and ambitious fledgling employees. For instance, he made an unqualified person who knows nothing about intelligence a deputy undersecretary purely for ideological reasons, and that person disclosed a major MİT operation to a domestic and foreign audience at an event organized by the Institute of Strategic Thinking (SDE).

This created much uneasiness within MİT. It is even said that some MİT employees have lost their lives due to such partisanship and ineptitude. At least some MİT employees are concerned about it. Therefore, the agency actually does not work. Other state agencies are prevented from collecting intelligence about ISIL and jihadists because only MİT is authorized to do so.

Erdogan vs Putin

Russia has the right to make a military response after the downing of a Russian warplane earlier this week by NATO member Turkey, lower house speaker Sergei Naryshkin said on Friday. Speaking in an interview with Romanian television station Digi24, Naryshkin, who spoke in Russian and was translated by the broadcaster, said: "This is intentional murder of our soldiers and this deed must be punished."

The shooting down of the Russian warplane by the Turkish air force on Tuesday was one of the most serious clashes between a NATO member and Russia, and further complicated international efforts to battle Islamic State of Iraq and the Levant (ISIL) militants.

"We know those who did this and they must be judged. At the same time, the response from the Russian side will surely follow, in line with international law. And aside from this, Russia has also the right to military response," added Naryshkin, who was attending a meeting of the Parliamentary Assembly of the Black Sea Economic Cooperation (PABSEC) in Bucharest.

Naryshkin, who said economic measures against Turkey might be on the cards, said Moscow had allocated additional military resources on Thursday to boost the security of Russian warplanes. "Even yesterday, military resources were allocated, (for) the S400 Triumph, which is the most advanced missile defence system, with the role to maintain flight safety of Russian planes, of our military and air forces whose task is to destroy terrorist infrastructure of the so-called ISIL and other organizations operating in Syria."

Moreover, the incident will further isolate Turkey in ongoing talks among major powers to find a political solution to Syria's four-and-a-half-year civil war. The location of the incident brings into question a possible proxy war taking place between Turkey and Russia. The incident took place in a mountainous area in northern Syria near the Turkish-Syrian border in the Yayladağı district of Hatay province, across the border from the Turkmen Mountains in Syria where an intensive bombing campaign by Syrian and Russian warplanes has been under way. Turkmens have ties of ethnic kinship with Turkey, which earlier warned Russia against ongoing assaults on Turkmen areas.

Hence, the developments that have culminated with Turkey downing a Russian fighter have indicated that a proxy war is developing between Turkey and

Russia that has nothing to do with the Islamic State in Iraq and the Levant (ISIL). On one side there is Turkey and the groups it supports, including the Turkmens. On the other, there is Russia and the Syrian regime.

Matters, however, are becoming increasingly uncomfortable for Turkey because regime forces are now just a few kilometers from the Turkish-Syrian border around Hatay province. Regime forces backed by Russian fighters have also continued bombing Turkmen areas in northern Syria where the Russian jet was downed by Turkish F-16s, capturing a strategic mountain in the region.

Putin's answer

In retaliation to the downing of its aircraft, Russia announced a series of economic, political and military measures against Turkey. Moscow has urged Russian tourists not to visit Turkey and mutual contacts have been canceled. Russia ranks second after Germany in terms of the number of tourists visiting Turkey, reaching 4.5 million last year.

As part of military measures, Russia has announced the deployment of the Slava-class guided missile cruiser Moskva off the Syrian coast, close to Turkish shores, and has stated that its strike aircraft in Syria will now be escorted by fighter aircraft.

In return, Turkey has increased the number of its F-16s deployed along the Syrian border from 14 to 18, while dispatching its Fırtına self-propelled guns to the area. Although Turkey and Russia enjoy close trade and economic ties, with the former buying more than half of its gas from the latter, while Turkish contracting work in Russia has a volume of around $60 billion, differing policies on Syria have, in fact, been straining ties between the two.

Turkey backs opposition forces in Syria, while Russia fights alongside the forces of Assad, whose downfall Ankara seeks. Moreover, Russia has been opting to hit other opposition groups, complicating the 60-member, US-led coalition strategy of defeating ISIL in Syria and Iraq. The downing of the Russian aircraft is not expected to change Russian policies in the region. Instead, Turkey has the most to lose, mainly through soft power mechanisms, because Moscow has already begun enforcing measures such as halting the entry of Turkish goods into the country.

Moreover, the Russians have already begun to embarrass the Turkish government by releasing information they have about Turkey's alleged support for ISIL, provided they have something tangible. In fact, Russian President Vladimir Putin has claimed that unnamed Turkish officials were benefiting from ISIL oil sales.

"Now, 'the gloves are off,' so to speak, so I expect that diplomatic niceties are over. This will get interesting now as Turkey's relationship with ISIL might be under the Russian microscope," commented a Western diplomat. At the end of the day, the Turkish government was careless in engaging the Russian aircraft because it does not serve the national interest.

S-400 missiles

The bitter verbal and military clash between Moscow and Ankara spiraled further Friday, Nov. 27. Russian Lt.-Gen. Evgeny Buzhinsky announced that following the downing of the Russian jet by Turkey, "Russia will have to resort to electronic jamming and other warfare equipment, including special aircraft with special equipment on board to protect our pilots from being struck by missiles."

This was after Turkish Prime Minister Tayyip Erdogan warned Vladimir Putin "not to play with fire." The tension between Moscow and Ankara was further ramped up by the following steps:

- Turkey suspended its flights over Syria as part of its partnership with the US for air strikes against the Islamic State. Ankara decided to avoid the risk of being shot down by the highly advanced Russian S-300 and S-400 anti-air missile systems newly deployed to Syria.

- The Russian Foreign Minister Sergei Lavrov said that visa-free travel for Turkish citizens would be suspended starting from Jan. 1. Thursday, the Russian police detained 39 Turkish visitors attending an agricultural exhibition on the grounds that they had no licenses to contract business in Russia. Moscow also announced tightened controls on Turkish imports of food and farm products, and advised Russian holidaymakers to give Turkey a wide berth.

- More than 1,000 trucks loaded with Turkish farm produce and industrial products for the Russian market are stuck at the Georgian-Russian border.

-       While threatening the Russian leader, Erdogan also asked to meet him at the climate conference in Paris next week. He must first apologize for the downing of the Russian warplane, Putin's aide Yuri Ushakov said Friday. Ushakov added that in Paris, Putin will meet Israeli Prime Minister Binyamin Netanyahu to discuss the Syrian crisis and Israeli-Palestinian conflict. He will also meet German Chancellor Angela Merkel for talks about Syria and Ukraine.

The Russian leader said at a press conference with visiting French President Francois Hollande, "The American side, which leads the coalition that Turkey belongs to, knew about the location and time of our planes' flights, and we were hit exactly there and at that time." Such incidents are "…absolutely unacceptable," he went on to say. "And we proceed from the position that there will be no repeat of this, otherwise we'll have no need of cooperation with anybody, any coalition, any country."

In the last two days, Putin has been found saying one thing and doing another: Although he declared that Russia would not go to war with Turkey for "stabbing it in the back, since Wednesday night, Nov. 25, Russian heavy bombers and warplanes have been hitting every Turkish vehicle moving or stationary inside Syria."

They bombed the Bab al-Hawa border crossing, located on the Turkey-Syria frontier, as well trailers and tractors parked in an area belonging to the Turkish Humanitarian Relief Foundation, on the Syrian side of the border. It was this group (a terrorist association in disguise) that five years ago organized a flotilla to break Israel's blockade of the Gaza Strip. The lead-ship the Marmara was boarded by Israeli troops and 12 "aid workers" were killed in a clash, an incident that sparked a major clash between Ankara and Jerusalem. Erdogan then insisted he had never heard of the organization although their strong links were uncovered.

Putin has made no allegations. He simply sent his bombers to destroy the organization's vehicles and plough up their parking area on the Syrian side of the border. He also refuses to take calls from Erdogan. All these circumstances are features of a very active war waged between the two countries - albeit on Syrian soil - since Turkish warplanes downed the Russian Su-24.
In addition to punishing the Turkish leader, Russia's massive military operations in Syria aim to degrade the rebel groups fighting the Assad regime. Heavy bombing sorties this week on the Syrian-Turkish border are cutting off tens of thousands of rebels from their only source of fresh supplies of weapons,

ammo, food and fighters, leaving them without a line of retreat and nowhere to send their wounded.

After a week or two of intensive Russian air strikes against Turkish supply convoys crossing into Syria, experts expect Syrian army, Iranian and Hizballah forces to use the rebels' plight for an all-out offensive to destroy them.

Still, there is hope in some quarters that the Russian leader may change course. After meeting Putin at the Kremlin on Nov. 26, President Hollande touted their agreement to confine themselves to striking ISIS targets in Syria, not rebels. However, Russian military actions in Syria this week again showed Putin saying one thing and doing the opposite.

His bombers are not only settling accounts with Erdogan, but continuing to attack the Syrian rebel groups which received military aid from the US, France, Saudi Arabia, the UAE and Israel, both in northern Syria and also in the south, only a few kilometers from Syria's borders with Israel and Jordan.

However, the biggest damage Turkey may incur in the fallout of the fallen jet may come after the statements made by Russian leaders, which claim that they will take the issue of ISIL's financial avenues to the UN Security Council -- and that may cause Turkey a much-unneeded headache.

President Vladimir Putin called the downing of the jet a stab in the back administered by "the accomplices of terrorists," referring to Turkey and ISIL. Russian Foreign Minister Sergei Lavrov echoed Putin, when he said that the Turkish action came after Russian planes successfully targeted the oil infrastructure used by ISIL.

More importantly, Lavrov alleged that Turkey benefited from the oil trade and said Russia will ask the UN Security Council to examine information on how terrorists are financed. President Recep Tayyip Erdoğan defied those claims saying, "Those who claim we [AK Party] have brought petrol from Daesh [the Arabic term for ISIL], are required to prove their claims, otherwise I will call them [Russian leaders] slanderers."

This is not the first time Turkey has been accused of intermediating ISIL's oil. In July a senior Western official claimed that information gathered at the compound of Abu Sayyaf, ISIL's officer responsible for oil smuggling operations, pointed to high-level contacts between Turkish officials and high-ranking ISIL members, according to a report by the UK-based Guardian newspaper.

Turkey, which only started to take an active part in the international coalition against ISIL, reluctantly, and after two years, has also been accused of turning a blind eye to the crossing of militants into Syria to join ISIL, if not openly facilitating militants' border crossings to join ISIL in Syria.

While giving voice to veiled criticisms of Turkey's dubious dealings with ISIL, Western officials had refrained, until very recently, from directly critiquing Turkish authorities. Russia's recent disclosures indicate that Turkey may be the target of international scrutiny.

Speech of the Russian Deputy Defence Minister Anatoly Antonov

International terrorism is the world's biggest threat today. It is not an imaginary threat. It is very real, and many countries, particularly Russia, have firsthand experience of suffering from it.The notorious Islamic State is the absolute leader of international terrorism.But there are ways to combat the raging monster of international terrorism, and defeat it. Russian Aerospace Forces have evidently demonstrated that over the past two months.

We are convinced that, in order to defeat ISIS, it is instrumental to deal a crushing blow to its sources of funding, as Russian President Vladimir Putin has pointed out on many occasions. Terrorism without money is a beast without its fangs.Illegal oil revenues are one of the main sources of income for the terrorists in Syria. According to some reports, they make about $2 billion a year on illegal oil trade.

Turkey is the main destination for the oil stolen from its legitimate owners, which are Syria and Iraq. Turkey resells this oil. The appalling part about it is that the country's top political leadership is involved in the illegal business — President Erdogan and his family.We have warned on many occasions how dangerous it is to court terrorists. It is the same as pouring gasoline on fire. Fire may spread onto other countries, and that is exactly what we are seeing in the Middle East.

Today, we will present to you only part of the available facts that prove there is a single team at work in the region, composed of extremists and the Turkish elites conspiring to steal oil from their neighbors. Oil is transported to Turkey in industrial quantities along the "rolling pipelines" made up of thousands of tanker trucks.

We are certain that Turkey is the destination for that stolen oil, and today we will present you with irrefutable facts to prove it. We have a lot of media people with us today, and many more of your colleagues will see broadcasts of this briefing. In view of this, there is one thing I would like to tell you.

We appreciate the work of journalists. We know there are many brave, courageous people in the press community, who do their job with integrity. Today, we showed you how illegal oil trade is carried out, resulting in the funding of terrorism. We have presented you with hard evidence, which we believe could be used for journalist investigations.

We are confident that, with your help, truth will prevail. We know how much Erdogan's words are worth. He has already been caught red-handed by Turkish journalists, who have unearthed arms and munitions shipments from Turkey to the extremists, masked as humanitarian convoys. For that, those journalists have been jailed.

Turkish leaders, including Mr. Erdogan, would not step down or admit anything even if their faces were smeared with stolen oil. Maybe I am being a bit too blunt, but our comrades in arms have fallen at the hands of the Turkish military. The Turkish leadership has demonstrated extreme cynicism. Look at what they are doing! They have invaded the territory of another country and are brazenly plundering it. And if the hosts are standing in their way, they must be removed.

I would like to emphasize that Erdogan's resignation is not our goal. It's up to the people of Turkey to decide. Our purpose is fighting terrorism. Our objective is to shut down the sources of financing of terrorism. We call upon all those present here to join us in this effort. We are prepared to make your findings available to the public. We will continue to present you and the general public with evidence related to the financing of international terrorism.

Maybe, I would be too straightforward, but the control over this larcenous business can be trusted only to the closest people. It is interesting that no one in the West do not ask themselves a question, why the son of the Turkish President is the head of one of the largest energy companies and the son-in-law – the Minister of Energy and Natural Resources?

There are no opinions in the western media on this matter, but I am sure that the truth cannot be hidden. Of course, the dirty oil dollars will work. I am sure that there will appear conversations that all the data demonstrated here is a fake. Well, if there is nothing to hide, let the journalists visit those areas, which are shown during the briefing.

It is evident that it was just a part of published information about heinous crimes committed by the Turkish elite, who were financing the international terrorism directly. Any sober-minded journalist is considered to fight the plague of XXI century.

The global experience has repeatedly proved that objective journalism can be an effective and dangerous weapon against different finance corruption schemes. We encourage the colleagues for conducting a journalistic investigation on disclosure of schemes of financial support providing and delivering oil products from terrorists to the customers. Moreover, oil produced by the terrorists is transferred to other regions from the Turkish ports.

The Russian Defence Ministry will continue publishing materials concerning delivering oil products by terrorists to the foreign countries and informing about operations carried out by the Russian Aerospace Forces. Let's join our efforts.
We will be liquidating income sources of terrorism in Syria. Join us and do the same out of the Syrian borders.

Russian boots in Syria

The positioning of Russian aircraft in Syria gives the Kremlin an ability to shape and control U.S. and Western operations in both Syria and Iraq out of all proportion to the size of the Russian force. It can compel the U.S. to accept a de facto combined coalition with Russia, Syria, Iran, and Lebanese Hezbollah, possibly in support of indiscriminate operations against any and all regime opponents, not just ISIS and Jabhat al-Nusra. It may portend the establishment of a permanent Russian air and naval base in the Eastern Mediterranean. Russian forces have prepared and trained to conduct close air support and possibly special operations in Syria, and may begin doing so within days.

The deployment of Russian military forces to Syria is a major geostrategic inflection. Its significance goes far beyond the situation in Syria. It may well herald, in fact, a new era in global geopolitics and security. Russian forces are establishing an airbase likely to become capable of conducting operations throughout the Levant and the Eastern Mediterranean. It would be the first time in history that Russia had an outpost on land for projecting force beyond the confines of the Black Sea. The U.S. and NATO must consider and respond to this development recognizing its true stakes.

The Obama Administration remains inexplicably bewildered, however. Secretary of State John Kerry stated on 22 September 2015 that the Russian equipment that had arrived in Syria was there to protect Russian forces. "We don't yet have clarity with respect to the Russian effort," he noted in a press conference. After Kerry's meeting with Russian Foreign Minister Sergei Lavrov on 27 September 2015, the State Department stated: "Again, we're just at the beginning of trying to understand what the Russians' intentions are in Syria, in Iraq, and to try to see if there are mutually beneficial ways forward here."

Understanding the Kremlin's intentions at a basic level is not really very hard, though. Russian President Vladimir Putin certainly means to deter the U.S.-led coalition from attacking the forces of Syrian President Bashar al Assad, establishing any sort of no-fly zone, or taking any meaningful action that might harm Assad's forces. He also means to forge a counter-alliance consisting of Russia, Iran, Iraq, Syria, and Lebanese Hezbollah and demonstrate that his coalition is more effective than the West's. He intends, finally, to establish a permanent foothold in the Middle East from which he can threaten NATO's southern flank directly, project power into the Mediterranean and the Arab

World, and generally re-create Russia's aura as a global power. He may have more complicated objectives in mind as well, but the State Department should be able at least to recognize these.

Americans should not fall for Putin's "active measures," a phrase he used in his interview with Charlie Rose on 60 Minutes to dismiss as falsehoods descriptions of the Assad regime's brutality against the Syrian people. One must reckon with such an aptitude for falsehood when hearing Putin state, "we do not have any obsession with being a superpower in the international arena." And one must hear the threat in statements such as, "Russia will not participate in any troop operations in the territory of Syria or in any other states. Well, at least we don't plan on it right now....

The Russian deployment severely constrains Western options within Syria and may come to challenge America's ability to continue to operate in Iraq as well. Russian aircraft flying around Syria give Moscow absolute veto power over any attempt to establish any sort of no-fly zone or ISIS-free zone, unless the U.S. and its partners are prepared to risk aerial combat with the Russian Air Force. Russian planes can escort Syrian Air Force (SAF) aircraft on missions, fly combat air patrols (CAP) to protect Syrian helicopters engaged in barrel-bombing, and harass U.S. or NATO aircraft or drones attempting to enforce ISIS-free zones.

Putin is likely trying to guarantee that the U.S. cannot attack the Assad regime effectively now or in the future. The Russian presence alone helps to deter any strikes against Assad. If the U.S. begins to coordinate its air operations with the Russians and the Russians remain tightly allied with Assad, it stands to reason that Moscow will pass along to Damascus warning of any potential U.S. attack. Considering the increasing closeness of the Russia-Iran relationship, we can assume that Putin would provide a similar benefit to Iranian and Lebanese Hezbollah forces on the ground in Syria. The Iraqi military has already announced that it will share intelligence with Syria, Russia, and Iran.

The composition of Russian forces deployed to Syria is absurdly large to be simply protecting Russian civilian and military positions already there. It is, rather, consistent with the mission of providing air support to Assad regime ground forces fighting against the rebels. Su-25 (Frogfoot) ground-attack aircraft comprise the majority of the fixed-wing airframes visible on the ground at Bassel al Assad airfield near Latakia on the Syrian coast.

These planes are similar to U.S. Air Force A-10s in that they were designed to fly low and slow to provide close-air support (CAS) to ground forces engaged with enemy units. The Mi-24 Hind helicopter is a large attack platform that performs a role similar to that of the U.S. Apache, except that the Hind is much larger and, unlike the Apache, can carry troops and supplies as well as conduct ground-attack missions.

These are among the premier Russian airframes for supporting troops in contact. They have limited combat radii (400 kilometers or less) and so would not be ideal for operations beyond the line from roughly Qusayr in the south to Idlib in the north from their current position. They could be moved to other Syrian regime airbases, particularly Damascus and Der ez Zour to support operations in southern or eastern Syria. They pose a very limited threat to U.S., forces, Turkey, Jordan, or Israel from Latakia.

Moscow has also positioned a smaller number of Su-24 Fencer and Su-30 Flanker multirole fighters at Latakia, however. The Fencer is an old airframe used mainly for longer-range ground-attack missions. Its combat radius is sufficient to cover much of Syria from the base at Latakia and to range into the Eastern Mediterranean as well.

It can conduct long-range strike missions against specific targets or aerial reconnaissance. It is not a serious threat to the ability of U.S., NATO, or Israeli air forces to operate freely throughout the region, however, nor is it particularly survivable against advanced surface-to-air missiles. The Flanker is another story entirely. Its radius of action is several thousand kilometers, and it is very well-designed for aerial maneuvering, making it much more able to avoid SAMs and theoretically more capable of contesting airspace against limited numbers of less-proficient Western aircraft. It can be used for strike operations anywhere throughout the Levant and can also perform reconnaissance missions over a wide area.

The Fencers and Flankers are a sensible part of an air posture aimed exclusively at supporting the Assad regime, despite their advanced capabilities and long ranges that might appear to transcend local requirements. Long ranges also translate into the ability to stay airborne for a long time waiting for targets to appear—or to conduct reconnaissance over a given area. The more advanced technical capabilities, particularly of the Flankers, could well allow the Russians to provide much more timely and accurate support to ground forces than the Frogfoots could do, particularly at short notice far from their base. The air package visible on the ground so far, therefore, remains entirely consistent with an exclusively local mission.

U.S. forces undertaking a similar mission would likely bring to bear a mix of aircraft with similar capabilities, ranging from A-10s to advanced and long-range F-15s and F/A-18s.

The U.S. would similarly undertake to expand the ground support facilities at an airbase it intended to use for a protracted support mission, as the Russians are doing. Satellite imagery shows fuel and weapons storage facilities, radomes, logistics areas, and a relatively small complement of (probably) T-90 tanks, advanced BTR-80 armored personnel carriers, and artillery—all consistent with the requirements to keep combat aircraft flying and to secure the airfield against possible terrorist or even insurgent attacks.

Such U.S. activities nevertheless distress regional competitors even when they are aimed entirely at narrowly-constrained local operations. The Iranian military felt itself surrounded when American aircraft were operating out of bases in both Afghanistan and Iran, and even built out additional airfields of its own along the Afghan border to defend against the possibility that U.S. planes would one day fly west rather than east

The U.S. and its NATO and non-NATO partners should take a similar view of the development of the Bassel al Assad airfield into a major Russian airbase. Moscow may well intend at this point nothing more than helping keep Assad in power, but the airfeld, particularly if advanced, long-range, multi-role fighters like the Flanker stay there, gives Vladimir Putin dramatic new capabilities against Turkey, Israel, and the U.S. Sixth Fleet.

The location and orientation of the airfield is particularly problematic in this regard, should Putin choose to use it as a way of increasing tensions with the West outside of Ukraine. The airbase is less than 50 kilometers from the Turkish border and the runways point north-south. A supersonic fighter, such as the Flanker, taking off to the north could be in Turkish airspace within minutes. Worse still, it could be almost impossible to tell if such a fighter intended to cross into Turkey or turn east to operate against rebels until the very last moment. Turkish Air Force aircraft and the U.S. and European NATO planes deployed in Turkey would have very little time to decide whether to intercept the Russian planes or allow them to fly into Turkey.

Such considerations are far from theoretical, considering the aggressiveness with which Russian military aircraft have been regularly oveflying the Baltic countries, Sweden, and Finland. The Bassel al-Assad airbase allows Putin to extend this pattern to Turkey, Israel, Jordan, and Saudi Arabia if he chose.

It also would allow his aircraft to shadow the U.S. Sixth Fleet around the Eastern Mediterranean. He could force Turkey and its NATO allies to establish standing combat air patrols along the southern Turkish border. If he kept the tension very high, the risk of mistakes and accidental weapons releases would also increase. The Russian invasion of Crimea and crypto-invasion of Ukraine has forced the U.S. and Europeans to think about potential territorial violations in northern or eastern Europe that might invoke the Article V collective defense provisions requiring all allies to come to the defense of a threatened member.

They have prepared for such contingencies through the pre-deployment of units and armor in order to deter or respond. Turkey is also a NATO ally, and Russia's presence on the Turkish border gives Putin the ability to test whether NATO will indeed invoke and support Article V in a very different context for which the alliance is much less prepared.

The presence of the Flankers in Latakia could also allow Putin to expand his interference into Iraq. Flankers or even Fencers could pursue ISIS fighters across the border, which they cross freely, to short distances at first, but ultimately deeper into Anbar, Ninewah, and Salah-ad-Din Provinces as well— even over Baghdad International Airport. He might work with his Iranian allies to cause the Iraqi government to invite or, at least, consent to Russian air operations against ISIS in Iraq. Iraq, after all, has no ability of its own to contest such operations even though it retains full legal authority over its own airspace.

If U.S. aircraft wanted to intercept Russian planes flying into Iraq, they would require the permission of the Iraqi government to do so. It is highly unlikely that any Iraqi government would put itself so clearly on the side of the U.S. and against the Russians and Iranians under the current circumstances. The U.S. might well end itself obliged to contend with competing Russian air operations over both Iraq and Syria.

That will not be easy to do. Coordinating the activities of many high-performance aircraft in a confined space is an intricate and difficult job under the best of circumstances. Differences in approach between the U.S. Marine Corps and the U.S. Air Force and Navy, in fact, were sufficient to make it desirable to designate Marine-only airspace in Iraq and Afghanistan. How will American and Russian aircraft conflict their operations? The easiest and most tempting way will be to designate, at least informally, areas in which

Russian aircraft but not Western aircraft fly, and vice-versa. But Putin can force continued renegotiation of such delineations at any time simply by ordering his planes to fly beyond their allotted zone. If he causes them to operate broadly across Syria or into Iraq he can attempt to compel the U.S. to establish de facto a more integrated approach to air operations—one that might effectively require U.S. aircraft to tell the Russians of planned operations in advance.

Putin may be positioning himself, therefore, to compel the U.S. to merge its coalition with his simply in order to mitigate the risks caused by having a lot of combat aircraft flying around. Putin can thus try to take effective control of U.S. air operations in Iraq and Syria without ever having to issue an order. Such an idea is not theoretical either.

It would be an implementation of the doctrine of "reflexive control" that is well and prominently established in current Russian military thinking and is in active use in Russian operations against Ukraine. The idea behind reflexive control is to shape the environment in such a way that the enemy chooses Russia's preferred course of action voluntarily, because it is easiest and all the others appear much more difficult and risky, if not impossible. Reflexive control allows a much weaker force to constrain and even control the activities of a much stronger force. It has worked magnificently in Ukraine, and Putin may well be trying to expand it to the Levant and Iraq.

The U.S. already seems to be falling into this trap. A senior State Department official offering a read-out of the September 27 discussion between Secretary Kerry and Foreign Minister Lavrov said, "if the Russians are going to be more engaged in this theater, we have to de-conflict militarily."

De-confliction is a form of military cooperation that gives the less-responsible party leverage over the more-responsible party. Western air forces are not likely to be willing to take risks that Russian aircraft might. Thus Moscow will control what "de-confliction" actually means in the skies over Syria...or Iraq. This is part of reflexive control at work.

The Russian military has just completed a major annual exercise, Center-2015, which it claims involved 95,000 troops. The kinds of training it reportedly executed offer some useful clues about the types of activities its forces might be prepared to undertake in Syria, although the fact that it claims its forces conducted certain types of training does not mean they did, and the fact that they trained does not mean that they could execute in combat. The breadth and specificity of the claims are nevertheless interesting in what they reveal about possible Russian intentions or, at least, capabilities, for operations in Syria.

Russia exercised its Hind attack helicopters extensively, for example. They practiced conducting rocket and bombing runs against ground targets and providing air cover to ground forces flying very-low-altitude nap-of-the-earth missions. They þred their unguided rockets and cannons against targets mimicking columns of military equipment. They practiced flying with one engine off (simulating its failure in flight) at 200 meters.These are the kinds of skills that would be required if the Russians intended to provide close air support to Syrian, Iranian, or Lebanese Hezbollahi troops in contact with rebel forces.

Russian special forces units, known as Spetsnaz, have also been honing their skills. A group from the Russian military base in Abkhazia (which Russia seized from Georgia in the 2008 war) practiced ambushing and seizing a source, attacking another facility based on his information, and then returning to base to conduct document exploitation of the captured material. A combined force of Spetsnaz and military police practiced fighting "illegal armed formations" in an urban setting. The exercise included freeing ten hostages and destroying the bad guys, while the military police worked to re-establish order and control road movements. Russian reconnaissance units are also practicing operations in mountainous terrain both in North Ossetia (in the Caucasus) and in Tajikistan (where a Russian military force is permanently based).

Russian airborne forces practiced air-dropping into enemy areas to conduct reconnaissance and the destruction of illegal armed groups. They exercised in different drop zones each time, from low altitudes, and into areas unknown to the troops.All of these advanced skills would be valuable should the Russians deploy Spetsnaz or other elite formations into Syria to conduct missions similar to those executed by U.S. Special Forces against high-value targets.

The Russians have also been practicing air operations of many varieties. Their fighters have exercised escort missions for long-range bombers (which would also be applicable to escorting any other kind of aircraft facing potential air threats, such as Assad's air force should the West declare a no-fly zone).

The Russian Ministry of Defense reported on September 21/2015 seemingly apropos of nothing, that forces of the Southern Military District had conducted more than 20 exercises "of various scales" with the "newest ground-attack aircraft Su-25SM", which the Russians call "Grach" or "Rook," and NATO calls Frogfoot.

These exercises included attacking enemy aircraft on the ground, "bases of illegal armed formations," and weapons depots. Frogfoot crews in particular practiced destroying concealed insurgent bases in forested and mountainous regions, as well as emergency actions in the case of equipment failure, and concealed movement to avoid the attacks of hostile fighters. They conducted these training exercises at low altitude and with an eye to defending themselves against anti-aircraft weapons that the enemy might have.

The crews of Su-24 Fencer aircraft practiced aerial refueling, a skill that could be very important indeed if the Russians intend to keep those aircraft flying over Syria for extended periods of time.

All of these exercises support operations in which Russian forces are already engaged in Ukraine, of course. They are also good preparation for counter-terrorism operations against the ISIS affiliate in the Caucasus. It is easy to argue that Putin is only preparing to help the U.S. accomplish something we have been too timid to do—defeat ISIS. Russian aircraft and helicopters will presumably not face the same extreme restrictions on dropping weapons when they might cause civilian casualties or when they are not certain of the target that hamper American crews. And Russia's alliance with Assad virtually ensures much more effective coordination of ground and air operations against whatever rebels the Syrian regime chooses to fight. Might Russia's intervention not work out for the U.S. after all?

The answer is absolutely not. Putin is not simply intervening to attack ISIS. His stated goal and posture is to support the Assad regime and Bashar al Assad in particular. The deployment of Russian forces into Syria therefore effectively guarantees that Assad can remain in power for as long as Putin chooses to back him, thus obviating the need for Assad to make any meaningful concessions to the opposition. Assad's forces had been reeling from the advances of multiple rebel groups and running out of reinforcements. His regime might have faced collapse, he might have been pushed aside, or he might have felt compelled to negotiate seriously with his Syrian opponents.

Now he is likely to become extremely intransigent. The only path to ending the war thus offered by this Russian adventure is the crushing of the majority Sunni Arab population in Syria by the combined forces of Assad, Iran, Lebanese Hezbollah, and the Kremlin. It is hard to see that approach being successful. The Russians, after all, tried something like it in Afghanistan in the 1980s. The conditions in Syria today are not more propitious than they were then—and Russia is nothing like as strong militarily as was the Soviet Union at the height of its power. No, the advent of Russian reinforcements is likely only to cement a brutal stalemate that has driven millions of people from their homes, radicalized the region, caused a humanitarian apocalypse, and turned Syria into a magnet for global jihadists.

Any serious plan for bringing peace, ultimately, to Syria requires separating supporters of ISIS and al Qaeda affiliate Jabhat al Nusra from the bulk of the Syrian Sunni Arab population now working with them for lack of any better alternatives. That approach requires differentiating among the various groups fighting against Assad, identifying which ones might be lured away, and determining what would be required to lure them. Putin, it seems clear, has no interest whatsoever in such an approach. He told U.S. networks that "provision of military support to illegal structures runs counter to the principles of modern international law and the United Nations Charter," and made it clear that he regards the only "legitimate government entities" in Syria to be the organs of Assad's government.

It is likely, therefore, that Russian support for Assad will take the form of an indiscriminate attack against Assad's opponents, regardless of the degree of their affiliation with ISIS or JN. Such an effort will tend to unify the Syrian opposition with the jihadists against the Russians and Assad. If the U.S. appears to support Russia—a position the Obama Administration seems to be steadily drifting toward—it will solidify the idea that all of the Western powers are united with Iran behind Assad and that only al Qaeda and ISIS offer international support for the struggle against the Alawite government. A blank-check support for the Assad regime of the sort Putin is ready to provide, in other words, is very likely to backfire, further radicalizing the conflict and permitting the continued commitment of war crimes by the Assad regime.

The Russian deployment to Syria is a serious blow to the U.S., its allies, and its prospects for developing and executing any plausible strategy to defeat ISIS and al Qaeda in the Levant and Iraq. It is likely the thin edge of the wedge, moreover, that will offer Putin greater opportunities to disrupt American operations in the Middle East and the Mediterranean. The path of least resistance for the U.S. will be gradually coming to terms with the new reality and making a virtue of necessity by cooperating, reluctantly at first and then more enthusiastically, with the Russian-Iranian-Syrian axis that is now forming.

It will, in other words, continue the trend of realigning the American geostrategic position the Middle East fundamentally. More remarkably, it may represent the opening of a new Russian flank against NATO and against America's ability to operate in the region. If so, it will be much easier to resist or defect this Russian adventure now, at its beginning and when it is very limited, than to reverse it some years hence after it has taken form root.

The battle begins

Before dawn on Thursday, Sept. 24/2015, Russian marines went into battle for the first time since their deployment to Syria. Russian Marine Brigade 810 fought with Syrian army and Hizballah special forces in an attack or ISIS forces at the Kweiris airbase, east of Aleppo.

This operation runs contrary to the assurances of President Vladimir Putin to Prime Minister Binyamin Netaryahu on Sept. 21/2015 – just three days ago - that Russian forces in Syria were only there to defend Russian interests and would not engaged in combat with the Syrian army, Hizballah or Iranian troops. The ISIS force defending the air base is dominated by Chechen fighters under the command of Abu Omar al-Shishani, who is considered one of the terrorist organization's leading commanders in the last two years. The 27-year-old al-Shishani hails from the Chechen enclave of Pankisi in Georgia, like many others who joined ISIS from 2012.

However, targeting Chechen fighters was not the only reason for the order given by Russian command in Syria to attack the air base. The Russian mission in Syria would be to break the Syrian rebel siege on Aleppo, Syria's second-largest city. As their first step, the Russians would have to prevent the cutoff of highway 5, running from Aleppo to Damascus, and keep it open for Syrian army reinforcements and military equipment to the city.

The build-up at Latakia

It's been evident since late August that Israel expected the imminent deployment of Russian fighter squadrons - the Americans chose to stall for a few days before giving any response to these early stories, mindful presumably that President Putin was about to commit on the ground in a way President Obama has dreaded doing since the outbreak of the Syrian civil war four years ago. From 20 August shipments of equipment from Black Sea ports, via the Bosphorus, to the Syrian port of Tartous started picking up.

The operation followed a logical military pattern: secure the Latakia airfield; improve its facilities; create a defence against possible air attack; and lastly, bring in your combat aircraft. Then dozens of flights by heavy Antonov cargo planes started augmenting the sea lift.

The Russians had moved in 28 combat jets (12 Su24 bombers, 12 Su25 ground attack aircraft and 4 Su-30 multi-role fighters), two types of drones, and 20 helicopters (a mix of gunships and troop carriers). Some reports suggest that the deployment is getting so large that it will need more than one airfield for its operations, and indeed the latest satellite pictures of the Syrian coastal region suggest that other military facilities may be under preparation for further deployments.

Pentagon officials were briefing on Monday, that the drones were already operating, presumably searching for targets, and that offensive air operations could be expected "within days". The Russians, in a fortnight, have moved in a striking force of roughly equivalent power to the few dozen surviving capable aircraft at Syria's disposal - but with more modern guided weapons and surveillance systems. This initiative, just like the Kremlin's moves in Ukraine last year, strikes at a delicate transatlantic seam.

The deployment of some of Russia's most advanced ground attack planes and fighter jets as well as multiple air defense systems at the base near the ancestral home of President Bashar al-Assad appears to leave little doubt about Moscow's goal to establish a military outpost in the Middle East. The planes are protected by at least two or possibly three SA-22 surface-to-air, antiaircraft systems, and unarmed Predator-like surveillance drones are being used to fly reconnaissance missions.

With competent pilots and with an effective command and control process, the addition of these aircraft could prove very effective depending on the desired objectives for their use. In addition, a total of 15 Russian Hip transport and Hind attack helicopters are also now stationed at the base, doubling the number of those aircraft from last week. For use in possible ground attacks, the Russians now also have nine T-90 tanks and more than 500 marines, up from more than 200 last week.

The operation to move dozens of combat aircraft and hundreds of troops to the aid of President Bashar al-Assad must have been given the green light some weeks ago, but think of what's been happening during the past 10 days as reports emerged of the Russians appearing at an air base near the Assad stronghold of Latakia.

White House's "no way" policy

A major overhaul of the Obama administration's program to train and equip moderate Syrian rebels is expected to be announced in the coming days, according to several administration officials. The move comes after the program has fallen far short of its goals. A top U.S. general told the Senate on Wednesday that of the thousands the Pentagon was supposed to train in the first year, only four or five are in place on the battlefield. One leading option to dramatically reshape the train-and-equip program would be to place several hundred trained rebels with other groups of Syrian fighters to fight ISIS.

The trained rebels might not fight ISIS directly, as the program originally intended, but instead would help by providing communications, intelligence and targeting information, officials said, though they would not call in airstrikes on their own. Standard procedure continues to be that coalition forces verify all information before airstrikes are conducted.

The administration is looking at potentially placing the trained rebels with groups of Syrian Arabs now living in the areas between Raqqa and the Turkish border, as well as alongside some Kurds in the area. Officials said that there may be a loose coalition of hundreds of Syrian Arabs willing to join forces.

No final decision has been made, and other options remain under consideration. But the overhaul underscores the conclusion inside the administration that the program as it currently exists "is a big mess" and must be changed, one official told CNN.

A review of the effort has been underway since the initial group of some 54 rebels put into northern Syria this summer came under attack and are no longer a functioning fighting force. That attack demonstrated that units have to be larger so the forces can protect themselves, officials said.

The fate of the original effort to train and equip more than 5,000 moderate rebels in the first year was the subject of a fiery hearing before the Senate Armed Services Committee when the top U.S. general in charge of fighting ISIS acknowledged the current status of the initial 54 trained by the United States.

With American policy stalled and arguments about the degree to which its bombing campaign has blunted Islamic State (IS), the president's envoy, retired General John Allen, and several other senior officials have decided to step down. Gen Allen was known to believe the US should harden its position on the overthrow of President Assad, and in the need for a safe zone in the north of Syria - instead the prospect seems to be slipping away of either happening.

The US general running Central Command, the Pentagon's Middle East arm, went through humiliating testimony in front of the Senate Armed Services Committee in which he had to admit that the number of Syrian rebels trained under a $500m (£325m) US program who had actually made it into the field could be counted on the fingers of one hand, and that plans for a safe area in northern Syria to protect civilians would be meaningless without ground troops, but he could not recommend the commitment of US soldiers on such a mission.

IS has been spreading its influence among Muslim communities in Russia's North Caucasus, and many of the Russians in its ranks are believed to be Chechens. An anti-Moscow insurgency continues in the region. The main nationalities of IS volunteers from Central Asia are Uzbek, Kazakh and Turkmen.

Russia's "Syria stake"

US Secretary of Defence Ashton Carter and Russia's Defence Minister Sergei Shoigu have held their first talks to discuss the conflict in Syria. The phone call between the two men which took place on Friday, with Russian state media saying it proved the two sides had common ground, while the Pentagon said the ministers discussed how the US and Russia could avoid accidentally clashing on the ground.

Russia's reported increased military presence in Syria has raised concerns in the US for some time. First and foremost are what the leadership perceives as security concerns. The Kremlin argues that the fall of Syrian President Bashar al-Assad would bring radical Islamists to power in Syria and that this in turn would lead to further destabilisation in the Middle East and consequently affect Russia's Muslim regions.

Russia points to Western-backed changes of government in Iraq and Libya, which have led to violence and instability affecting the region as a whole. Moscow is also concerned about the possible return to Russia of the 2,000 or more Russian-speakers currently fighting against Assad's forces.

Russia's economic and military interests also play a role. Ambitions to extend the reach of the Russian navy mean Moscow needs to safeguard the supply point in Tartus, while Russian energy companies are interested in the possible oil and gas reserves along Syria's coastline.

For these reasons, Moscow's "master plan" is to ensure the survival of the Assad regime, and recent reports of its decision to increase military support to Damascus should therefore not have come as a surprise to the West. The Kremlin is not unwavering in its loyalty to President Assad. On the contrary, his inflexibility irritates the Kremlin and has created mistrust on several occasions prior to the current conflict, including in the early 2000s, when the Syrian government refused to extradite Chechen rebels.

Russian contacts with the Syrian opposition demonstrate that Moscow is keeping its options open. But the Russian government would probably show more flexibility if the opposition offered to preserve some of Russia's political and economic influence in a post-Assad Syria, and to prevent an influx of jihadist groups from Syria to Russia's Muslim regions.

In June 2015, while confirming Moscow's support for Damascus, President Putin stated that the Kremlin was "ready to work with the president [Assad] to ensure political transformation, so that all Syrians have access to the instruments of power".

In this vein, the Kremlin has adopted a two-track approach. On the one hand it is intensifying dialogue with the international community on options for the national reconciliation process in Syria. Meanwhile, it is increasing the volume and quality of military supplies to the Syrian regime to ensure it survives long enough for the Kremlin to achieve a diplomatic breakthrough commensurate with its interests.

Russia's reaction

Russia's reaction would be likely to be overwhelmingly negative. In 2013, when the US and its partners were considering options for military intervention, Foreign Minister Sergei Lavrov and Defence Minister Shoigu said Moscow would adopt an asymmetric response to any attack on Assad, to make the West "learn its lesson". The increased supplies of arms and weapons systems provided by Moscow will make any military operation against Damascus more challenging. Despite the presence of Russian military advisers and other troops, any direct military confrontation between Russia and Western forces in Syria is unlikely though.

This telephone call, initiated by the Russian side, shows that Moscow does not want to escalate confrontation with the West over Syria beyond the current level without what it sees as good reason. Currently, the Russian authorities are doing their best to clarify their position and partly allay Western concerns. As part of possible trust-building measures they even offered to launch direct negotiations with the US on how to deal with the so-called Islamic State (IS).
Russia's endgame

The confrontation between Russia and the West over Ukraine has contributed to Moscow's heightened engagement in the Middle East. The Kremlin believes that good relations with states in the region can help Russia avoid international isolation and compensate for the negative effect of US and EU sanctions.

If necessary, the Kremlin can also use its leverage with other states in the region, such as Iran and Egypt, to put additional pressure on Western countries. For example, in March 2014, in the wake of the Ukrainian crisis, Russia announced it was reconsidering its participation in the negotiations between Iran and the P5+1 (the five permanent members of the UN Security Council - China, France, Russia, the UK and the US - plus Germany). This was enough to keep Washington concerned about this possibility for the rest of 2014.

"We don't want to die there"

Mainly non commissioned troops refused to deploy to Syria due to their fear of ISIS. One of the soldiers, a lieutenant named Alexei, said, "We don't want to go Syria, we don't want to die there."

The group complained that the military had hid their destination from them. They were due to be shipped off on September 17, but 10 days later they were told they would be deployed to a hot region with a very different climate than what they were used to, and that there would be poisonous animals at the new place, but the specific region was not named.

At first, the soldiers assumed they were being sent to eastern Ukraine. But On September 16, the army told them they would be sent to Latakia and that they may have to participate in the fighting alongside Syrian troops.

The troops were required to sign confidentiality agreements, and were told that if they didn't sign – their families would not receive compensation if they were wounded or killed in the fighting. The soldiers were also warned that if they didn't sign – they would face criminal charges.

The soldiers were surprised to receive new weapons and equipment with their serial numbers removed. The soldiers were also instructed on how to behave if they were captured.Mothers of soldiers had been sent to Syria, said that their sons had been sent to fight a war that was not theirs: "People there are driven like cattle to the slaughter." The soldiers complained that they felt like mercenaries.

Alex Tanzer, an expert on Russian media, explained that President Vladimir Putin passed a law in recent months which banned the publication of names of soldiers killed in action. The law was passed as a result of the public outcry caused by the war in Ukraine. The outcry has been renewed by the soldiers who are being sent to Syria. The Russian Defense Ministry declined to comment on the report.

Russia prepared to bolster Assad

Recent sightings of brand new Russian armoured vehicles in Syria, of types never previously supplied to its ally, suggest that with the Assad regime suffering serious reverses, Moscow is intent on redressing the military balance.

On 20 August, a heavily-laden Alligator class landing ship of the Russian Navy, the Nikolay Filchenkov, was seen passing southwards through the Bosphorus.

On board, according to experts who have analysed the images, were trucks and armoured vehicles. The ship was believed to be on its way to Syria. Subsequently, the Syrian army has released video material that shows seemingly brand new BTR-82A infantry combat vehicles in action or on exercises - a variant of the vehicle that has never before been supplied to the Syrian military.

The vehicles appear to be in a Russian paint scheme and thus may have been taken straight from Russian army stocks. Separate images have emerged of Russian Tigre military utility vehicles; again a type that has not been exported to Syria before. Caution must always be used when analysing this kind of material.

But Joseph Dempsey, an expert at the International Institute for Strategic Studies in London, says that the images "if authentic, provide strong evidence of the BTR-82A and Tigr being in Syria". The delivery of these weapons raises all sorts of questions.

Syria did receive a small number of the related BTR-80 armoured personnel carrier in late 2013/early 2014 but the BTR-82A has a more modern and very different turret and weapons station.

Russia is one of the Syrian president's few foreign allies. It has long been a major arms supplier to Syria and, in the current crisis, it has given the Syrian regime important diplomatic support. Russia was instrumental in helping to negotiate the deal in 2013 under which the Assad regime gave up its chemical weapons.

Russia has long maintained a small naval base on the Syrian coast at Tartus. It represents a toehold for Russian influence in the region that peaked during the 1970s at the height of the Cold War. However, the Syrian crisis has alarmed Moscow. It is every bit as concerned by the rise of the murderous religious radicals of the so-called Islamic State (IS) movement as is the West.

Russia did not respond to the upheavals of the "Arab Spring" with the enthusiasm of many Western governments. And in retrospect, given that hopes for a democratic surge through the region have collapsed, Russia's hard-headed pragmatism looks to be a little more realistic than much of the West's "aspirational" diplomacy.

The Syria crisis also provides Russia with an opportunity. Its ties to the Assad regime make it a key player. Russian Foreign Minister Sergei Lavrov has forcefully reiterated Russia's position that the departure of Mr Assad cannot be a condition for any peace deal.

Such demands, he says, are "totally unrealistic and counterproductive". Russia insists that it is working to create what it calls a "broad anti-terrorist front" to counter IS. But the crucial thing for Russia is that the Assad regime must survive, whatever Mr Assad's personal fate in the longer term.

Much of the attention over recent weeks has focused on Russia's diplomatic efforts regarding Syria; its talks with senior Saudi and Iranian officials, for example. But, in the meantime, things have not been going well for Mr Assad on the ground, with his opponents pressing ever closer to the Alawite heartland - the coastal basin to the east of the Mediterranean, inland from Latakia and Tartus.

Amidst the uncertainty, a host of rumours are flying round of a much greater Russian role. Russia has denied that it recently delivered advanced warplanes to Syria. Some Israeli analysts, for example, believe that Russia is preparing to use its own aircraft against IS and might even be willing to play a greater role on the ground if the Assad regime's fortunes do not change.

This for now may be little more than speculation. The Russians themselves have denied that any aircraft have been deployed to Syria to prepare for strikes against IS. One expert, Ruslan Pukhov, a spokesman for Russia's arms industry, believes that what the Syrian forces require right now is "ammunition, light weapons, communications and UAVs [drones]"

Israel in panic

With Russia apparently beefing up its military presence in Syria, some countries are getting nervous about what could happen -- including Israel. Israeli Prime Minister Benjamin Netanyahu visited Russian President Vladimir Putin to discuss "the Middle East peace process and the fight against the global terrorist threat,".

But in a rare move, Netanyahu brought several top Israeli military and security officials with him to Moscow. Israel Defense Forces Chief of Staff Lt. Gen. Gadi Eizenkot, IDF Director of Military Intelligence Maj. Gen. Hertzi HaLevi and National Security Adviser Yossi Cohen accompanied the Prime Minster.

The meeting, which was closed to the media, came after satellite pictures showed a rapid buildup of an air force base in Syria, with loads of Russian military equipment moving in. Among the Russian equipment are advanced Russian Sukhoi Flanker fighter jets. Afterward, Netanyahu called the talks "substantive" -- noting that both countries had agreed to "a joint mechanism for preventing misunderstandings between our forces" in and around Syria.

He said there was a "very big" need to prevent such "misunderstandings." "Israel is constantly working to prevent the transfer of advanced and deadly weaponry from Syrian territory to Hezbollah," said Netanyahu, who also alluded to a threat from the Golan Heights.

"Israel is taking action and, when it does so, it is important for everyone -- including Russia -- to know that we are taking action." The hotline will enable the two sides to ask to clarify events, without offering their reasons for doing so. In other words, the hotline will be used at a time when Russian or Israeli military operations in Syria are underway, and senior officers are acting to avert a probable clash between the two military forces - or after the event.

In the first instance, it will be important to cut the clashes short without delay to avert an escalation of hostilities. Besides the technical arrangements for operating the hotline, the two deputy chiefs of staff will need to meet, get to know each other, and agree on a framework of military topics for discussion. This process could take several weeks.

In other words, the issue at hand is not coordination of military operations, but rather a mechanism that goes into action fast to assess collisions after the event and determine how to prevent them in the future.

In any case, Israel is constrained from full military coordination with the Russian military, especially in the Syrian theater, by the IDF's commitment to joint operations with the US and Jordanian army via US Central Command Forward-Jordan. The IDF moreover maintains mechanisms for coordinating its air, naval and missile operations with the US military.

Russia, for its part, coordinates its military operations in Syria with its close ally, Iran, which is also Israel's sworn enemy. The Russian chief of staff was not in uniform when he received Gen. Eisenkot. This was a demonstration of the Russian intention to downgrade the military aspect of the Israeli-Russian talks.

Before flying out of Moscow, Netanyahu announced that he had briefed Washington fully on its talks with Putin, thus ascertaining that those talks in no way impaired any aspect of Israeli-US military cooperation. According to initial reports, Prime Minister Binyamin Netanyahu and President Vladimir Putin talked mostly at cross-purposes when they met in the presidential residence outside Moscow Monday, Sept. 21/2015

Netanyahu, who brought with him an impressive party of top Israeli generals, presented his host with intelligence evidence to demonstrate that Iran – under the cover of the Syrian army – is trying to "build a second terrorist front against us from the Golan Heights."

He indicated that Israel would be forced to resort to military action to counter this front and asked to see Putin in order to avert collisions between Israeli and Russian forces on Syrian soil. Putin greeted these words with slippery evasions. Syria is in no state to open up an additional front, he said, and Moscow s main goal in its involvement in Syria is to defend that country.

The point the Israeli prime minister tried to make was that Israel's security was at stake here - not Syria's. He stressed that Iran and Syria were arming the radical Islamic organization Hizballah with "advanced weaponry that is directed at us, and has already been fired at us."

But Putin sidestepped this too, remarking that that he is aware that Israel has been fired upon from Syria, and has condemned that, but added that those weapons were "locally produced." While the two leaders were still talking, US officials disclosed that Russia had started drone surveillance missions in Syria.

On Saturday, Sept. 19/2015 just two days before Israeli Prime Minister Binyamin Netanyahu's summit with Russian President Vladimir Putin at the presidential dacha outside Moscow, troops at the Russian base outside the coastal Syrian city of Latakia were seen preparing to deploy batteries of advanced S-300 anti-aircraft missiles. Their presence in Syria will raise major questions, one of which is this: against which air power are they deployed, given the fact that the Islamic State has no air force.

Their deployment therefore poses troubling ramifications for the ongoing Syrian civil war as well as the region as a whole. For Israel, the placement of S-300 missiles in Syria is problematic for three reasons:

1. They seriously reduce the Israeli Air Force's freedom of action in Lebanese and Syrian airspace.

2. Following a spate of contradictory and muddled statements about Moscow's intentions to withhold the S-300s from Syria and Iran – an apparent smoke screen -, it turns out that they are coming to Syria after all.

3. The Russians say they are building up military strength in Syria to fight ISIS. But neither ISIS nor any other regional power poses an air threat to the Russian deployment. So the state-of-the-art air defense missile delivered to Syria, to which Iran too has access, does pose a threat to Israel's security.

Its deployment in Syria appears to signal that Putin has a long game for his military buildup in Syria - more far-reaching that it would appear. Each day brings news of more Russian forces arriving in Syria. At first, reports said several hundred marines were being deployed, but now preparations are being made for 2,000 of them.

A similar process is occurring with the deployment of anti-aircraft missiles. Initially, reports said that Moscow was providing Syria with the SA-22, known as the Pantsir-S1, but those missiles never arrived. Now, it appears that the S-300 is to be deployed instead.

The arrival of four advanced multi-role Sukhoi 30SM (Flanker) tactical jets in Latakia on Sept. 18/2015 has also raised eyebrows. It came just hours after US Defense Secretary Ashton Carter met with Russian Defense Minister Sergei Shoigu in an effort to prevent collisions between US and Russian forces operating in Syria. As those jets are intended for air-to-air combat, observers wonder which forces are to be targeted. The same question hangs over the half a dozen MiG-31 interceptors, which landed in Damascus earlier this month.

In another development that was only noticed in very few circles in the West and Israel, Iranian Gen. Yahya Rahim Safavi, military advisor of Iran's supreme leader Ayatollah Ali Khamenei, said on 'Friday, Sept. 18/2015: "Russia moves in coordination with Iran in some regional issues including Syria."

In other words, the US and Israel, which are attempting to coordinate their military steps with those of Russia, have already fallen behind. Reports in Israel over the last few days have claimed that Putin was keen on holding the summit even more than Netanyahu, and that the Israeli Air Force had started setting up a mechanism for liaison with the Russian Air Force in order to prevent inadvertent collisions.

There is no doubt that Netanyahu is making a bold statement by bringing to the Kremlin meeting the IDF chief of staff Lt. Gen. Gady Eisenkot and the head of military intelligence, Maj. Gen. Hertzi Halevi. This is the first time such high-ranking military officers have participated in a meeting of the Israeli and Russian leaders.

Putin will no doubt parrot Obama in assuring Netanyahu of Russia's abiding commitment to Israel's security. But he will not waver in his steps for strengthening Iran's foothold in Syria, any more than Obama has.

The enhancement of President Bashar Assad's military capabilities by an injection of sophisticated weapons is part and parcel of Putin's project, and a share of those arms will undoubtedly be allotted to Assad's ally, Hizballah.

Lacking most of all is a consensus on which terrorist organizations pose the paramount threat. For Obama, it is the Islamic State of Iraq and the Levant - ISIS; for Netanyahu, ISIS and Hizballah are equally dangerous; whereas Putin lumps ISIS and other Syrian Islamist rebel groups in the same category, especially the Nusra Front, which has Russian Chechen recruits and therefore poses a direct threat to Moscow.

Putin warns Israel

Russian President Vladimir Putin is concerned about Israel's repeated attacks in Syria after talking for an hour and a half with President Barack Obama early Tuesday, Sept. 29/2015 on the sidelines of the UN General Assembly in New York. Putin agreed that Israel's security concerns must be taken into account in Syria, but he was worried by the IDF's periodic strikes on positions in the embattled territory.

The message the Russian president issued, straight after his meeting with Obama, was that Moscow would not put up with Israeli strikes in Syria, even in response to an attack.

During the meeting between Putin – Netanyahou in Moscow, Israel's prime minister disclosed his knowledge that Gen. Azadi had come to replace Gen. Ali Allah Dadi, who died on Jan 18 in an Israeli air strike against a convoy carrying Iranian Guards and Hizballah commanders traveling near Quneitra. They were there to survey a site for mounting a terrorist campaign inside Israel.

The Israeli air strike nipped this plan in the bud. But Iran and Hizballah never gave up, and Gen. Azadi was assigned to finish setting up the terror machine and getting it up and running. The Russian leader explained that Israel's attacks on Iranian military targets presented a problem because they weakened Bashar Assad.

As matter stand therefore, Russia and Israel are on a collision course: While Israel views Gen. Azadi as a menacing adversary, Putin regards him as part of the Russian-Iranian axis in Syria and wants Israel to keep its hands off him. This point is of such paramount importance to the Russian leader's plans for Syria that he made a big deal of it at the highest international forum - almost as a sequel to his first meeting with President Obama in more than a year.

He was signaling strongly that the arrangement for the Russian and Israeli armies to coordinate their operations in Syria is unworkable and he was losing patience with Israel's "security concerns" in so far as they impeded his plans with Iran for Syria.

Israel's gas fields

More than a fortnight ago, Russian President Vladimir put a proposition to Israel for Moscow to undertake responsibility for guarding Israel's Mediterranean gas fields, along with the offer of a Russian investment of $7-10 billion for developing Leviathan, the largest well, and building a pipeline to Turkey for exporting the gas to Europe. The offer was made to Prime Minister Binyamin Netanyahu in confidential phone conversations and through quiet envoys.

Russian President put a proposition to Israel for Moscow to undertake responsibility for guarding Israel's Mediterranean gas fields, along with the offer of a Russian investment of $7-10 billion for developing Leviathan, the largest well, and building a pipeline to Turkey for exporting the gas to Europe.

The offer was made to Prime Minister Binyamin Netanyahu in confidential phone conversations and through quiet envoys.

At the time, Putin did not share with Netanyahu his plans for an imminent buildup of marines, air force units, warships and missiles in Syria, although the plan had been worked out in detail with Tehran in late July. The Russian ruler put it this way: Leviathan abuts on the fringes of Lebanon's economic water zone and is therefore vulnerable to potential sabotage by Iran, Syria or Hizballah, whether by commando or rocket attack.

A multibillion Russian investment in the field would make it a Russian project which neither Syria nor Hizballah would dare attack, even though it belongs to Israel. But now the situation has assumed a different face. Russian forces are streaming to Latakia, and Moscow has declared the area from Tartous, Syria up to Cyprus closed to shipping and air traffic from Sept. 15 to Oct. 7 in view of a "military exercise including test firings of guided missiles" from Russian warships.

When he offered a shield for Israeli gas fields in late August, The Russian ruler knew that implementation would rest with Russian military forces on the spot, rather than Iranian and Syrian reluctance to harm Russian interests.

Then, on Aug. 30, Netanyahu discussed the new Russian proposition with Italian Prime Minister Matteo Renzi when they met in Florence, in the context of the former Italian Prime Minister Silvio Berlusconi's involvement in Middle Eastern and European energy business and his close ties with Putin. Berlusconi and Netanyahu are also good friends. The Israeli prime minister never explicitly confirmed to Putin that he would consider the Russian transaction.

He hesitated because he sensed that a deal with Moscow for gas projects would be unacceptable to Washington and Noble Energy of Texas, which holds a 39.66 percent share in the consortium controlling Leviathan, as well as stakes in the smaller Tanin and Tamar gas wells.

Meanwhile, two Israeli ministers, Moshe Kahlon, finance, and Arye Deri, economy, consistently obstructed the final government go-ahead for gas production, tactics which also held Netanyahu back from his reply to Putin.

But when the fresh influx of Russian troops and hardware to Syria became known, Netanyahu began to appreciate that, not only had Israel's military and strategic situation with regard to Syria and the eastern Mediterranean been stood on its head, so too had foreign investment prospects for development projects in Israeli gas.

Israel's strategic landscape had in fact changed radically in four respects:

1. Its government can no longer accept as a working hypothesis (which never, incidentally, held up) the short term expectancy of the Assad regime. The injection of Russian military might, combined with the Iranian Revolutionary Guards forces, have given Assad a substantial lease of life.

The Israel Defense Forces must therefore revamp its posture on the Syrian front, and reassess its sponsorship of the select rebel groups which are holding the line in southern Syria against hostile Iranian or Hizballah cross-border attacks on northern Israel.

The changing attitude was suggested in views heard in the last couple of days from top Israeli security officials, who now say that leaving Assad in office might be the better option, after all.

2. The new Russian ground, air and sea buildup taking shape in Syria provides a shield not just for the Assad regime but also Hizballah. This too calls for changes in Israel's military posture.

3. The Russian military presence in Syria seriously inhibits Israel's flexibility for launching military action against Iranian or Hizballah targets when needed.

4. Three aspects of the new situation stand out prominently:

a) The Russian air force and navy are the strongest foreign military force in the eastern Mediterranean. The US deploys nothing comparable.

b) Israel's military strength is substantial but no one is looking for a military clash with the Russians, although this did occur four decades ago, when Israel was fighting for its life against Russian-backed Arab invasions.

c) In view of the prevalence of the Russian military presence in the eastern Mediterranean, it is hard to see any foreign investor coming forward to sink billions of dollars in Israeli gas.

d) Although Russia called Saturday, Sept. 12/2015 for "military-to-military cooperation with the United States" to avert "unintended incidents" amid its naval "exercises" off the coast of Syria, the tone of the call was cynical. It is more than likely that Moscow may revert to the original Putin offer of a Russian defense shield for Israeli gas fields. But with such strong Russian cards in place in Syria, he may well stiffen his terms for this deal.

Iran's operations in Syria

The Islamic Republic of Iran has conducted an extensive, expensive, and integrated effort to keep President Bashar al-Assad in power as long as possible while setting conditions to retain its ability to use Syrian territory and assets to pursue its regional interests should Assad fall.

The Iranian security and intelligence services are advising and assisting the Syrian military in order to preserve Bashar al-Assad's hold on power. These efforts have evolved into an expeditionary training mission using Islamic Revolutionary Guards Corps (IRGC) Ground Forces, Quds Force, intelligence services, and law enforcement forces. The deployment of IRGC Ground Forces to conflict abroad is a notable expansion of Iran's willingness and ability to project military force beyond its borders.

Iran has been providing essential military supplies to Assad, primarily by air. Opposition gains in Syria have interdicted many ground resupply routes between Baghdad and Damascus, and the relative paucity of Iranian port-visits in Syria suggests that Iran's sea-lanes to Syria are more symbolic than practical. The air line of communication between Iran and Syria is thus a key vulnerability for Iranian strategy in Syria.

Iran would not be able to maintain its current level of support to Assad if this air route were interdicted through a no-fly zone or rebel capture of Syrian airfields.

Iran is also assisting pro-government shabiha militias, partly to hedge against Assad's fall or the contraction of the regime into Damascus and a coastal Alawite enclave. These militias will become even more dependent on Tehran in such a scenario, allowing Iran to maintain some ability to operate in and project force from Syria.

Lebanese Hezbollah began to take on a more direct combat role in Syria as the Assad regime began losing control over Syrian territory in 2012. Hezbollah has supported Assad with a robust, well-trained force whose involvement in the conflict aligns with Iranian strategic interests as Secretary General Hassan Nasrallah acknowledged on April 30 in Tehran. Hezbollah's commitment is not without limitations, however, because Nasrallah must carefully calibrate his support to Assad with his domestic responsibilities in order constituency in Lebanon.

Iraqi Shi'a militants are also fighting in Syria in support of Assad. Their presence became overt in 2012 with the formation of the Abu al-Fadl al-Abbas Brigade, a pro-government militia that is a conglomerate of Syrian and foreign Shi'a fighters, including members of Lebanese Hezbollah and Iraq-based Asa'ib Ahl al-Haq and Kata'ib Hezbollah. Like other paramilitary forces operating in Syria, these militants escalated their involvement as the conflict descended into civil war. The open participation of Iraqi Shi'a militants in Syria is an alarming indicator of the expansion of sectarian conflict throughout the region.

The Syrian conflict has already constrained Iran's influence in the Levant, and the fall of the Assad regime would further reduce Tehran's ability to project power. Iran's hedging strategy aims to ensure, however, that it can continue to pursue its vital interests if and when the regime collapses, using parts of Syria as a base as long as the Syrian opposition fails to establish full control over all of Syrian territory.

Iran has provided support to Syria's chemical weapons programs, including the deployment of Iranian scientists, the supply of equipment and precursor chemicals, and technical training. Syria has been Iran's strategic partner in deterring Israel from attacking Iran's proxies or its nuclear program. Iran's strategy in Syria aims to keep President Bashar al-Assad in power as long as possible while setting conditions to ensure Tehran's ability to use Syrian territory and assets to pursue its regional interests should Assad fall. Iran has conducted an extensive, expensive, and integrated effort to achieve these objectives.

Iranian training and support to the Syrian state security apparatus is intended to prolong Assad's grip on power. This effort consists of an advisory and assistance mission to support the Assad regime's security forces. Iran has conducted this foreign internal defense mission in Syria using its regular Islamic Revolutionary Guards Corps (IRGC) forces alongside the IRGC Quds Force and other clandestine services, marking a new kind of Iranian expeditionary military strategy. These missions initially supported Assad's counterinsurgency campaign, which attempted to restore state control throughout Syria. As Assad began to lose control over eastern and northern Syria in the summer of 2012, the Iranian advisory and assistance mission continued to reinforce Assad's geographically consolidated grip on central and southern Syria.

Iran is also hedging against the failure of this strategy by complementing its support for state security institutions with assistance to pro-government militias in order to develop proxies that will survive Assad. This aspect of Iran's approach is congruent with Tehran's longstanding efforts in Lebanon and Iraq, where it also built Shi'a militias to ensure that its interests were protected even in the absence of effective or pliable host states. These paramilitary forces have become increasingly important to Iran and the Assad regime as the nature of the conflict has devolved from counterinsurgency to civil war. As Syrian state military capabilities continue to deteriorate, these militias may form the framework for Iran's continued influence and activity in Syria and the region.

The Syrian conflict has already constrained Iran's influence in the Levant, and the fall of the Assad regime would further reduce Tehran's ability to project power. Iran's hedging strategy aims to ensure, however, that it can continue to pursue its vital interests if and when the regime collapses, using parts of Syria as a base as long as the Syrian opposition fails to establish full control over all of Syrian territory.

This strategy is meant to guarantee that the mostly Alawite remnants of the Assad regime continue to provide support for Iranian activity in the Levant even if an opposition government takes power in Damascus. By encouraging convergence between pro-regime militias and loyalist remnants of the Assad regime by supporting both the official and the paramilitary components of Assad's forces, Iran is working to preserve its short-term interests while laying the foundations for long-term influence and access in the Levant.

Few observers doubt Iranian involvement in Syria. The scope and nature of that involvement, however, has been difficult to describe or pinpoint. Iran has once again demonstrated its ability to work within low intensity conflict environments while successfully obfuscating details about its operations, as it did in Iraq during the latter half of the Iraq War. Iranian media sources provide only limited insight, and often only in rare public slips, and most Syrian opposition accusations of Iranian involvement lack credibility. Utilizing only open-source material, it is difficult and in many cases impossible to verify press reports or public announcements independently.

The information below derives from a broad range of sources, including U.S. Department of the Treasury designations, Western and Iranian news outlets, and social media, which have been placed in context to form assessments based on the indicators available and past behavior. Advisory Mission Iran has made a concerted effort to advise the Syrian military in order to preserve Bashar al-Assad's hold on power. Both the IRGC Quds Force (IRGC-QF) and elements of the conventional IRGC Ground Forces (IRGC-GF), as well as several Iranian intelligence organizations, have trained and advised elements of Assad's state military and security services. These organizations all have distinct operational strengths that complement one another in support of Assad.

Top-level Support to the Syrian Army Iran's primary foreign military arm, IRGC-QF, appears to be leading this effort. The U.S. Department of the Treasury (USDOT) designated IRGC-QF Commander Major General Qassem Suleimani and Operations and Training Commander Mohsen Chizari in May 2011 for their role in "the violent repression against the Syrian people."

The Quds Force is responsible for Iran's external operations, and Commander Suleimani played a prominent role managing Iranian activity in Iraq, so it is not surprising that he has taken a leadership role in Iran's Syria policy. Former Syrian Prime Minister Riad Hijab said in a news conference after his defection that "Syria is occupied by the Iranian regime.

The person who runs the country is not Bashar al-Assad but Qassem Suleimani, the head of Iranian regime's Quds Force." Hyperbole aside, Hijab's accusation underscores Suleimani's leading role in Syria. Mohsen Chizari was presumably directing Quds Force training efforts, as his title implies, although the USDOT designation does not specify.

Chizari is also known to have facilitated militant activities in Iraq. U.S. forces captured Chizari and another IRGC-QF commander inside the compound of Iraqi Shi'a leader Abdul Aziz al-Hakim in 2006.4 U.S. defense officials reported at the time that the two men had been found with information related to the movement of sophisticated weapons, including shaped explosive charges, into Iraq.

The Iraqi government promptly expelled the two IRGC-QF commanders rather than detain them, claiming that they were protected by diplomatic immunity. The extent of IRGC-QF involvement in Syria became clearer in February

2013 when Iranian Brigadier General Hassan Shateri was assassinated in the Damascus countryside while traveling to Beirut, after having travelled to Aleppo. Shateri was a senior Quds Force commander who had been operating covertly in Lebanon since 2006 as the head of Iran's Committee for the Reconstruction of Southern Lebanon under the alias Hessam Khoshnevis. Prior to his time in Lebanon, Shateri had operated in Afghanistan and Iraq. The presence of such a high-ranking commander inside Syria highlights Tehran's commitment to achieving its objectives in the country, as well as its potential vulnerabilities should Assad fall.

Shateri's mission in Syria may have been related to the al-Sa`r chemical weapons and SCUD missile facility near Aleppo. Iranian personnel have been involved in the operations of al-Sa`r since at least 2005; a number were killed in an explosion at the facility in 2007. Rebels had made significant gains near al-Sa`r days prior to Shateri's assassination. It is reasonable to conclude that Iran would dispatch a team to sanitize the base of documents or materials that could have revealed aspects of Iran's WMD programs before the rebels seized them.

Shateri's presence in such a dangerous location shows, in any case, that the IRGC-QF is deeply involved in Syria at the highest levels. Iranian support to Syrian security forces may include training new military units. In a leaked video of a Syrian Republican Guard briefing in Baba Amr, the Brigadier General giving the briefing tells his troops, "we are forming the 416th Special Forces Battalion and they are being trained now by domestic and foreign trainers."

The leaked video does not specify the location of the training, but the Syrian Special Forces training complex in al-Dreij, situated between the capital and Zabadani, is a likely facility.

Although Russia or Lebanese Hezbollah could have provided the foreign trainers referenced here, Iran is the prime candidate, as there is further evidence that it has provided other trainers.

The conventional Ground Forces of the IRGC are also involved in this advisory and assistance mission within Syria. The January 2013 release of 48 Iranian nationals kidnapped near Damascus in August 2012 revealed that IRGC-GF personnel have been operating inside of Syria since at least that time. Among be deliberately selecting trainers from the elements of the ground forces most prepared for counterinsurgency.

The IRGC-QF and the IRGC-GF typically operate separately due to their distinct missions but appear to be working together in this case. There is no available open-source information indicating the exact nature of their cooperation or command and control; however, despite a report in September 2012 that former IRGC Greater Tehran unit commander BG Hossein Hamedani is leading Iran's advisory mission, it is more likely that Qassem Suleimani commands Iran's overall effort. As a three-star major general, Suleimani outranks Hamedani and all other IRGC-GF commanders, and the QF has historically led Iran's external operations. If Suleimani is in charge of the effort, it appears that he is able both to draw on non-QF IRGC units and resources to all capability gaps and to draw on specific expertise to support IRGC-QF efforts.

Some activities of the Syrian armed forces have been congruent with strategic concepts promoted by senior Quds Force officials, although we cannot assess what specific influence Iranian advisors have had on the Syrian military or leadership. Assad's decision to commit the majority of his security forces to secure key urban areas, for example, may have been influenced by Iranian advice.

Qassem Suleimani said in January 2012, for example, that "the mass movement in Syria has not been in the cities but rather has been, and continues to be, in the villages.... Therefore, Syria's illness is not an illness that will destroy the government." Suleimani concluded that Assad could contain the conflict by preventing the opposition from gaining territory in Syria's urban centers. Indeed, Assad has concentrated his forces in cities while the opposition has flourished in rural areas. Although Assad's forces have lost control of many neighborhoods even in key cities, they had prevented the opposition from taking control of any provincial capital until rebels seized the eastern desert city of al-Raqqa in March 2013.

Specific military operations have served the interests of both IRGC-QF and the Assad regime, and may have been driven by Iranian advice. The Assad regime mounted a string of major offensives in the first quarter of 2012, beginning with the Damascus suburb of Zabadani, even though the opposition had a greater presence in Homs. The regime may have chosen to begin in Zabadani for two reasons, not mutually exclusive: First, because it is closer to the capital, sitting approximately forty kilometers northwest of

Damascus, and second, because Zabadani functions as a critical line of supply to Hezbollah in Lebanon. Zabadani was the staging area for the IRGC's deployment to Lebanon in 1982; the IRGC even moved the kidnapped president of the American University of Beirut through Zabadani on the way to Tehran the following year.

Just weeks into the 2011 uprising, a United Press International report identified Zabadani as "IRGC's main support facility for Hezbollah." Qassem Suleimani is only known to have visited Assad in Damascus twice since the beginning of the conflict, and one of those visits occurred just a few days prior to the Zabadani operation. It is possible that Suleimani's January 2012 visit was related to the imperative of recapturing Zabadani. Assad's decision to prioritize Zabadani may have rejected Iranian advice or pressure as much as his own perception of the regime's best interests.

Some of the Syrian regime's urban counterinsurgency practices may also reject Iranian advice that derived from lessons learned in Iraq. After clearing Zabadani, the regime laid siege to Homs, forcing rebels to retreat by the beginning of March 2012. Assad garrisoned the city with a large contingent of his forces and began to construct a concrete wall around the former rebel stronghold. A reporter who visited the wall described it as a ten-foot high cement barrier, around which soldiers and secret police guard a few narrow gaps in the wall and arrest military-aged males who attempt to pass through it.

In 2008, American forces constructed a similar cement barrier around the Shi'a enclave of Sadr City, Baghdad to cut insurgents' supplies and limit their movements. Iranian observers working with proxies in Sadr City at that time would have seen the effectiveness of the campaign first-hand and could have advised the Assad regime to adopt a similar approach.

The Assad regime has not been a perfect partner, however. Iranian senior leaders have been frustrated at times by the Assad regime's approach to the opposition. Quds Force Commander Suleimani implicitly criticized the Syrian military as recently as February 2013 during an address honoring Iran-Iraq War-era IRGC commanders. After a lengthy exposition on the courage, religiosity, of Iran's martyred commanders, Suleimani concluded his speech by stating, "If the government and country of Syria had just one Hemmat and Kharrazi [war-era martyrs] of their own, their condition would not be [as it is now] and we would not have seen any of the events [that we have seen] in that country. The missing link in these countries is the absence of individuals that we had in abundance during the Sacred Defense."

This critique followed Shateri's assassination and may have reflected Suleimani's resentment toward the regime whose failings allowed his subordinate to be killed. Quds Force Deputy Commander Brigadier General Esmail Ghaani also issued an implicit criticism of the Assad regime two days after the May 25, 2012 Houla massacre, during which Assad's forces killed an estimated 90 people.

Apparently frustrated with Assad's propensity to respond disproportionately to protests, Ghaani told an Iranian media outlet, "If the Islamic Republic were not present in Syria, many more of its people would have been killed." Qassem Suleimani is said to have echoed his deputy's frustrations in September 2012. According to an Iranian nationalist opposition source, Suleimani said at that time, "We tell Assad to send the police to the streets and suddenly he dispatches the army!"

The IRGC has clearly been providing advice and coordination, but it is unlikely that they have assumed a direct combat role. The only evidence to the contrary has emerged from Syrian defectors and opposition leaders, who have accused Iran of deploying snipers to assist in crackdowns on protests and military operations.

Regardless of whether Iran is involved in direct combat, Iranian top-level coordination with Assad's military forces is evident and demonstrates the energy and resources that Tehran is expending in order to achieve its strategic objectives in Syria.

Intelligence Support

Assad's need for Iranian intelligence support likely became more urgent as the regime sought to suppress protests throughout Syria in the spring of 2011. A series of U.S. Department of the Treasury (USDOT) designations beginning at that time indicate that a range of Iranian organizations have been involved in the effort, including Law Enforcement Forces (LEF), the Ministry of Intelligence and Security (MOIS), and the large defense contractor Iran Electronics Industries (IEI). These designations also shed some light on the relationships between Syrian and Iranian state security institutions.

Tehran dispatched LEF personnel to advise and assist Assad beginning in early 2011. According to the USDOT designation, LEF Deputy Commander Brigadier General Ahmad Reza Radan "travelled to Damascus [in April 2011] where he met with Syrian security services and provided expertise to aid in the Syrian government's crackdown."

The designation further states that the LEF "provided material support to the Syrian General Intelligence Directorate (GID) and dispatched personnel to Damascus…to assist the Syrian government in suppressing the Syrian people."

The U.S. Department of the Treasury had previously designated LEF for its "role in the government crackdown on protesters in the aftermath of [Iran's] June 2009 election," during which the LEF gained extensive experience neutralizing popular unrest.

Since that episode, addressing internal unrest has become a primary mission for the Islamic Republic's security apparatus more broadly. It is understandable, then, that the Iranians drew on the LEF's combination of recent experience, training, and technological know-how to support Assad's early efforts to control popular protests.

The deployment of LEF personnel in support of Assad is noteworthy, however, because it demonstrates that Iranian strategy toward Syria has been formulated and is being implemented by the senior-most leadership of the Islamic Republic. The LEF fall under the control of the Interior Ministry and are not in the chain-of-command of the IRGC or the regular armed forces. The Interior Minister in theory reports to President Mahmoud Ahmadinejad.

In practice, however, the LEF, like all Iranian security services, is overseen by the Supreme National Security Council (SNSC), which reports to the Supreme Leader. It is very likely, therefore, that the SNSC developed a plan for supporting Assad that the Supreme Leader would then have approved and that this plan is now being executed. The presence of LEF officers in Syria is the clearest possible evidence that Iran's whole-of-government strategy in Syria is being controlled directly by Khamenei rather than Suleimani, the IRGC, or any other single individual or entity in Iran.

Available evidence indicates that Iran's intelligence support has been routed primarily through the Syrian General Intelligence Directorate. Syria has four overlapping intelligence agencies, all of which enjoy broad mandates to monitor and neutralize internal and external threats to the regime, and all of which report directly to President Assad. It is unclear whether Iran maintains direct relations with other Syrian intelligence agencies, or whether the GID acts as the sole conduit for Iranian intelligence support.

Although GID is primarily responsible for external intelligence, its powerful internal security branch was headed for decades by Mohammed Nasif Kheirbek, a close advisor to Hafez al-Assad. The Kheirbek family is one of three families that make up the inner core of the Assad regime and hold leadership roles throughout the intelligence and security apparatuses.

Mohammed Nasif later became the Deputy Director of GID, and he acted as a special assistant to President Assad for intelligence and security by the beginning of the uprising. Mohammed Nasif Kheirbek has been identified as the interlocutor between Assad and the Iranian regime. According to one report, Kheirbek travelled to Tehran during the summer of 2011 to negotiate Iranian assistance to establish a new military compound and supply depot at Latakia airport.

Kheirbek's identification as the primary contact for Syria's relationship with Iran reinforces the assessment that GID acts as the principal conduit for Iranian intelligence support to Syria's security apparatus.

Military Resupply

Aerial resupply is the most critical component of Iranian material support to SyriaUSDOT designations have shed light on the significance of commercial airlines in these operations. Other evidence suggests that Iranian Air Force jets have supplemented this effort and that Iran has relatively limited access to ground and sea lines of communication.

USDOT has sanctioned three Iranian airlines since the beginning of the conflict for transporting military equipment and personnel from Iran to Syria. In June 2011, USDOT designated Iran Air for transporting military equipment that included "missile or rocket components to Syria."

According to the designation, the IRGC disguises military equipment as "medicine or generic spare parts" in order to transport the illicit cargo. Yas Air was designated in March 2012 for transporting IRGC-QF personnel and weapons, including small arms, ammunition, rockets, anti-aircraft guns, and mortar shells. The designation describes a series of IRGC-QF-coordinated Yas Air Flights in March 2011, at the very outset of the conflict, which transported weapons to Hezbollah and Syrian officials.

Iranian air supply to Syria pre-dated the uprising, as Damascus has long been used as the main Iranian hub to supply Lebanese Hezbollah. Iran Air has facilitated shipments for Iran's Ministry of Defense and Armed Forces Logistics (MODAFL) and the IRGC since at least 2000.

A UN report on illegal arms transfers found that Syria was the top destination for illicit arms shipments from Iran. These arms were then often passed on to Lebanese and Palestinian militants.

Iranian aircraft also transport personnel for advise-and-assist missions in Syria. The U.S. Treasury Department sanctioned Mahan Air in October 2011 for providing "travel services for IRGC-QF personnel ‡own to and from Iran and Syria for military training."

One ground resupply route between Baghdad and Damascus remains a viable corridor for Iranian material support to the Syrian regime. Iran has been "increasing their support [to Assad] for the last three, four months through Iraq's airspace and now trucks," an anonymous Western diplomat told Reuters in mid-March, "And the Iraqis are really looking the other way." As depicted on the map, the four primary Syria-Iraq border crossing points are Rabia-Yaarabiya in the north,

Iran has also deployed naval vessels through the Suez Canal to Syrian ports of call, demonstrating the plausibility of a sea line of communication. In February 2011, before the uprising began, Iranian naval vessels transited the Suez Canal for the Syrian forces. The U.S. Department of Defense, however, denied that the ships had docked or delivered cargo. The relative infrequency of these voyages suggests that Iran's sea lanes to Syria are more symbolic than practical.

An unofficial sea line of communication utilizing commercial vessels is more plausible but still problematic. In February 2013, the Syrian Economic Task Force reported that tankers belonging to Iranian oil companies frequently traversed the Suez Canal to ship oil between Syria and Iran. Two ships in particular were identified, which had reagged repeatedly in recent months. The report suggested that the Iranian ships were primarily moving Syrian crude to Iran, perhaps to offset Iranian investment in Assad's regime.

If the operational landscape significantly degrades Iran's ability to transport equipment and personnel via ground and air routes, however, Iran could look to make use of this established alternate point of access to transport weapons, equipment, and personnel.

Given the limitations of sea lines of communication, however, air shipments remain Iran's most feasible method of supplying the Assad regime. Shipping weapons by ground is much less expensive than maintaining an air bridge, but the constraints of the current operational environment in eastern Syria and western Iraq will place increasing significance on air shipments. The deployment of Iranian heavy transport aircraft and the unrestricted air corridor over Iraq enables continuous Iranian air supply to Syria. A U.S. intelligence report in September indicated that air shipments were occurring "on an almost daily basis."

As the battle for Syria continues and Assad consolidates forces around well-secured military airbases, the use of military-grade cargo planes for cross-border shipments will remain Iran's ability to support Assad with personnel and equipment is inextricably linked to the maintenance of this air corridor, making it a key vulnerability for Iranian strategy in Syria.

Ethnic Cleansing

The group that calls itself the Islamic State (IS) has carried out ethnic cleansing on a historic scale in northern Iraq. IS has systematically targeted non-Arab and non-Sunni Muslim communities, killing or abducting hundreds, possibly thousands, and forcing more than 830,000 others to flee the areas it has captured since 10 June 2014.

Ethnic and religious minorities – Assyrian Christians, Turkmen Shi'a, Shabak Shi'a, Yezidis, Kakai and Sabean Mandaeans – have lived together in the Nineveh province, much of it now under IS control, for centuries. Today, only those who were unable to flee when IS fighters seized the area remain trapped there, under threat of death if they do not convert to Islam.

Hundreds, possibly thousands, of Yezidis, most of them women and children from the Sinjar region, were abducted as they fled the IS takeover in early August 2014. At the time of writing, they continue to be held by the IS and, with a few exceptions, little is known of their fate or whereabouts. Some of those who managed to make contact with their families said they are being pressured to convert to Islam and some have reported that some of the women and children – both girls and boys – from their families were taken to unknown locations by their captors. Some families say their detained relatives have also told them there have been cases of rape and sexual abuse of detained women and children.

Hundreds of Yezidi men from towns and villages in the Sinjar region, which put up armed resistance in a bid to repel the IS advance, were captured and shot dead in cold blood, scores in large groups, others individually, seemingly in reprisal for resisting and to dissuade others from doing so. It is from these towns and villages that most of the women and children were abducted.

Scores of Yezidi men who were captured on 3 August 2014, when IS fighters stormed the Sinjar region, were shown converting to Islam in a video distributed on social media around 20 August 2014, in which an IS commander says that those who do not want to convert can die of hunger and thirst "on the mountain" (a reference to Mount Sinjar, where Yezidi fighters and some civilians have been sheltering since 3 August, surrounded by IS fighters). There is little doubt that those shown in the video converted to save their lives and in the hope of being freed. However, even those who converted have so far not been allowed to leave.

Although the overwhelming majority of the people of these minority communities managed to flee before IS fighters reached their towns and villages, they escaped with their lives and nothing else. They had to leave their homes and everything they owned behind and even the little they could carry – especially money and jewellery – was often taken from them by IS fighters manning checkpoints on the perimeters of the areas they control.

Their homes have since been appropriated or looted by IS fighters and their supporters among the local Sunni population, and their places of worship destroyed. While the IS has mainly targeted the minority communities, many Arab Sunni Muslims known or believed to oppose the IS or to have worked with the government and security forces, or previously with the US army (present in Iraq until 2011), have likewise been forced to flee to avoid being killed, and their homes have been appropriated or destroyed.

Since 10 June 2014, more than 830,000 people, have been forced from their homes in IS-controlled parts of northern Iraq, 6 resulting in a humanitarian crisis which prompted the UN to declare its highest level of emergency on 14 August. Most of the displaced are sheltering in the semi-autonomous region of Iraqi Kurdistan, under the control of the Kurdistan Regional Government (KRG), with small numbers sheltering across the borders in Syria and Turkey.

The humanitarian conditions for the overwhelming majority of the hundreds of thousands of displaced are dire – lacking shelter, many sleep in building sites, makeshift encampments and parks with no sanitation, others in schools, halls and other public buildings. KRG officials have admitted that they are overwhelmed and unable to cope, while the response of the international community has been slow and inadequate, though the UN's recent designation of the crisis as its highest level of emergency should result in prompter action from the relevant international humanitarian agencies.

The forced displacement of Iraq's ethnic and religious minorities, including some of the region's oldest communities, is a tragedy of historic proportions. Amnesty International's field investigations have concluded that the IS is systematically and deliberately carrying out a program of ethnic cleansing in the areas under its control. This is not only destroying lives, but also causing irreparable damage to the fabric of Iraq's society, and fuelling inter-ethnic, sectarian and inter-religious tensions in the region and beyond.

Entire communities in large swathes of territories in northern Iraq were abandoned to their fate without protection from attacks by the IS when the Shi'a-dominated Iraqi army and security forces fled the area in June. The scale and gravity of the abuses and the urgency of the situation demand a swift and robust response – not only to provide humanitarian assistance to those displaced and otherwise affected by the conflict but also to ensure the protection of vulnerable communities who risk being wiped off the map of Iraq. States have an obligation to provide equal protection to all communities within their borders.

Successive Iraqi central governments have failed to do so. Further, they have contributed to the worsening of the situation in recent months by tolerating, encouraging and arming sectarian militias, in particular Shi'a militias in and around the capital, Baghdad, and in other parts of the country. In responding to the current crisis, the Iraqi central government and the KRG (whose armed forces now control some of the areas abandoned by the Iraqi army) must prioritize measures to ensure the protection of the civilian population regardless of religion or ethnicity.

The new Iraqi central government, whose formation is currently being negotiated, must prioritize the establishment of non-sectarian government, military and security institutions that are both willing and able to restore security and the rule of law and to provide protection and recourse for all sectors of the population without discrimination. At the same time, it should disarm and disband militias responsible for extrajudicial executions and other gross violations and bring perpetrators to justice.

A witness to one such mass killing in Solagh, a village south-east of Sinjar city, told that on the morning of 3 August, as he was trying to flee towards Mount Sinjar, he saw vehicles with IS fighters in them approaching, and managed to conceal himself. From his hiding place he saw them take some civilians from a house in the western outskirts of Solagh: "A white Toyota pick-up stopped by the house of my neighbour, Salah Mrad Noura, who raised a white flag to indicate they were peaceful civilians. The pick-up had some 14 IS men on the back. They took out some 30 people from my neighbour's house: men, women and children. They put the women and children, some 20 of them, on the back of another vehicle which had come, a large white Kia, and marched the men, about nine of them, to the nearby wadi [dry river bed]. There they made them kneel and shot them in the back. They were all killed; I watched from my hiding place for a long time and none of them moved. I know two of those killed: my neighbor Salah Mrad Noura, who was about 80 years old, and his son Kheiro, aged about 45 or 50."

On the morning of Friday 15 August the nightmare that had haunted the residents of Kocho (also known as Kuju) for the previous 12 days came to pass, when IS fighters killed at least a hundred, and possibly many more, of the village's men and boys and abducted all the women and children. Since the IS had taken control of the Sinjar region on 3 August, many of the residents of the small Yezidi hamlet, with its population of about 1,200, had been trapped in the village some 15 km south of the town of Sinjar, unable to flee and in constant fear of being abducted or killed.

Survivors of the massacre told that the IS fighters assembled the village residents at the secondary school, on the northern outskirts of the village, where they separated men and boys from women and younger children. The men were then bundled into pick-up vehicles – some 15-20 in each vehicle – and driven away to different nearby locations, where they were shot.

Elias Salah, a 59-year-old nurse, told: "IS militants initially spoke to our Sheikh [community leader] and said that if we handed over our weapons we would not be harmed. So, we gave them our weapons but still feared they would kill us. Some of them demanded that we convert to Islam, which we refused to do, and threatened to kill us if we did not. Then later we were told that, following interventions by Sunni Muslim tribal chiefs from Mosul, we would be spared. But we were under siege and not allowed to leave.... At 11-11.30am [on Friday 15 August] IS militants called all the residents to the secondary school, which has been their headquarters since they came to the village two weeks ago. There they asked that we hand over our money and our mobile phones, and that the women hand over their jewellery.

"After about 15 minutes they brought vehicles and started to fill them up with men and boys. They pushed about 20 of us onto the back of a Kia pick-up vehicle and drove us about one kilometre east of the village. They got us off the vehicle by the pool and made us crouch on the ground in a tight cluster and one of them photographed us. I thought then they'd let us go after that, but they opened fire at us from behind. I was hit in the left knee, but the bullet only grazed my knee. I let myself fall forward, as if I were dead, and I stayed there face down without moving. When the shooting stopped I kept still and after they left, I ran away. Five or six others were also alive and they also ran from the place. The rest were all killed. I know two of them, they were right next to me: Khider Matto Qasem, 28, and Ravo Mokri Salah, about 80 years old.

"I don't know who the others were; I was too scared to look around, I couldn't focus. I don't know what happened to my family, my wife, my seven children (my two daughters and my five sons; the youngest is only 14), my son's wife and their two children; I don't know if they are dead or alive or where they are. "I only now learned from one of the survivors from another group that my brother Amin and his 10-year-old son 'Asem were both killed, God bless them. I can't contact anyone as they took our mobile phones and so I have lost all the numbers. After the killings I ran to Mount Sinjar. There were other survivors who also ran away. I saw five others; one of them, Rafid Sa'id, was badly injured. I found him later on Mount Sinjar; the only escape route."

Khider Hasan, a 17-year-old student, who escaped with what looked like superficial bullet wounds to his back, told that he was also part of the first group of men and boys taken to the village's outskirts and shot.

"There was no order, they [the IS militants] just filled up vehicles indiscriminately. My cousin Ghaleb Elias and I were pushed into the same vehicle. We were next to each other as they lined us up face down on the ground. He was killed. He was the same age as me, and worked as a labourer, mostly in construction. I have no news of what happened to my parents and my four brothers and six sisters. Did they kill them? Did they abduct them? I don't know anything about them.

"After the IS armed men who shot us left I ran away, stopping to hide when I thought someone might see me or when I could not walk any more. I had to walk many hours to reach Mount Sinjar."

Another survivor, Khaled Mrad, a 32-year-old shop owner and father of three, told: "IS militants, who had been controlling the village since 3 August, had promised repeatedly that we would be allowed to leave. I thought this was the day as I followed many people from the village... When we reached the school, the women and children were sent to the upper floor and we the men were kept on the ground floor. IS militants told us to hand over our money, our phones and any gold. Then they started to fill pick-up vehicles with men and to drive away.

"I was still thinking that they were going to take us to the mountain as had been promised. About four vehicles left, two at a time. Then I was put in a vehicle with about 20 other men. We stopped near the last house on the edge of the village and they got us off the vehicle, I knew that they were going to kill us as this was not the way to the mountain. We were on the edge of a hill and as I looked down I saw a group of bodies below by the wadi.

"They told us to stand in line and one of the men in our group, the son of the Sheikh, told them 'this is not what was agreed; you were going to take us to the mountain'. They shot him multiple times. We threw ourselves to the ground and they shot at us for several minutes and then they left. I was shot three times, twice in the left arm and once in the left hip. After they left, another man, Nadir Ibrahim and I got up. All the others were dead or dying.

"Nadir and I walked for about three kilometres and then I heard a car come and I hid in some straw nearby but Nadir was behind me and did not manage to hide on time and was shot dead. I stayed hidden in the straw for several hours, until the evening, and then I kept walking towards the mountain."

Later that night, on the way to the mountain, Khaled met up with his younger brother, Said, and another man, Ali Abbas Ismail, who had been part of another truckload and had also survived. Said, 23, was shot five times, three times in his left knee, once in the left hip and once in the left shoulder.

At the hospital where the brothers were being treated for their injuries, Said showed a bullet doctors had just removed from his knee. Khaled and Said are lucky to have survived, but are now grieving for their seven brothers who are believed to have been killed in the massacre. Elias, Jallu, Pessi, Masa'ud, Hajji, Kheiri, and Nawaf, aged between 41 and 22, were also at the school and have not been heard of since.

"It has been two weeks.12 There is just the two of us left now. Those who survived have by now made it back and my brothers are not among them. I think they are all dead. I hope that they died quickly, that they did not lie there in pain for hours," Khaled said as he broke down in tears. But some of the victims of the 15 August massacre were not killed instantly, and died of their injuries hours, possibly days, later, having been left for dead and being too seriously wounded to drag themselves away.

Salem, another survivor, who managed to hide near the massacre site for 12 days thanks to the help of a Muslim neighbour, told: "Some could not move and could not save themselves; they lay in agony waiting to die. They died a horrible death. I managed to drag myself away and was saved by a Muslim neighbor; he risked his life to save me; he is more than a brother to me. For 12 days he brought me food and water every night. I could not walk and had no hope of getting away and it was becoming increasingly dangerous for him to continue to keep me there. He gave me a phone so that I could speak with my relatives (in the mountain and in Kurdistan) and after 12 days he managed to get me a donkey so that I could ride to the mountain, and from there I was evacuated through Syria and on to Kurdistan."

Another survivor, Khalaf Hodeida, a 32-year-old father of three young children, told: "I was in the third car-load. Before me, they [IS militants] took away two other vehicles full of men and youth. We were driven a very short distance east, maybe 200-300 metres. We were 20 or 25 crammed in the back of the pick-up, I don't know for sure. When we got there they made us stand in a row and then one of them shouted 'Allahu Akbar' ['God is Great'] and then there was shooting. There were maybe 10 of them, but they were behind us. I don't know how many of them opened fire. I was hit twice, in the left hip and the left calf.

"After the shooting stopped I heard the vehicles leave and another man and I got up and ran. I went in one direction and he in the other. I don't know where he is now. I don't know where anyone is, my children, my family. Where are they? Have they taken them? How can I find them?

"Among those killed near me was Amin Salah, the brother of Elias [the nurse who survived the first group killing], and his son 'Asem, aged 10-12, and seven others whose names I know and another 10 or 12 whose names I don't know because I could not see properly. I was so terrified; I kept my head down and when it became quiet and I was sure they had left I just ran away."

Many of the hundreds of women and children who were abducted from Kocho on 15 August are currently held in and around Tal 'Afar – halfway between Sinjar and Mosul – where IS groups are holding other abducted Yezidi civilians. Amnesty International had been in contact with Kocho residents before the massacre, who said that the village then had a population of more than 1,200. The organization has been unable to contact them since 13 August. Relatives of some of the abducted women and children have told Amnesty International that they have not been able to make contact with them since they were abducted and are extremely concerned for their safety.

In the afternoon of 3 August scores of men and boys were summarily killed on the edge of the village of Qiniyeh, south-east of the town of Sinjar. Amnesty International spoke to several survivors and witnesses of the massacre, all of whom gave very similar accounts. They were interviewed separately and in some cases did not know each other.

According to their statements, a large group of some 300 or more Yezidis, most of them from the nearby village of Tal Qasab and many from the same extended family and tribe, became trapped in Qiniyeh as they were making their way to Mount Sinjar. Most of them were women and children, but there were also scores of men, many of whom had earlier engaged in armed clashes with IS fighters, in an attempt to prevent them from storming their villages.

Once they realized they had no hope of halting the IS advance they fled north towards Mount Sinjar, getting stuck in Qiniyeh. There, IS fighters caught up with them, separated the women and children from the men and boys and took a group of up to 85-90 men and boys – including boys as young as 12 – and shot most of them dead. The massacre seems to have been carried out to punish those who had, or were suspected of having, tried to repel the IS attack on their villages, and/or to dissuade others from putting up any resistance to IS advances.

A few people survived the massacre, and some others managed to escape in the melee as they were being marched to the killing site. Amnesty International spoke to some of the survivors. Fawas Safel gave a list of 28 men from his family who have been missing since the massacre. He believes they have all been killed:

"My family and I fled Tal Qasab in the morning [of 3 August]. There was a huge number of people fleeing towards the mountain [Mount Sinjar]. Those who had cars could go on more easily. We did not have a car so we stopped in Qiniyeh, at a farm on the edge of the village.

We were more than 200, mostly women and children. A military vehicle came with some IS militants. They asked us for weapons and we said that we did not have any. We did have weapons but we had hidden them around the area. They said that they would search the area and if they found weapons or if we tried to run away they would kill us and if not they would not harm us. I was in a group with 72 other men and boys and we stayed put, without trying to run away.

"They left and after half an hour a convoy of IS vehicles came, 10 or 12 of them; about four saloon cars and the rest pick-ups. They again asked for weapons and we said we had none. They told us to hand over our mobile phones. They sent a Yezidi man who was with them to collect the phones from the women. Then they put us into two lines: men and boys in one line and women and children in the other.

They marched us (men and boys) towards the mountain, about 15 minutes' walk away. We stopped at a place where there was a big hole, by the wadi, we were on the edge of the hole. They opened fire and some people tried to run away. I let myself fall in the hole, and others fell on top of me. I stayed still. After the continuous fire stopped, IS militants fired individual shots at those they saw were not yet dead. After they left – I don't know how much time passed exactly – I got up and so did my friend Ezzedin Amin and we ran away. Neither of us were injured. We walked to the mountain and there we found three others who had also escaped alive from the massacre. They were injured, one very lightly and two more seriously."

Another villager, Mohsen Elias, told: After the Peshmerga who used to protect our villages fled in the night between 2 and 3 August, me and many other men from the village [Tal Qasab] took our weapons (most of us had Kalashnikovs, for the protection of our families) and clashed with IS militants. At about 7 or 8am we ran out of ammunition and ran away toward the mountain (Mount Sinjar). We stopped in the village of Qiniyeh, near the foot of the mountain. We were about 90 men and youths and with us were more than 100 women and children from our families.

"At about 1pm or so IS militants came and spoke to us and said that they were only looking for Peshmerga and asked if we had weapons and said they would kill anyone found to have weapons. We had hidden our weapons and said we had none. They said we could go home soon and left. After half an hour some 20 IS vehicles came and surrounded us. My relative Nasser Elias tried to run away and they shot him dead.

They split us into two groups, men and boys of 12 and older in one group and women and younger children in another group. They started to load the women and children in the vehicles and made us (men and boys) walk to the nearby wadi. The youngest of the group was my brother Nusrat, 12 years old. We were made to squat by the edge of the wadi, which was deep. They told us to convert to Islam and we refused.

One grabbed me by my shirt from behind and pulled me up and tried to shoot me but his weapon did not fire. My brother Nusrat was scared and was crying. They opened fire from behind us. I fell into the wadi and was not injured. My brother Nusrat was right next to me and was killed. My father, Elias, and my four brothers, Faysal, Ma'amun, Sa'id and Sofian, were all killed. Most of the other men and boys were also killed, including more than 43 of my relatives.

After the IS men left I waited and then ran away to the mountain. I only know four others who survived: my neighbour Fawas, Khalaf Mirze and his son 'Ayad (Khalaf had been shot in the back, shoulder and leg, and 'Ayad in the shoulder) and another man called Ziad. I don't know if any others survived." Hawwas Hashem, another of those who had stopped in Qiniyeh, told Amnesty International that he had hidden himself nearby:

After hours of clashes with the IS militants who were attacking our village we were overpowered and fled toward the mountain. Many of us stopped in Qiniyeh; there had been no clashes there and we thought we would be safe. There were many families,men, women and children. Hundreds all together. The IS men left and after a while they came back with several vehicles. Four of the vehicles surrounded the house where I was with my family.

I ran away and hid in a nearby hill. From there I could see what was happening. It was early afternoon – broad daylight. They brought all the people out of the houses and divided the men from the women and children. They put the women and children in vehicles and drove away and marched the men and some young boys to the wadi nearby. They made them kneel or crouch along the edge of the wadi, and shot them in the back. I counted about 67 who were killed and some others survived and ran away after the IS militants left. Then I ran away from the hill to Mount Sinjar."

The names and details provided by the survivors, relatives of some of those killed and witnesses indicate that some 65-70, possibly up to 80-85, men and boys were shot dead on the edge of the village of Qiniyeh. Many more are reported to have been killed in smaller groups further away from the village, most as they were trying to flee to Mount Sinjar and some after they were captured near the foot of the mountain as they came down to fetch water and food for themselves and their families who were stranded there.

Some 50-60 men, who were fleeing towards Sinjar Mountain with scores of women and children from their families, were rounded up and shot dead by IS fighters near the Qahtanya/Sinjar crossroad on the morning of 3 August, two of the survivors told Amnesty International.

One of them, Dakhil Sabri, said: "As I was walking to the mountain with my wife and other families we stopped by a farm to look for water. Several cars with IS armed men came by. Five stopped right where we were and some others further back. They grouped all of the men and pushed us to the ground.

Some tried to get away. One was shot several times; even as he collapsed to the ground they continued to shoot at him. "In the melee, I managed to slip into a small animal pen and hid there. I heard a lot of shooting for several minutes and then silence and then the armed men left taking the women and children with them. After they left I came out of my hiding place. All the men were dead except for me and two others who had also managed to hide. We escaped to the mountain.

My wife, Dilo, who is pregnant, was among the women and children who were taken away. Until recently she was held in the school in Tal 'Afar but now I am not sure if she is still there or has been moved to another place."

Rape and abuse

There are allegations that many of the women and girls who have been abducted by IS fighters, notably girls in their teens and early 20s, have been subjected to rape or sexual abuse, forced to marry fighters, or sold into sexual slavery.

Most of the families who are in contact with female relatives detained by IS fighters have told that their relatives have not been subjected to such abuse but that they believe that others have, notably those who were moved to undisclosed locations and have not been heard from since. Women and girls who recently managed to escape IS captivity have told that many others had been removed from their places of detention and sent away to be forcibly married; they were told that if they refused they would be sold. They said that they had still refused to be married and had managed to escape before their captors could carry out their threats, but that they do not know what had happened to other women and girls who had been threatened with a similar fate.

Ahmed Navef told that 18 women and children from his family had been taken on 3 August and held by the IS. Two of the girls, he said, disappeared on 20 August, and a third committed suicide at about the same time. "Jihan, age 16, and Ghalia, 15, went missing from the place where they were detained in Tal 'Afar," he said, "and we heard that 19-year-old Jilan killed herself rather than be forced to marry."

"They took us to Bi'aj and the following day they took all the women and children to another place. I later learned that they had been taken to Mosul. My grandfather was released after four days and the other men and I were taken to Tal Banat and held there for another three days. They told us that we would be killed if we did not convert to Islam. Then they told us we would be released.

"On 10 August me and nine others escaped. We walked for 10-12 hours to reach the mountain. While we were detained they took a group of boys aged about 12-15years who were held with us to another place; maybe they took them for military training. My uncle who did not manage to escape is still being held, now in Tal 'Afar in a place with many other men.

The women and children from my family – my 70-year-old grandmother, four of my aunts and their 11 children – who were taken with me, are still detained, also in Tal 'Afar but in a separate place, not together with my uncle. Among them there is a little baby and a 12-year-old boy with a disability. We sometimes receive news via another family who is in contact with their detained female relatives."

With few exceptions, nothing is known of the fate of the men who have been captured by IS fighters. Sawsan Hassa, a 30-year-old mother of six, told Amnesty International that she has not been able to obtain any information about her husband, Kheir Kasso, 30, who was abducted on 3 August in Qahtanya:

"I was visiting my parents in Khana Sor (north-west of Sinjar) with my children when my husband called me. He had remained at home in Qahtanya. He said that the area was being attacked by IS and everyone was fleeing. He said that he would go back home to get our ID cards and documents and would then flee toward the mountain.

"The last time we spoke he was running and was out of breath. Something was happening. He only managed to mumble that he would not be able to speak anymore. I think he was caught then. I have not managed to speak to him again or to find out anything from anyone about him. I don't know if he is still alive or if they [IS] have killed him. I have six children who are asking about their father. What do I tell them?" Kheir's sister, Marine Kasso, told Amnesty International that her two sons, Faraj 15, and Walid 18, went missing at the same time. She fears that they too have been killed.

Most of the members of non-Muslim communities being held by IS who have been able to communicate with their families have reported consistent pressures on them by their captors to convert to Islam. The pressures have ranged from promises of freedom to threats that they will be killed if they do not convert.

In Kocho, where scores of male residents were murdered on 15 August, residents reported being told that they would be killed if they did not convert. In a video distributed on social media around 20 August showing scores of Yezidi men who were captured on 3 August converting to Islam, an IS commander states that those who do not want to convert can die of hunger and thirst "on the mountain" (a reference to Mount Sinjar, where Yezidi fighters and some civilians have been sheltering since 3 August, surrounded by IS fighters).

Some have told that they converted in order to save their lives and have not been allowed to leave the areas they are trapped in. A member of one such family told the organization on 30 August:

"We are in a very difficult situation. We agreed to convert because we thought this would solve our problem but the pressure on us is increasing. We are under surveillance and cannot leave. We cannot just try to leave on our own; we are scared of what could happen to us. Can someone come to get us out of here? It is too dangerous for us here. We need help please."

This situation contrasts with an earlier case, in June 2014, of a group of Yezidi men in the Sinjar region, most of them members of the Iraqi security forces, who were captured by the IS and pressured into converting to Islam. On this occasion, a ransom was demanded and the men were released when it was paid.

As part of its ethnic cleansing policy, the IS has also reinforced its message to ethnic and religious minorities that there is no place for them in Iraq by systematically destroying their places of worship and cultural heritage. Since taking control of Mosul on 10 June, the IS have systematically destroyed and damaged places of worship of r on Sunni Muslim communities.

Among the first targets were Shi'a mosques blown up in Mosul and Tal 'Afar in June; the same month, the Christian Tahira (Immaculate) Church in Mosul had a statue of the Virgin Mary removed from its roof. In July, the tomb of the Prophet Jonah in Mosul was demolished and, in August, the Shi'a Imam Redha Maqam (a Shi'a shrine) near Bartalla, the Yezidi Three Sisters Temples in Bashiqa and SheikhMand Temple in Sinjar, and the Kakai Mazar Yad Gar and Sayed Hayyas Temples in al-Hamdaniya were all destroyed.

Yezidis at camps

ISIS forces took several thousand Yezidi civilians into custody in northern Iraq's Nineveh province in August 2014, according to Kurdistan officials and community leaders. Witnesses said that fighters systematically separated young women and adolescent girls from their families and other captives and moved them from one location to another inside Iraq and Syria.

The Yezidis live in Iraq's Nineveh province on land claimed by both the Kurdistan regional government and the Iraqi central government. They practice an ancient monotheistic religion, and Yezidis say they have been persecuted for hundreds of years because many consider them "heretics."

Violent attacks against Yezidis by Sunni Arab extremists escalated after the US-led invasion of Iraq in 2003. On August 14, 2007, four simultaneous truck bombings killed more than 300 Yezidis and wounded more than 700 in Sinjar district communities. Some Yezidi activists also faced intimidation and threats from Kurdistan government forces.

Kurdistan authorities consider Yezidis to be Kurds and, therefore, Yezidi lands part of the Kurdistan region of Iraq. Thousands of Yezidi families have f ed to Syria, Jordan, and elsewhere. Since 2003, but before the latest attack by ISIS, their numbers in Iraq had dropped from about 700,000 to 500,000. There are probably fewer now.

No one knows how many Yezidis have been killed by ISIS – they're still uncovering mass graves. Very little information comes out of ISIS-controlled areas. Every family has been affected, has had a husband or son killed, a daughter abducted, or has had to flee.

The main camp, Khanke, near Dohuk, houses more than 18,000 Yazidis, mainly from around the city of Sinjar, about a two-and-a-half hour drive away. The Yezidis are living in a virtual sea of displaced person tents and nearby unfinished buildings, which lack doors and heat, perched on windswept hills. The views from the hilltops are stunning on a sunny day, but there's little to protect the people there from the cold.

One girl said ISIS members, wanting to find out who "desecrated" their Quran, handcuffed and blindfolded her and two other girls, beat them with a cable, and then fired a gunshot into the air. Apparently, the girl told, one of the many cats in the house had ripped the Quran.

Most of the girls said they were transferred from one place to another, ultimately living in big houses or halls with between 5 and 60 other girls. During the course of the day, ISIS fighters would come in, pick a girl to take, and if she refused, she'd be slapped or beaten.

Virginity is a huge issue across the region. There is a stigma attached to the abducted women because they could have experienced sexual violence from the ISIS fighters – and it extends to their families. In conflicts around the world, communities retaliate against women who are victims of sexual violence. Husbands leave wives, families abandon daughters.

Yezidi religious leader, Baba Sheikh, instructed the community to welcome back and not harm those who were abducted, forced to convert, or raped. Because of this, most families have welcomed back their female relatives. They already had so many family members killed or abducted by ISIS, they just want their families back. One of the most common sentiments was that their biggest wish is to be reunited with their families, as they don't know how to be whole without them.

One girl was abducted at 15, and after being moved from place to place she lived in a house with other girls who were forcibly married off or sold one-by-one. She and a friend attempted suicide together but an ISIS member caught them and stopped them. When her friend was picked to be taken by an ISIS member, the girl begged the men to take her too, so she could stay with her friend. They agreed and took both girls to another house. There, two other men told them, "You are sold to us." They then beat and raped them for five days until they escaped, breaking through the door while the men were away fighting.

When she first came to the camp, she looked like a ghost. She was reunited with her parents, who were traumatized after their only son, Noor's brother, was executed in front of them. But Noor had her parents' support. She said that she'd been to the hospital a few times, is receiving regular counseling, and is taking a sewing class. Her friend that she escaped with lives in a separate camp, and her father has taken her there to visit. Sometimes NGO activists take her out of the camp for social activities like going to the mall.

About half the women and girls who spoke to Human Rights Watch said the ISIS fighters pressured them to convert to Islam. Zara, 13, said she was held captive in a three-story house in Mosul with girls ages 10 to 15: "When they came to select the girls, they would pull them away. The girls would cry and faint, they would have to take them by force. They made us convert to Islam and we al had to say the shahada [Islamic creed]. They said, "You Yezidis are kufar [infidels], you must repeat these words after the leader." They gathered us all in one place and made us repeat after him. After we said the shahada, he said you have now been converted to our religion and our religion is the correct one. We didn't dare not say the shahada."

ISIS fighters held Noor, 16, in various places including Mosul. "The leader of this group asked us to convert to Islam and read the Quran," she said. "We were forced to read the Quran and we started to pray slowly. We started to behave like actors."

Crimes Against Humanity

Rape and other forms of sexual violence, sexual slavery, cruel treatment, and other abuses committed during an armed conflict violate the laws of war. International criminal courts have ruled that rape and other sexual violence may also amount to torture.

Those who commit serious violations of the laws of war with criminal intent are responsible for war crimes. Commanders and civilian leaders may be prosecuted for war crimes as a matter of command responsibility when they knew or should have known about the commission of war crimes and took insufficient measures to prevent them or punish those responsible.

The mass rape and other serious abuses by ISIS against Yezidi civilians may be crimes against humanity. Crimes against humanity are serious offenses, including rape, sexual slavery, enslavement, unlawful imprisonment, persecution of a religious group, and other inhumane acts intentionally causing great suffering, that are part of a widespread or systematic attack on a civilian population.

"Widespread" refers to the scale of the acts or the number of victims. "Systematic" concerns "a pattern or methodical plan." ISIS public statements concerning enslavement, forced marriage, and abuse of captured women, as well as the organized sale of Yezidi women and girls, indicate a widespread practice and a systematic plan of action by ISIS.

Narin, the 20-year-old woman from Sinjar, told that she was abducted on August 3 and given as a "gift" to an ISIS fighter, who tried to force her to marry him: "I wasn't raped – [the ISIS member] didn't touch me because I told him I was sick.... I got a forensic gynecological exam in Dohuk, which cleared me of abuse. I wasn't comfortable during this exam, and [the doctor] didn't explain what she was doing to me beforehand."

Yezidi Women

Isis fighters are committing widespread, organized and systematic rape and sexual assault on Yazidi women and girls in what may amount to a crime against humanity.

Fighters from Europe are among those from Iraq, Syria, other countries in the Middle East and Central Asia abusing girls and women, according to harrowing accounts from victims. Girls as young as 12 after they escaped their captors in northern Iraq, described being gang-raped by brutal fighters multiple times. Many had witnessed other women and young girls being sexually assaulted.

A doctor in charge of treating survivors in Dohuk said at least 70 of the 105 female survivors she had treated appeared to have been raped while being held hostage by the extremist group.

One woman, Rashida, described militants choosing women by drawing their names out of a "lottery". The 31-year-old says she tried to kill herself by swallowing a toxic chemical after being ordered by the fighter who picked her name to bathe.

Two girls described the abuse of their 16-year-old sister by four men over a period of several months. Their sister, who was allowed to visit them, recounted a Ukrainian fighter beating her, raping her, giving her electric shocks and denying her food. The 16-year-old girl is still being held hostage by Isis.

Jalila was 12 when she was separated from her family in August 2014 as they tried to flee Isis' advance. After being stopped by a group of Arab men, she was handed over to Isis and later taken to a house in Syria, where other young girls were being held.

"The men would come and select us," she told. "When they came, they would tell us to stand up and then examine our bodies. They would tell us to show our hair and sometimes they beat the girls if they refused. They wore dishdashas [ankle length garments], and had long beards and hair."

She said an Isis fighter selected and dragged her out of the house when she tried to fight him off. "I told him not to touch me and begged him to let me go," she said. "I told him to take me to my mother. I was a young girl, and I asked him, 'What do you want from me?' He spent three days having sex with me."
Another 12-year-old said she was abducted by Isis in August, who then took her to a school in Tal Afar which was being used to hold Yazidi captives and separated her from her family.

She said an older fighter assured her he would not harm her, and then raped her repeatedly. "He was sleeping in the same place with me and told me not be afraid because I was like his daughter," she said. "One day I woke up and my legs were covered in blood."

Another woman, Leila, said she was brutally punished when she was discovered trying to kill herself. "After they realized what I was doing, they beat me with a long piece of wood and with their fists," she said. "My eyes were swollen shut and my arms turned blue. They handcuffed me to the sink, and cut my clothes with a knife and washed me. They took me out of the bathroom, brought in [my friend] and raped her in the room in front of me." Leila was raped shortly after this ordeal.

Many victims were struggling to access psychological help, counselling, tests for sexually transmitted infections, emergency contraception and in cases of pregnancy, safe and legal abortion.

"Isis forces have committed organized rape, sexual assault, and other horrific crimes against Yezidi women and girls," said Liesl Gerntholtz, women's rights director at Human Rights Watch. "Those fortunate enough to have escaped need to be treated for the unimaginable trauma they endured."

Isis considers Yazidis heretical and published an article in its propaganda magazine Dabiq attempting to justify the practice of selling them using theological rulings of early Islam.Yazidi women released by Isis were gang-raped in public by fighters and tortured by their captors, according to distressing accounts of their ordeals.

Hundreds of women and children were abducted from the town of Sinjar, in northern Iraq, and held hostage by Isis for over eight months. Some were sold to fighters as sex slaves or given as 'prizes'. Many were beaten and forced to convert to Islam.

Ziyad Shammo Khalaf, who works with the Yazda organization to support Yazidi victims, said children were separated from their mothers and "distributed among houses" in Mosul and Tal Afar. "If you come and sit with the girls you will find different stories from girl to girl. A lot of them have been sold to Isis fighters, they have been raped in [...] public, and by more than two or three people at a time," he told. "They were tortured, beaten and subject to any type of violence."

Other Yazidi survivors have also given disturbing accounts of their treatment by Isis, with one women describing how militants were forcing hostages to give their blood for transfusions.

Amnesty International's Donatella Rovera, who spoke to more than 40 former captives in northern Iraq, said: "Hundreds of Yezidi women and girls have had their lives shattered by the horrors of sexual violence and sexual slavery in Islamic State captivity. Many of those held as sexual slaves are children - girls aged 14, 15 or even younger. Islamic State fighters are using rape as a weapon in attacks amounting to war crimes and crimes against humanity."

The horrors endured in Islamic State captivity have left these women and girls so severely traumatized that some have been driven to end their own lives. Nineteen-year-old Jilan committed suicide while being held captive in Mosul because she feared she would be raped, her brother told Amnesty. One of the girls, who managed to escape, was held in the same room as Jilan and 20 others, including two girls aged ten and 12.

"One day we were given clothes that looked like dance costumes and were told to bathe and wear those clothes. Jilan killed herself in the bathroom. She cut her wrists and hanged herself. She was very beautiful; I think she knew she was going to be taken away by a man and that is why she killed herself."

Wafa, 27, another former captive, told Amnesty how she and her sister attempted to end their lives one night after their captor threatened them with forced marriage. They tried to strangle themselves with scarves but two girls sleeping in the same room awoke and stopped them.

Wafa said: "We tied the scarves around our necks and pulled away from each other as hard as we could, until I fainted ... I could not speak for several days after that."

The majority of the perpetrators are Iraqi and Syrian men; many of them are Islamic State fighters but others are believed to be supporters of the group. Several former captives said they had been held in family homes where they lived with their captors' wives and children. Many Yezidi survivors are doubly affected as they are also struggling to cope with the loss of dozens of their relatives who either remain in captivity or have been killed by the Islamic State.

Randa, a 16-year-old girl from a village near Mount Sinjar, was abducted with scores of her family members including her heavily-pregnant mother. Randa was "sold" or given as a "gift" to a man twice her age who raped her. She described the impact of her ordeal:

"It is so painful what they did to me and to my family. Da'esh [Islamic State] has ruined our lives ... What will happen to my family? I don't know if I will ever see them again."

The trauma of survivors of sexual violence is further exacerbated by the stigma surrounding rape. Survivors feel that their "honour" and that of their families has been tarnished and fear that their standing in society will be diminished as a result. Meanwhile, many survivors of sexual violence are still not receiving the full help and support they desperately need.

Donatella Rovera added: "The physical and psychological toll of the horrifying sexual violence these women have endured is catastrophic. Many of them have been tortured and treated as chattel. Even those who have managed to escape remain deeply traumatized. The Kurdistan Regional Government, UN and other humanitarian organizations who are providing medical and other support services to survivors of sexual violence must step up their efforts. They must ensure they are swiftly and proactively reaching out to all those who may need them, and that women and girls are made aware of the support available to them."

A Yazidi teenager who was captured and held by Isis militants has claimed women are being forced to give blood to save the lives of wounded fighters. The woman, identified only as Hamshe, described how militants were forcing hostages to give their blood for transfusions. Hamshe said she was held by Isis militants for 28 days, who she says also killed her husband, father in-law and brother in-law. She recounted a militant taking her to his house and locked her inside his room. He then warned that he would deny her food or water if she refused to marry him. "I can never forget when they separated the men and women from each other," she said. "It was very painful to witness women and girls being taken as war spoils. They forced the Yazidi girls to donate blood to Isis wounded fighters. Which God allows these acts?"

Another 21-year-old survivor recalled seeing women being repeatedly raped and tortured by militants. She told: "I saw babies separated from their mothers. Some children were five and six years old when they were taken from their families. They killed our fathers, uncles and everyone. There is no horror I haven't experienced. There is nothing worse than rape. One of the leaders took a 13 year-old girl to his house, locked the room and told his children she is a Yazidi girl who converted to Islam, that he will teach her how to pray and read the Koran. In fact he was raping her during that time. She told me she was there for three days and said 'I was raped all that time'."

Hamshe said she fled her captors one night as they slept outside the room she was being held in. "One night my baby was crying from thirst. I knocked at the door and saw all the guards sleeping outside. I took a bottle of water from them and I ran away with my baby and walked for four hours," she explained.

19 women have been executed for refusing to have sex with ISIS fanatics. A Kurdish official revealed that the women were being held hostage in Islamic State's stronghold of Mosul, Iraq. Said Mimousini, a spokesman for the Kurdish Democratic Party in Mosul told Iraqi News that the women were sentenced to death because they refused to "participate in the practice of sexual jihad".

The young women - Bushra, 21, Munira, 17, and Noor, 22 – whose names have been changed to protect their identity said they were forced to marry ISIS fighters. They described being tied up, gang raped and burnt with cigarettes. Bushra tried to kill herself when she was sold to an ISIS extremist. She said: "The man who had bought me took me to hospital. He told me he was going to rape me that same day, however ill I made myself. He took me home, tied up my hands and feet, and raped me.

A UN envoy named Bangura, investigating Islamic State's sex trade has said that one woman can be bought by six different men as 'girls get peddled like barrels of petrol'.

Bangura said: "They [ISIS] have a machinery... They have a manual on how you treat these women. They have a marriage bureau which organizes all of these 'marriages' and the sale of women... They have a price list."

She also verified a disturbing ISIS document which suggested the extremists sell the Yazidi and Christian women and children they have abducted. The price for Yazidi or Christian women between the age of 40 - 50 is $43 (£27)

It then gives the prices of women and children by age, with one to nine-year-olds costing the most - around £110. The older the women, the lower the price. The pamphlet - published on October 16 - goes on to say: 'Customers are allowed to purchase only three items with the exception of customers from Turkey, Syria and Gulf countries.

Bangura said the fighters get to choose first and then 'wealthy Middle-Easterners are allowed to. The UN envoy has previously said the Yazidi virgins are sent to slave auctions in Islamic State's de facto capital of Raqqa in Syria, where they are stripped naked and sold to the highest bidder.

An ISIS video released in November last year appeared to show an ISIS 'sex slave market' where fighters can choose among different Yazidi girls who are priced according to 'desirable' physical features.

In October, a Yazidi woman held captive in a brothel in Iraq managed to contact members of NGO Compassion4Kurdistan and told them she was raped around 30 times a day by the insurgents. The Yazidi woman has begged the West to bomb the brothel where she is being detained and repeatedly raped by terror group Islamic State.

The unidentified woman alleged she was raped dozens of times in a phone call with activists from Compassion4Kurdistan, which aims to raise awareness of IS' persecution of the Yazidi community in Iraq.

"If you know where we are please bomb us... There is no life after this. I'm going to kill myself anyway - others have killed themselves this morning," she was quoted as saying. "I've been raped 30 times and it's not even lunchtime. I can't go to the toilet. Please bomb us."

The woman's phone call came just a few days after the UN said that IS' persecution of the Yazidi community is "an attempt to commit genocide." The militants, whose insurgence in Iraq and Syria has claimed thousands of lives since June 2014, admitted last October that they are Yazidi.

UN officials issued a joint statement in October condemning "the explicit targeting of women and children and the barbaric acts the Islamic State has perpetrated on minorities in areas under its control. "We remind all armed groups that acts of sexual violence are grave human rights violations that can be considered as war crimes and crimes against humanity."

The statement followed a UN study about IS sex slavery markets, in which a 13-year-old Yazidi girl gave her account of what happened to her after she was abducted by IS from her village in August."She stated that IS took hundreds of women who had not been able to flee to Jabal Sinjar," said the report. "The girl stated that she was raped several times by several IS fighters, before she was sold to a market."

At least 2,500 women and children have been imprisoned, sexually abused and sold for around $10 each by Isis slavers. The slave markets in the al-Quds area of Mosul in Iraq and Raqqa in Syria have been used as a way of attracting new recruits to Islamic State, the UN said.

Women who were captured at the end of August managed to contact the UN, having kept hold of their mobile phones. They reported being subject to sexual assaults. The UN study is based on claims made in 450 interviews with Iraqi witnesses to alleged war crimes.

UN high commissioner for human Rights Zeid Ra'ad al Hussein told: "The array of violations and abuses perpetrated by ISIL and associated armed groups is staggering, and many of their acts may amount to war crimes or crimes against humanity."

One 13-year-old Yazidi girl gave a harrowing account of what happened to her after she was abducted by Isis from her village on 3 August 2014. "She stated that ISIL [Islamic State] took hundreds of women who had not been able to flee to Jabal Sinjar," stated the report. "The girl stated that she was raped several times by several ISIL fighters, before she was sold to a market."

One Yazidi woman was given to 10 Islamic State men. "We were sold for $10 or $12. Who could accept that behaviour? Can God accept that?" the woman told. "It's a shame to rape a woman, but when she is raped by 10 men... what is this? They are animals, they are not humans. Because of them I am afraid all the time."

She managed to flee her captors with the help of sympathetic local residents and sought safety in Mosul.A 17-year-old woman said she was being held captive with 40 other Yazidi women by Islamic State fighters.

"I beg you not to publish my name because I'm so ashamed of what they are doing to me. There's a part of me that just wants to die. But there is another part of me that still hopes that I will be saved and that I will be able to embrace my parents once again," she told.

The newspaper was able to interview her by calling her on her mobile phone, after being given the number by her parents, who are in a refugee camp in Iraqi Kurdistan.

"We've asked our jailers to shoot us dead, to kill us, but we are too valuable for them. They keep telling us that we are unbelievers because we are non-Muslims and that we are their property, like war booty. They say we are like goats bought at a market."

Price List

An ISIS "price list" first appeared about eight months ago, and was purported to be genuine. The pamphlet detailed the cost to the buyer for children, young girls and women for use as sex slaves. Since that time, the list has been confirmed to be real.

The thought of selling human beings as slaves is abhorrent to most people, and selling someone as a sex slave is unspeakably terrible, but the Islamic State, in its twisted ideology, thinks nothing of doing exactly that.

The list circulated by ISIS is for the pleasure of their own fighters, as well as the rich from the Middle East. While the "prices" listed are accurate, the actual cost of an individual slave is often a lot more because outsiders can bid on an individual, and this can amount to thousands of dollars.

For the Islamic State fighters, the price in Iraqi dinars for boys and girls aged one to nine are equal to about $165. An adolescent girl fetches $124, and women over 20 years of age are even cheaper. But outsiders have first choice, simply because they will pay more hard cash.

Zainab Bangura, the UN's Special Representative of the Secretary-General for Sexual Violence in Conflict, says she had seen the list put out by the terrorist group in April, and it reflects genuine transactions.

"The girls get peddled like barrels of petrol. One girl can be sold and bought by five or six different men. Sometimes these fighters sell the girls back to their families for thousands of dollars of ransom,".

Sadly, this is not the first time ISIS has spoken about the use of women as slaves. In 2014, the group distributed a pamphlet on female slaves, and how they were treated while at the same time using the Koran to justify the women's treatment as well as other crimes.

Kayla Mueller

Kayla Mueller, the U.S. aid worker killed this year while being held hostage by Islamic State militants, was raped repeatedly by the group's leader, Abu Bakr al-Baghdadi, while in captivity in Syria, U.S. officials said.

Her parents, Carl and Marsha Mueller, were told by U.S. government officials that their daughter had been raped by al-Baghdadi and tortured during her captivity, family spokeswoman Emily Lenzner told. Mueller was 26 at the time of her death. "We can confirm that the Mueller family learned in June of Kayla's treatment from the FBI," Lenzner said.

Islamic State said in February that Mueller, of Prescott, Arizona, was killed when Jordanian fighter jets bombed a building where she was being held outside Raqqa, a stronghold in Syria of the Islamist militant group. Jordanian and U.S. officials have expressed doubt about Islamic State's account of her death following 18 months as a hostage.

Mueller was seized in August 2013 while leaving a hospital in Aleppo in northern Syria. Al-Baghdadi personally brought Mueller to be imprisoned inside the home of Abu Sayyaf, a Tunisian Islamic State figure killed in a U.S. raid in May.

The information about al-Baghdadi's actions came from many sources including U.S. interviews with at least two teenage Yezidi girls held as sex slaves in Sayyaf's compound and the interrogation of Sayyaf's wife, Umm Sayyaf, who was captured by U.S. forces in the raid in which her husband was killed.

Mueller went to Turkey in December 2012 to work for a Turkish organization providing humanitarian aid to Syrian refugees along the Syrian border. Islamic State has beheaded numerous hostages, including three Americans. Its forces control wide swathes of territory in Iraq and Syria.

Lenzner said Mueller's parents were told at a meeting in Washington of Mueller's abuse by al-Baghdadi and her torture while held captive. Lenzner was not clear about whether al-Baghdadi was responsible for torturing Mueller. Mueller's family declined to comment directly. "The family is so exhausted at this point, they need some time," Lenzner said.

National Security Council Spokeswoman Bernadette Meehan said the family received "a private message from Kayla's [ISIS] captors containing additional information." The information was later reviewed by United States intelligence.

While the government has not formally commented on the form of information the family received, anonymous government officials told a photograph of

Mueller was reviewed, in which her face and shoulders are visible. ISIS first claimed Mueller had died as the result of a Jordanian airstrike. The terrorist organization distributed photographs of a building they said held Mueller. In the photos, the building is in rubble, however, the photograph of Mueller reportedly seen by government officials did not picture any rubble. The cause of her death remains unknown.

Mueller spent over a year in captivity; she was captured in Aleppo, Syria in 2013. During that time, her family received a video of her, forcibly filmed by her captors, as proof of life. They also received a letter, made public after the announcement of her death.

The letter was carried out of captivity by a fellow hostage who was released on or after November 11, 2014. She asks the family not to negotiate on her behalf, "If there is any other option take it, even if it takes more time," she writes. Mueller also urges her family to contact "these women" and "seek their advice," their names were redacted. Based on the context of the letter, they may have been fellow captives.

In the message, she offers a rare glimpse into life as a female captive with ISIS. She said she was not mistreated and had "put on weight in fact." In an interview, Didier François, a French reporter who was held hostage by ISIS in the same building as Mueller, said women were given slightly more room to move around in. However, "being a woman doesn't make it easier," he said of ISIS captivity.

Sinai

A Russian civilian plane with 217 passengers and 7 crew aboard crashed over Sinai early Saturday morning, Oct. 31, shortly after taking off from the Sinai resort town of Sharm el-Sheikh for St. Petersburg.

Initial reporting on the fate of the plane was confused and is still not completely clear. It was first reported to be missing after contact was lost with Egyptian air control; it was then said to be safely on its way to Russia over Turkey. Russian aviation sources then reported the A321 to be missing over Cypriot air space. Finally, the Egyptian prime minister's office Egyptian prime minister's office confirmed that a Russian passenger plane had crashed in central Sinai and a cabinet level crisis committee had been formed to deal with the crash.

The airliner owned by the small airline Kogalymavia disappeared from screen 23 minutes after takeoff from Sharm el-Sheikh. There were many families with children aboard.

The first claim by Russian aviation sources that the plane had gone missing over Cyprus was an attempt to draw attention from the likelihood that it was shot down over Sinai, where the former Ansar al-Maqdis, which has renamed itself ISIS-Sinai, maintains its main strongholds.

On board the plane were 17 children, along with 200 adults and seven crew, said aviation authorities. There are no signs of survivors. Confirming the deliberate attempt at confusion, Moscow and Cairo both stated that the plane had disappeared from the radar 23 minutes after takeoff from Sharm El-Sheikh.

This is refuted by the discovery of the wreckage, a few minutes ago, completely gutted and destroyed, and a short distance away near Bir Al-Hassaneh, in the central Sinai Jabal al-Halal mountain range, where Ansar Beit al-Miqdas terrorists are holed up and which is almost inaccessible to rescue teams.

It is to this stronghold that ISIS sent officers, former senior members of Saddam Hussein's army, to set up a major campaign against the Egyptian army, along with advanced anti-air missile systems smuggled into Sinai and the Gaza Strip from Libya for this campaign.

In another attempt to disguise the cause of the disaster, Russian and Egyptian officials now say that the pilot of the Russian plane reported a technical fault after takeoff and asked to be rerouted to Cairo or El-Arish. Russian and Egyptian officials have meanwhile announced they are forming commissions of inquiry to investigate the cause of the tragedy. Official condolences were relayed to the waiting families the airport.

The Sinai branch of the Islamic State has developed a highly competent intelligence-gathering network operated by local Bedouin tribesmen who track the slightest movements in the Peninsula. The Egyptian army and the American troops serving at the big the Multinational Force base there are fully aware of the round-the-clock surveillance maintained by the terrorists at Egyptian resorts, using staff at hotels, restaurants and the local airfield as inside informers.

Ansar has never yet harmed the tourist traffic in Sinai. But once ISIS decided to use it to hit back at Russia's intensified military intervention in the Syrian conflict, the Islamists would not have found it hard to find out when the Russian airliner was due to take off from the Red Sea resort, chart its route north along the western coast of the Gulf of Aqaba up to Dahab and then turn west towards central Sinai and head for the Mediterranean. All the terrorists had to do was to lay a missile ambush for the plane from the Jabal Halal eminence of 876 meters (2,865 ft).

Russian sources following the forensic examination of the bodies and partial remains of the victims flown to St. Petersburg report that they show evidence of an explosion in the plane before it plummeted to the ground. Further testing is required to establish the cause of the explosion.

A US infrared satellite detected a heat flash at the same time and same vicinity over Sinai where the Russian plane went down. A US defense official added that the same satellite would have been able to track the tell-tale heat trail of a missile from the ground. "The speculation that this plane was brought down by a missile is off the table," the official said.

Another official said, "the plane disintegrated at a very high altitude." The general consensus ahead of the Egyptian and Russian probes is that a sudden, catastrophic explosion caused the crash - whether from a bomb inside, "external impact" – as the Metrojet company claims - or from faulty fuel. Russian fuel experts found nothing wrong with the fuel.

An Egyptian physician who inspected the scene of the disaster found that one out of every five bodies he saw had been incinerated to death from a fire that may have started in the passenger's cabin and spread to the rest of the plane. Egyptian experts reported that "the large number of separate body fragments" could indicate that a strong explosion occurred onboard before the aircraft hit the ground. They were scattered across a radius of 8-10 square kilometers from the wreckage.

Russian and Egyptian sources tracking the examination of the two black boxes found evidence that the calamity occurred too rapidly for the pilots or crew to send an SOS or even say a few words.

As the probe of the air catastrophe began Tuesday and Wednesday, Moscow and Cairo were increasingly at odds on their findings. The Russians asserted that the plane must have broken up into two parts as a result of a strong explosion, whereas Egyptian officials remained intent on playing down the claim of responsibility for the crash published Saturday by the Sinai wing of the Islamic State. They criticize the Russians as rushing to conclusions ahead of the probe.

Egyptian President Abdel-Fatteh El-Sisi arrived in London Wednesday for talks with British Prime Minister David Cameron. In interviews prior to his arrival, the Egyptian president said that he will demand that David Cameron "complete his mission in Libya to prevent the country being dominated by Islamists." By "mission," El-Sisi was referring to the UK's role in the coalition which toppled Muammar Qaddafi in 2011.

Egypt faces an acute problem from Libya's transformation in the last two years into the main supply source of smuggled arms and fighters for the Islamist terrorists operating in Egypt and Sinai. While neither the Egyptians or the Russians are willing to admit this, it is highly likely that the missile or explosives which brought down the Russian airliner Saturday came from Libya.

Press release

"The fighters of the Islamic State were able to down a Russian plane over Sinai province that was carrying over 220 Russian crusaders. They were all killed, thanks be to God," said a statement from the Sinai affiliate of ISIS

The terrorists' statement went on to say: "You should know, Russians and your allies, that you have no security on Muslim land or its airspace... The daily murder of scores of innocents in Syria by your air bombardments will bring upon you disasters... Just as you kill, so you will be killed..." |

In an audio recording release via social networks, ISIS repeated its claim of responsibility for the downing of a Russian airliner over the Sinai Peninsula on Saturday, adding that it will soon reveal how it shot down the jet. The message also challenged the government of Egypt to prove that ISIS was not responsible for the crash.

Britain has canceled flights indefinitely to and from Sharm el-Sheikh due to security concerns after the downing of the Russian airliner, leaving 20,000 British holidaymakers stranded there. Downing Street has cited an explosive device as the possible cause of the Russian jet's crash over Sinai killing all 224 people aboard. PM David Cameron has called a second Cobra (emergency cabinet) meeting to review the situation ahead of his lunch date with visiting Egyptian president Abdel-Fatteh El-Sisi. Foreign Secretary Philip Hammond says that plans are in place to evacuate the tourists.

Background

Ansar Beit al-Maqdis (ABM), also known as the Sinai Province, is a Salafi jihadist group that formed in Egypt and the Gaza Strip in 2011. After authoritarian president Hosni Mubarak was ousted from power in Egypt in 2011, tribal communities in Sinai, which claimed that they were oppressed by the Egyptian government, drove security forces out of the region. In this power vacuum, members of the region's active militant population joined the militant group Al-Tawhid wa'al-Jihad to merge and form ABM.

ABM shares a similar ideology as Al Qaeda (AQ) and declared themselves AQ's wing in the Sinai in 2011. However, despite sharing similar ideology, ABM and AQ were never formal affiliates. Since its formation, judged to be at some point in 2011, the group seems to have gained support in the peninsula, seeming to breathe life into jihadi cells that had been neutralized by former campaigns in the Sinai.

This has been evidenced by the leadership of the group, many of whom are experienced militants who had previously been allied with other jihadi groups, particularly Tawhid wal-Jihad and the Mujahideen Shura Council (MSC) in the Environs of Jerusalem.

The group ingratiates itself to local population, calling on them to stand with Ansar Bayt al-Maqdis in their fight against the state. In a recent campaign, the group had been reported to be distributing fliers to local (and highly marginalized) populations that stated: "If you are not with us, do not be against us." In a recent statement, the group described itself as "your brothers...men from [Egypt]...perhaps your neighbors or relatives."

According to intelligence reports, the group is thought to have around 1,000 members, many of whom may have operated in other jihadi groups in the past. This number, however, is difficult to verify given the group's refusal to speak with members of the international press and the many reports of alleged killings or arrest of members from the Egyptian army.

Regardless of exact numbers, the group is known to be the strongest and best coordinated in Egypt, and it is in possession of advanced weaponry, including man-portable air-defense systems (MANPADS), rocket-propelled grenades, Grad rockets, and mortars. Additionally, since swearing Bay'a (an oath of allegiance) to the Islamic State on November 10, 2014, there has been a dramatic advance in the group's media capabilities and production, as well as an overall re-branding that showcases the strong tie to the greater Islamic State.

Egyptian security forces have launched a number of successful operations against Ansar Bayt al-Maqdis operatives, including a March 2014 raid that resulted in the death of six militants, the capture of eight others, and yielded a cache of weapons and strategic documents.

On April 9, 2014, the United States declared Ansar Bayt al-Maqdis a terrorist organization. Egypt followed suit shortly thereafter, declaring the group to be a terrorist organization on April 14, 2014.

Ansar Bayt al-Maqdis released a statement on July 25, 2014, lamenting the death of three of its leaders by an "Israeli drone;" Egyptian authorities vehemently denied the penetration of airspace. Despite these setbacks, the group continues to be active in the Sinai, releasing regular and frequent statements on social media.

On November 10, 2014, Ansar Bayt al-Maqdis formally swore allegiance (Bay'a) to the Islamic State, changing their name to Wilayat Sinai (Province of Sinai) which is the most significant, and potentially long-lasting recent development for the group. This allegiance provides the Islamic State with a "province" in Sinai, an extension of territory for their overall Caliphate, while also providing Ansar Bayt al-Maqdis with greater resources.

These resources are apparent when examining the increase in production value of Ansar Bayt al-Maqdis' media releases, that the Islamic State puts heavy focus upon, and also in the increased legitimacy and support the group receives from abroad. Evidence toward this point can be found in the media released statement calling for foreign fighters to travel to the Sinai to help solidify the Caliphate.

Attacks

Early statements from the Ansar Bayt al-Maqdis mainly targeted the Jewish population in nearby Israel, where the majority of the group's efforts were focused (with the exception of pipeline attacks on Egyptian soil).

Soon after the removal of President Muhammed Morsi, however, Ansar Bayt al-Maqdis shifted its attention to the Egyptian government for waging war against Islam. Since aligning themselves with the Islamic State, the group has adopted some, but not all of the Islamic State's ideology. The act of beheading enemies, especially those they deem as traitors has become more frequent since the group pledged themselves to the Islamic State, showing a clear evolution of their practices.

Despite claiming responsibility for the killing of American oil worker William Henderson, there is little evidence that Ansar Bayt al-Maqdis holds the intense anti-Western and sectarian ideologies of the Islamic State as a priority; the group's focus remains on Egyptian security forces.

Ansar Bayt al-Maqdis has attacked gas pipelines and a tourist bus in its efforts to wage economic war. The group has claimed responsibility for several pipeline attacks, as far back as February 5, 2011, and as late as January 17, 2014. In a highly coordinated attack on August 18, 2011, the group attacked a bus in Eilat, Israel, killing at least eight Israelis and three Egyptian security forces.

In its first attack after the ouster of President Muhammad Morsi, on September 5, 2013 Ansar Bayt al-Maqdis attempted to assassinate Minister of the Interior, Mohamed Ibrahim, but was unsuccessful. This attack was carried out by former

Egyptian military officer Walid Badr, who had traveled to wage jihad in Syria, was also known to have connections with the Muhammad Jamal Network.

The group's deadliest known attack to date was a December 24, 2013 attack on the Security Directorate building in Mansoura. This remains one of the deadliest attacks in Egypt in the past decade: 16 people were killed and 134 were injured in the bombing. This bombing also represented a moment of intense escalation in the Egyptian government's "war on terror;" despite not having been connected with the attack, the Muslim Brotherhood was declared a terrorist group the following day.

Also on the day after the Mansoura attack, Ansar Bayt al-Maqdis released a video of an attack on a helicopter. Militants used a man-portable air-defense system (MANPADS) to take down the aircraft, killing the five men on board.

In its first attack on tourists, an Ansar Bayt al-Maqdis suicide bomber attacked a bus of South Korean tourists traveling near the Israeli border on February 16, 2014. The attack killed three of the tourists and the Egyptian bus driver.

The group was engaged in a campaign against Israel during a period of the intense conflict between Israel and Gaza in July 2014. The group released videos of Grad and 107mm rocket attacks on the Israeli town of Eilat, two attacks on the village Bnei Netzarim, and an attack on an Israeli border military base.

In August, 2014, Ansar Bayt al-Maqdis turned its attention back to Egypt. The group released a video first documenting the murder of Egyptian police on August 18. Ten days later, on August 28, the group released a video in which they document the beheading of four Egyptian men they accuse of collaboration with Israeli intelligence. The August beheadings were the first violence of this type for the group, marking a chilling change in tactic that has endured through the posting of this profile in February 2015.

On October 24, 2014, Ansar Bayt al-Maqdis carried out what was its deadliest attack up until that point. The group detonated a car bomb at a heavily guarded security checkpoint in Sheikh Zuweid and then ambushed the guards who came to investigate the attack. Later the same day, they opened fire on a security checkpoint in Al-Arish. The attacks killed at least 33 Egyptian security forces and wounded as many. This was the at that point deadliest attack on the Egyptian military in decades.

On January 29, 2015, Ansar Bayt al-Maqdis carried out an attack reminiscent of their earlier October strike against the military. The group utilized suicide bombers, car bombs, mortars, and intense gunfire against a military base and nearby security buildings, a hotel, a police club, a newspaper office, and various security checkpoints through North Sinai. The result was over 30 dead Egyptian military members and many more wounded.

The scale and immense coordination of the attacks, along with the general escalation of their ability to strike at military targets points toward the group's overall cohesion. It might also point toward evidence that the widespread military crackdown on militants in the Sinai by the Egyptian military may not be experiencing the success that the military claim it has.

Ansar Bayt al-Maqdis has planted 21 bombs almost daily along several routes taken by the army and security officials in north Sinai in the areas stretching from el-Arish to Rafah and Sheikh Zuweid.

The security apparatus has succeeded in discovering and dismantling seven bombs, while 14 others exploded. Six bombs targeted military vehicles, killing four security men and wounding 24 others, some of whom were in critical condition, mostly soldiers and officers. Eight bombs exploded without hitting their target.

Ansar Bayt al-Maqdis is increasingly using bombs because they are unable to face the Egyptian army, which is better equipped and larger. As a result, the army outdoes them in direct confrontations, which it is well trained for.

Ansar Bayt al-Maqdis has lately succeeded in opening fronts inside other Egyptian districts, especially after pledging allegiance to IS. Several people who had always dreamed of the jihadist caliphate joined the group, in addition to defecting members from the Muslim Brotherhood, notably those holding a grudge against the state due to the Rabia and al-Nahda massacres.

In the evening of Friday, Nov. 28, Ansar Bayt al-Maqdis — or Wilayat Sinai as it is now called — claimed responsibility for the assassination of a colonel and two soldiers from the Egyptian army in the Suez bridge area in the heart of Cairo, and the killing of an officer and a soldier in Qalyubia governorate. The group declared in an online statement that the two attacks were carried out by a brigade affiliated to it and called the Martyr Abi Ubaidah al-Masri Brigade.

All the latest terrorist operations carried out by Ansar Bayt al-Maqdis confirm that the group relies on the remote targeting strategy in booby-trapping operations, assassinations or bombing of vital state infrastructure such as gas pipelines. This also confirms that the organization is avoiding direct confrontation with the Egyptian army, fearing the loss of its few members, according to sources close to the organization. Moreover, activists and observers in Sinai fear the increase in members of terrorist organizations in the future, if the state continues to fight terrorism with foul practices that harm civilians in the peninsula.

Regarding the bombing of the gas pipelines in Sinai, the jihadist source said that Ansar Bayt al-Maqdis will keep bombing gas pipelines for three reasons. First, the organization wants to regain its media momentum to prove that it is facing the tough military campaigns in Sinai. Second, it wants to cause losses to the army's economic structure — a structure that greatly relies on the huge profits from cement factories in the center of Sinai and uses gas in its work. Third, the organization wants to stop pumping gas exported to Jordan because the latter joined the anti-IS international alliance.

The Egyptian army's cement plants and other plants owned by businessmen close to the ruling regime in Cairo are suffering losses due to the suspension of production, which is described by one of the workers in these plants as a disaster. Meanwhile, the state is also suffering substantial losses. An officer at the Egyptian Natural Gas Co. (Gasco), the main operator in charge of gas repairs in Sinai, told that every time a pipeline is blown up, the repairs cost millions of Egyptian pounds paid from the state budget.

The Gasco source said that the losses also affected Jordan, which depends on Egyptian gas to generate electricity, stressing that it is impossible to secure the gas lines that are exposed and stretch over 100 kilometers (62 miles) in the vast desert. "This violates the economic contracts signed with Jordan and exposes the two countries to significant economic losses," he said.

One of the managers at the Sinai cement factory, in the industrial zone affected by the gas explosions in central Sinai, told "The citizens will incur the consequences of the losses and terrorist operations, including the bombing of the gas pipeline."

"The repeated bombings prompted the departments in charge of the operation of the plants — whether private or military plants — to raise the sale price by 25% as a result of the increase in the production cost. This increase came in response to attempts to replace gas with diesel, which is more costly, especially in terms of transportation to central Sinai," he added.

It is noteworthy that el-Arish's gas pipeline has been bombed 25 times since the regime of former President Hosni Mubarak was toppled.

All information and analyses from the field indicate that the coming phase will be very tough for Egypt, with the potential shift of violence from Sinai to the core of Egypt.

In a recent article published on the website Minbar al Tawhid wa'l Jihad, leading global jihad ideologue Sheikh Abu al Mundhir al Shinqiti called on Egypt's Muslims to wage jihad against Egyptian security forces, in particular within the Sinai Peninsula. According to Shinqiti, the Egyptian army "is an army of infidels and apostates" that is no different from the armies of the US, Israel, or the regime of Bashar al Assad in Syria.

"[B]elonging to this army is apostasy from Islam and a pledge of allegiance to the enemies of Allah. Belonging to this army is belonging to a sect that is at war with Allah," Shinqiti wrote. He further argued that "Muslim women married to a member of the army should know that their marriage is nullified because [their husbands] are apostates."

In the article, al Shinqiti also questioned the Muslim Brotherhood's approach to the July 2013 overthrow of Mohammed Morsi. Shinqiti also declared that anyone advocating non-violence "is a criminal thug who wants the Ummah to be eradicated and to be slaughtered."

According to Shinqiti, the Egyptian army must be fought as "peaceful change ... is now impossible." "Every attempt to avoid fighting the Egyptian Army is like treating a disease with the wrong medicine," he wrote. Shinqiti further called on Egyptian Muslims to "come and respond to the call of jihad ... come and shed blood for the sake of establishing Allah's law." Moreover, he declared jihad against the Egypt army to be "a religious duty and divine obligation."

"Every Muslim must support them according to his ability. Whoever is able to travel to them, fight with them, and increase their ranks, it is a duty to do so ...

whoever is unable must support them with money, by inciting to fight [with them], and by [helping to] prepare the fighters," Shinqiti stated.

With regard to ongoing Egyptian military operations in the Sinai, al Shinqiti contended that they are merely an attempt to protect Israel. "The goal of the security campaign that the tyrannical army in Egypt is directing in the Sinai is to protect Israel and its borders after jihadi groups in the Sinai became a real threat to it," Shinqiti wrote.

In addition, Shinqiti praised ongoing attacks by "your mujahideen brothers" in the Sinai and called on Egyptian Muslims to join them, "support them, increase their ranks, and be an aid and a champion of them." "[J]ihad in the Sinai is a great opportunity for you to gather and unite under a pure flag, unsullied by ignorant slogans," Shinqiti claimed.

Since the overthrow of Mohammed Morsi in early July 2013, there has been a plethora of statements from jihadists in response to the ongoing crackdown on the Muslim Brotherhood. For example, Harith bin Ghazi al Nadhari (also known as Muhammad al Murshidi), an official in al Qaeda in the Arabian Peninsula (AQAP), charged on Aug 25 that the Egyptian government was seeking "to return Egypt to the era of oppression, tyranny and the domination of the security and intelligence agencies."

On Aug. 17, jihadist ideologue Abu Sa'ad al 'Amili posted a series of tweets to his Twitter account urging Egyptian Muslims to prepare for an "open war." Likewise, Abdullah Muhammad Mahmoud of the jihadist Dawa'at al-Haq Foundation for Studies and Research warned Egyptian Muslims, in an article posted to jihadist forums on Aug. 14, that "if you don't do jihad today, then only blame yourselves tomorrow."

Similarly, on Aug. 15, Abu Hafs al Maqdisi, the leader of the Gaza-based Jaish a Ummah (Army of the Nation), called on Egyptians to wage "jihad" against Egyptian army commander General Abdul Fattah el Sisi. Four days ater, Shabaab, al Qaeda's affiliate in Somalia, urged Egyptian Muslims to "pick up arms and defend yourself." In addition, on Aug. 30, the Islamic State of Iraq and the Levant called on Egyptians to wage 'jihad' against army.

And on Aug. 22, al Salafiyya al Jihadiyya in Sinai released a statement that called on Muslims to fight the "apostate" Egyptian army. The communiqué was particularly notable as last fall the group said: "[T]he army and the police are not our targets and that our weapons are directed at the enemies and the enemies of our Ummah the Jews." More recently, in mid-May, the jihadist group said: "[T]he target of the Salafist Jihadist current in Sinai is the Zionist enemy and its operations are directed to them, and the Egyptian soldiers are not a target for us."

More recently, on Sept. 10, Ansar Jerusalem declared that "it is obligatory to repulse them [the Egyptian army] and fight them until the command of Allah is fulfilled." Similarly, on Sept. 15, the Salafi jihadist group declared: "We in Ansar Jerusalem and all the mujahideen in Sinai in Egypt as a whole stress that the blood of innocent Muslims will not go in vain."

In addition, on Sept. 22, the Ibn Taymiyyah Media Center (ITMC), a jihadist media unit tied to the Mujahideen Shura Council in the Environs of Jerusalem, called for jihadists to strike the Egyptian army. Now is the time for the "mujahideen to hit without fail so as to thwart those criminals from among the Egyptian army," the group said. And on Oct. 4, al Salafiyya al Jihadiyya in Sinai threatened to kill anyone found aiding Egyptian security forces.

Along with the calls for attacks, another theme that has been emphasized since the overthrow of Mohammed Morsi is the argument that the Muslim Brotherhood had made a mistake in engaging in the democratic process. This theme is a general jihadi talking point that al Qaeda and its affiliates, such as al Shabaab and al Qaeda in the Islamic Maghreb (AQIM), have pushed repeatedly since Morsi's ouster. In July, AQIM official Abu Abdul Ilah Ahmed al Jijeli said Morsi's overthrow should teach Egyptian Muslims "that the price for applying principles on the ground is a mountain of body parts and seas of blood, because evil must be killed and not shown mercy, and righteousness must be achieved by cutting the head of those who corrupt and not reason with them."

An essay released in July by Abu Muhammad al Maqdisi, a global jihadi ideologue and former mentor of Abu Musab al Zarqawi made a similar argument. In the essay, dated July 11, 2013, al Maqdisi contended that armed struggle was the only way to achieve the liberation of Muslim lands. Al Maqdisi further claimed that the ouster of Morsi proved "the soundness of the jihadi project and the choice of the ammunition box over the ballot box."

And in his most recent message, which was released to jihadist forums on Oct. 11, al Qaeda emir Ayman al Zawahiri concentrated on Egypt. In the audio message, Zawahiri called on Egyptian Muslims to unite and "rid Egypt of this criminal gang that jumped on power with iron and fire and took advantage of the concession of some factions in their drooling behind the mirage of the delusional reconciliation."

Egyptian Counter-terrorist Operations

On April 14, 2014 the Court for Urgent Matters officially labeled Ansar Bayt al-Maqdis a terrorist organization. In May 2014, Egypt's general prosecution referred 200 suspected Ansar Bayt al-Maqdis members to criminal court on charges of committing acts of terror. The Egyptian government has accused the Muslim Brotherhood of supporting militant attacks in Egypt but the Brotherhood has denied any such involvement.

Foreign Ministry spokesperson, Badr Abdel-Atty, said that Egypt had been in contact with many countries in an effort to explain the seriousness of the situation and the US State Department has designated Ansar Bayt al-Maqdis a "foreign terrorist organization."

Egypt joined the US-led international coalition, along with nine other Arab states, to combat the IS. So far, Egyptian officials have said that the country's military will not take part in any combat abroad against the IS and will confront the group using other means, including cutting funding sources or pushing an alternative religious discourse. It is unclear how ABM's declaration of allegiance to the Islamic State will affect Egypt's participation in the efforts against the IS.

The Egyptian military has targeted militant hideouts with helicopters and ground troops, killing scores of militants, according to army statements.

On May 23, 2014 the leader of Ansar Bayt al-Maqdis, Shadi al-Menei, was killed along with three senior members in a security operation. Security forces opened fire on the four men as they were in a car in central Sinai, purportedly preparing to carry out an attack on a gas pipeline.

In October 2014, Egyptian military forces arrested Walid Attalah, the leader of the military wing of Ansar Bayt al-Maqdis in North Sinai. Attalah is of Palestinian origin and received Egyptian citizenship during the era of ousted president, Mohamed Morsi. Attalah is suspected of orchestrating an RPG attack in North Sinai, which killed three policemen and injured seven others.

Following the attacks of October 24, 2014, Sinai was placed under a three-month state of emergency. President el-Sisi also ordered the creation of a 500-meter long buffer zone along the Egyptian border with Gaza in an attempt to quash the illegal tunnel trading between Sinai and the Gaza Strip. According to the Defense Ministry, the tunnels are an important method for "armed Takfiri groups to infiltrate Sinai to supply militants with arms, logistical assistance and shelter after staging their heinous attacks on the Egyptian army."

In a controversial move, the Egyptian army gave over 1,100 families who lived within the buffer zone only 48 hours to evacuate their houses. North Sinai's Governor Abdel Fattah Harhour stated that every family will receive EGP300 (US$40) in housing allowance for three months and further compensation will be given for demolished buildings. However, tribal leaders from the region have expressed their dissatisfaction with the sums offered.

ABM issued a statement on its alleged Twitter account condemning the Egyptian army's recent operations to form a buffer zone on the Rafah-Gaza border. Using strong language, as well as Quranic verses to justify its actions, the group said that the government's decision to evacuate hundreds of houses in the planned buffer zone was only helping the "Jews". The statement added that the buffer zone further tightened the ongoing Israeli blockade of the besieged Palestinian enclave. The group also called on local Sinai tribes to join the fight.

On January 31, 2015, Egypt's President Abdel Fattah al-Sisi established a unified command to combat terrorism east of the Suez Canal, following deadly militant attacks in Sinai. Egypt's Supreme Council of the Armed Forces (SCAF) announced the presidential decree establishing the command. Sisi promoted Third Field Army Commander Osama Roshdy Askar to lieutenant general, who will be in charge of the command.

Conclusions

In the wake of the June 2013 coup against the Mohamed Morsi government, Ansar Bayt al-Maqdis expanded its operations and attacks against security personnel. ABM has faced significant losses as a result of the campaign led by the Egyptian armed forces and it needs both financial and logistical support. Ansar Bayt al-Maqdis pledged its allegiance to the Islamic State in a bid to boost recruitment and bolster its fight against the Egyptian army.

The group also swore allegiance to the Islamic State's leader, Abu Bakr al-Baghdadi, and subsequently adopted the name Wilayat Sinai, representing the annexation of the group and its transformation into a province within al-Baghdadi's unrecognized Caliphate.

The announcement is the most significant pledge of support for the Islamic State in the region outside of Iraq and Syria, suggesting that the group's influence over militant groups is overshadowing its once dominant Al-Qaeda rivals.

A key factor for the IS at this stage is how it can use the sympathy of other Islamist groups, and prove that it is not affected by the international coalition's war and that it is still capable of recruiting new members. ABM's infamous reputation in Egypt made them a key target for IS recruitment.

On January 30, 2015, following the deadly attacks in North Sinai, the Egyptian army said that militant attacks will not deter the armed forces from their "holy duty of uprooting terrorism", and the Egyptian armed forces have responded by waging a military campaign throughout North Sinai, targeting terrorist hideouts using Apache helicopters and ground forces.

The main challenge facing President el-Sisi and the Egyptian security forces is to restore security and stability to Egypt. The latest terrorist in North Sinai proves that Egypt will have to fight a long war of attrition against radical Islamic groups in order to achieve this goal.

Baya

ABM made international headlines in November 2014 when the organization pledged allegiance to the Islamic State (IS) in a nine-minute audio speech released on Twitter. By declaring allegiance to IS, it is believed that ABM will receive resources such as weapons, oil, and money, allowing them to perpetrate additional attacks against the Sinai and Gaza Strip.

In their declaration of allegiance to IS in November 2014, ABM condemned the Muslim Brotherhood's attempts at democracy in Egypt by stating, "shameful peace will do you no good, nor will blasphemous democracy, and you have seen how it has claimed its upholders and their masters." The formal relationship between the groups is still unclear, but it is believed that IS provides ABM with weapons, money, and supplies.

Since it's inception, ABM has espoused a similar ideology AQ aiming to liberate Muslims from Western oppression based on radical Islam. While also supporting a Sunni interpretation of Shariah law, ABM has never been an official affiliate of AQ. ABM generally maintains a local focus in their goals, perpetrating attacks primarily in the Sinai Peninsula and the Gaza Strip. A main goal of the organization is to drive the Israeli government from Jerusalem. After the removal of Muslim Brotherhood candidate President Mohammed Morsi in 2013, ABM changed the focus of their attacks to Egyptian security and police forces as revenge for the oppression of Muslim militants.

On January 29, 2015 a series of deadly attacks involving car bombs, mortar fire and ambushes targeted several military and police sites in North Sinai. At least 44 people, including military and police personnel and civilians, were killed and 105 others were injured in the attacks.

This was the first major terrorist attack carried out by Ansar Bayt al-Maqdis, the Islamic State group's Egyptian affiliate, in the Sinai Province (Wilayat Sinai). The group claimed responsibility for the attacks via a Twitter account: "We executed extensive, simultaneous attacks in the cities of El-Arish, Sheikh Zuweid and Rafah". The group said it was retaliating against a government crackdown on supporters of former President Mohamed Morsi.

The deadly attacks in North Sinai suggested that Ansar Bayt al-Maqdis may be following the modus operandi of the Islamic State in Iraq and Syria. Ansar Bayt al-Maqdis (ABM), Egypt's most dangerous Islamic terrorist group, swore allegiance to the Islamic State on November 3, 2014. The group published a nearly 10-minute long recording on its Twitter account, which stated that: "After entrusting God we decided to swear allegiance to the emir of the faithful Abu Bakr Al-Baghdadi, caliph of the Muslims in Syria and Iraq and in other countries.". The recording was later suspended from the account along with other jihadist Web sites and forums.

The next day, ABM issued a short tweet denying the media reports that it had pledged allegiance to the Islamic State. In the tweet, ABM asked the media "to check the accuracy of their sources" and warned that all information from the group would only be released via its official social media sites.

Less than a week after denying the above reports, ABM released an audio clip in which it declared its support for the Islamic State, according to media reports. The nine-minute audio clip was posted on a Twitter account claiming to be ABM's official account. "In accordance with the teachings of the Prophet, we announce our pledge of allegiance to the caliph Ibrahim Ibn Awad ... to listen and obey him...and we call on all Muslims to pledge allegiance to him," a man who reportedly identified himself as part of the group's "information department" said in the recording, in which he referred to the Islamic State leader, Abu Bakr al-Baghdadi, by his adopted name.

The speaker reportedly said that al-Baghdadi was "chosen by God" to establish a new caliphate after "Muslims suffered decades of humiliation." A week later, the group used the same Twitter account to deny reports that it had aligned itself with the Islamic State. According to media reports, the speaker also urged Egyptians to rise up against "the tyrant," allegedly referring to President Abdel-Fattah el-Sisi. "What are you waiting for, after your honor has been aggressed upon and your sons ' blood has been shed at the hands of this tyrant and his soldiers?", the spokesperson reportedly said.

Shortly after ABM swore allegiance to the Islamic State, a jihadist Web site posted a statement that it attributed to Abu Mosa'ab al-Maqdisi, a prominent Jordanian jihadist scholar who is seen by many as a source of inspiration for the Islamic State, in which he called on Egyptian jihadists to "take the battle" to Cairo and not stay in the Sinai Peninsula. He added that they should target the economy and the tourism industry by attacking major companies and communication organizations, specifically the Suez Canal and Egyptian businessman, Naguib Sawiris.

Al-Maqdisi called on ABM to welcome "their immigrant foreign brother fighters" to Egypt while they can still access the country. He concluded with a warning that those who collude with police should be beheaded.

As a jihadist group that has pledged allegiance to the caliphate, ABM should eventually join the war against the international coalition led by the United States to fight the Islamic State in Iraq and Syria.

Ansar Bayt Al-Maqdis had previously sought inspiration and advice, and received financial aid from the Islamic State in return for the former's continued operations against the Egyptian army.

At the end of August 2013, Egyptian police forces in northern Sinai arrested an individual by the name of Adel Hebara, who they accused of belonging to the

Sinai Peninsula and participating in the second Rafah massacre, in which 25 Central Security Forces officers were killed.

In the case against Hebera, the court listened to several telephone calls between Hebara and an IS member in Syria, in which the latter promised to transfer $10,000 in return for the implementation of operations in the Sinai Peninsula and for an oath of allegiance to al-Baghdadi. Hebara accepted the conditions. The IS, for its part, sent messages through its Web site to the "brave mujahedeen of Sinai" in which it called on Sinai militants to keep fighting the Egyptian army and establish an Islamic state in the peninsula. The IS also criticized Al-Qaeda for not fighting against the Egyptian army.

The message stated: "Keep your faith in the religion of God, may he be praised, and know that you are in the right. Do not slacken, no matter how much people betray you or work against you. Our hearts, men and available resources are at your service, for we all fight to establish the rule of God's laws. God willing, we shall be one to cooperate in enforcing religion, and God will not divide us, neither through borders, nor nationalities, for we are with you in heart, substance, effort and money."

In September 2014, residents of border villages in Sinai near the cities of Sheikh Zuweid and Rafah reported seeing gunmen wave the black IS flag and carry banners emblazoned with "Islamic State," though the words Iraq and Levant were absent.

Links with Hamas

Analysts have debated the nature of ABM's relationship with several groups, including the Muslim Brotherhood, AQ, and IS. Some claim that ABM is the militant wing of the Muslim Brotherhood. Other analysts dispute this claim, saying that ABM instead is a militant alterative to the Muslim Brotherhood, seeking to draw disenfranchised Brotherhood members away from the group.

In addition, there is speculation about the relationship between ABM and AQ. While the two groups share a similar ideology, they were never formal affiliates. Until Ayman Zawahiri, AQ's leader, mentioned "our people in the Sinai" in January 2014, there had not even been confirmation that AQ recognized ABM. ABM's declaration of allegiance to IS could indicate a split between AQ and ABM. Some ABM cells in the Nile Valley remain loyal to AQ, which could possibly divide the group into two factions: one that remains loyal to AQ and one that is newly loyal to IS.

In September 2013, Egyptian Major General Ahmad Abd al-Halim stated that ABM is part of a larger organization working in the same sphere as Hamas. In addition, ABM's alleged use of smuggling tunnels along the eastern Egypt-Israel border is cited as a link with Hamas.

The question of whether Hamas' military wing cooperated with Wilayat Sinai (literally Sinai Province) is critical for Hamas. This issue is expected to impact not only the future of its relationship with Egypt, but the future of the movement overall. The largest terrorist attack in Sinai occurred when the leaders of the political wing thought the complicated relationship with the regime of Egyptian President Abdel Fattah al-Sisi was stabilizing and that improved relations and a calming of the tensions between them was on the horizon. Once again, however, an accusing finger is pointed toward Hamas, and its leaders are forced to defend themselves.

The leaders of the movement, Ismail Haniyeh, Mousa Abu Marzouk and Abu Obeida, the spokesman of the military wing, quickly denied any connection with the Sinai terror organization affiliated with the Islamic State (IS). In an interview with Al-Quds network, Abu Marzouk explained that everyone knows how his movement works in Gaza against what he called "the black extremism." He was referring to the surge of arrests in recent weeks carried out by Hamas of members of Salafist organizations in Gaza after Salafists had fired rockets toward Israel and tried to entangle his movement. Israel repeatedly states that it holds Hamas responsible for rockets fired at it.

Abu Marzouk, considered to have good relations with the Sisi regime, was sent on a defensive propaganda mission, while Khaled Meshaal, the leader of the movement, who is treated as persona non grata by Egypt, kept his silence. Any word from him would probably cause further damage to the complex relations.

Abu Marzouk, who has filled the leadership void in the movement ever since the crisis with Egypt, did his utmost to diminish the tension between the sides. He claimed that not only did Hamas have no interest in cooperating with the terrorists in Sinai, but the movement itself was harmed by the terror attack on its border. Abu Marzouk argued that every time the Egyptians intend to open the Rafah crossing a horrible attack happens and disrupts things. "This is detrimental to the security of Palestinians, especially those living in Gaza," he added, saying that the attacks hurt Hamas' relations with Egypt.

On the other hand, the coordinator of government activities in the territories, Maj. Gen. Yoav (Poli) Mordechai, was interviewed on Al Jazeera in Arabic and asserted that Israel has intelligence information that Hamas supports the Wilayat Sinai group, which carried out the attack, and even helped it with weapons. Mordechai added that Wael Faraj, a commander of a unit of Hamas' military wing, Izz ad-Din al-Qassam Brigades, smuggled injured fighters of the jihadi group to hospitals in Gaza and that the members of the military wing have close ties with the organization, which is affiliated with IS.

The Egyptian response to Hamas' alleged involvement was restrained. Sisi, who arrived for a tour of Sinai, did not rush to accuse members of al-Qassam Brigades of cooperation with the perpetrators of the attack, but the leaders of the movement also know that the crisis hasn't passed. The Egyptians haven't yet cleared the movement of responsibility, and Hamas believes Israel will try to convince Egypt that it has evidence of such cooperation. Hamas believes Israel wants to drive a wedge between Hamas and Cairo to destroy the bridge they have started to build into the heart of the Egyptian regime in the last few months.

In any case, the leaders of Hamas will find it hard to dispel all blame from themselves. In recent weeks, a number of people who were hurt in altercations with Egyptian security forces in Sinai have been brought to the al-Najjar hospital in Rafah in the Gaza Strip. The information about al-Qassam Brigades bringing these wounded persons to the hospital wasn't kept secret. Residents of Rafah saw how wounded people were brought in Hamas "military" vehicles and treated by a select medical staff.

A senior security figure in the Palestinian Authority, who is following events in Gaza, told that the cooperation of members of al-Qassam Brigades with many armed groups in the Sinai Peninsula is well-known to the leadership of the Palestinian Authority, Israeli intelligence, as well as Egyptian intelligence. He says the information shared by everyone isn't a working assumption, but well-founded and well-known, and that it includes the names of people active on both sides.

The activity of Faraj, which Mordechai revealed on Al Jazeera, is known and has taken place for a long time. According to the source, for years the leaders of the military wing carried out extensive smuggling operations with anyone who could help Hamas in Sinai before Israel's disengagement from Gaza (2005), but especially after the tightening of the siege on the Gaza Strip.

The close relations reached a peak after the fall of the Muslim Brotherhood regime in Egypt in July 2013, with the ascension of Sisi, a general who then headed the Egyptian military. After the Egyptian military sealed the smuggling tunnels with Egypt in Rafah and created a buffer zone, a strategic change occurred in the way in which Hamas' military wing perceived the Egyptian security forces. The Egyptian military is now perceived by the armed groups in Sinai and the Gaza Strip, including Hamas, as an enemy, and their goal has become to strike it and weaken its power in Sinai.

For years, a complicated and mutually beneficial relationship was built between Hamas members and jihadi activists on the Sinai Peninsula. Al-Qassam Brigades received aid from IS affiliates such as Wilayat Sinai, Aknaf Bayt al-Maqdis battalion and other terror organizations in smuggling arms, ammunition and raw materials such as fuel and building materials into Gaza. In exchange, Hamas provided a significant percentage of the arms smuggled from Sudan and Libya. Thus a reciprocal relationship was created that no one among the political leadership of Hamas will be able to uproot.

This utilitarian relationship structure is known and familiar to the heads of the political leadership of Hamas. Ever since Israel placed a siege on Gaza in June 2007, they encouraged the heads of al-Qassam Brigades to conduct the Saladin project — the creation of the smuggling tunnel network between Egypt and Israel. Any means were acceptable for that purpose, including the deliberate connection to "black extremism."

Islamic State's Affiliates

By now, many have seen the variations of maps that "Islamic State" (IS) activists have posted online showing aspirational future areas of conquest. This genre usually encompasses areas that have been under historical Caliphates shaded in black, including places such as Spain or Greece that do not even have a Muslim plurality of the population today. Ultimately, IS (as well as other Sunni jihadi groups) hopes the entire world comes under its dominion. This is nothing new.

All of this, is of course, contingent on any level of success and legitimacy, which at this juncture will be difficult in the face of most Muslims rejecting its "Caliphate" announcement as well other Islamist groups including pro-al-Qaeda jihadis.

The "Caliphate project" is a unique enterprise and one that does not necessarily play by the same rules most follow, since ultimately its goal is to overthrow the Westphalian nation-state model and the post-World War II American international system. The announcement of the renewed "Caliphate" could signal something more akin to a colonial project where the "Islamic state" seeks to incorporate non-contiguous territories. Already in Iraq and Syria, the areas it has taken control of are not all contiguous. Therefore, it is plausible that factions or groups in other locales could conceivably take territory and, having pledged bay'a (an oath of loyalty) to the Islamic State's self-proclaimed Caliph Abu Bakr al-Baghdadi, thereby expanding the State's Caliphate.

Unlike al-Qaeda, which has mainly used its foreign fighter contingents to train, plan, and then execute attacks in the West or Arab countries over the years, IS might have bigger plans for them. While IS would have no problem with dispatching foreign fighters for terrorist attacks out of theater (more on this below), they might also order their foreign fighter cadres to build up capacities for the expansion of its state once they return home. Further, it may also use them to infiltrate and subvert al-Qaeda branches and cells as part of its broader war with al-Qaeda for supremacy over the global jihadi movement.

The Islamic State's colonial Caliphate project would find the most fertile ground in the Northern Sinai, Eastern Libya, and some of the neighborhoods in poor areas of Western European cities that are Muslim-majority. None of this is inevitable. In fact, the Islamic State would have some serious difficulties in pulling it off, especially in Western Europe. But the jihadi movement has never let feasibility stand in the way of its ambitions. Like many jihadi strategists have proposed in the past, they would hope to set off a backlash that could lead to destabilization and chaos. This is exactly what jihadis thrive off. We have already seen failed attempts in England to establish "sharia zones" by local jihadis like the UK-based Anjem Choudary, who has cautiously spoken out in favor of the Caliphate claim.

Besides the Islamic State's ideological and narrative appeal, one of the biggest sources of its strength comes from its economic independence. Due to the spoils of war and criminal enterprises, they are far less reliant on private donors than al-Qaeda. Unlike al-Qaeda, the Islamic State has funding and can use its extra coffers to offer money to potential affiliates. It is a new center that can give resources to the periphery. In recent years, al-Qaeda has had more difficulty doing that.

The Islamic State's economic independence is also germane because many foreign fighters have criminal pasts and therefore would have experiences and have no issue with getting involved in criminal activities if and when they return home. Additionally, those outside the center of the Islamic State's gravity can leverage the criminal networks in locales like the Sinai and Libya. There has already been signs that jihadis have attempted to graft onto those criminal networks with varying success.

Similarly, one could see a scenario where Europe's foreign fighters — many of whom have deep criminal pasts — return home and set up business rackets and other illegal ventures in certain neighborhoods in areas where they are from and run them like mafia bosses or gangsters. This could lead to a chilling effect such as no-go zones where European police are not comfortable entering or operating.

Again, this is all hypothetical and not the current reality, but setting up such independent economic hubs in "statelets" could further the reach of the Islamic State, which has no time frame on its project. The success of such an undertaking would likely have an easier chance of working in the Sinai/Libya scenario due to lack of full state writ already.

Following the announcement of the Islamic State's self-proclaimed Caliphate, its leader Abu Bakr al-Baghdadi delivered a Ramadan address, which was filled with the usual jihadi platitudes. It also included specific "shout outs" to areas where Muslims are suffering and could be a clue to areas it hopes to expand its influence or compete with al-Qaeda.

For instance, Baghdadi specifically notes the suffering of Sunnis in Burma, the Philippines, Indonesia, Kashmir, Bosnia, the Caucasus, Palestine, Egypt, East Turkistan (China), Iran, France, Tunisia, and Central African Republic. There is already known public support for the Islamic State or has foreign fighter networks that have fed itself in Iraq and Syria in the Philippines, Indonesia, Bosnia, the Caucasus, Palestine, Egypt, Iran, France, and Tunisia. Therefore, if one wants to look to areas that are not in surrounding countries to Iraq or Syria these are potentially more immediate targets.

Closer to home, though, the Islamic State hopes to expand its reach in terms of linking up contiguous territory over "Sykes-Picot" borders. More recently, for the first time publicly the Islamic State has announced a presence in the Qalamoun region on the Lebanese-Syrian border as well as claiming responsibility for an attack in Beirut.

If it hopes to expand into Lebanon, it will have to compete with the Qaeda-aligned Abdullah Azzam Brigades, which has years of experience recruiting. Similarly, while there has been support in Ma'an, Jordan for the Islamic State, this is a minority sentiment in the broader Jordanian jihadi current, which has been closer to and more supportive of Jabhat al-Nusra in Syria.

The biggest prize beyond targeting Israel would be provoking violence against the Saudi regime and claiming Saudi territory. The majority of the 1,400+ Saudis that have gone to fight in Syria (and now Iraq) have joined the Islamic State rather than Jabhat al-Nusra. Additionally, hundreds in the last decade fought with the group when it was called al-Qaeda in Iraq. Among them, some then went onto fight with al-Qaeda in the Arabian Peninsula (AQAP). There are also number of its foreign fighters that have returned home and other soft support inside the Kingdom.

Therefore, it is possible that the Islamic State may rely on those already inside Saudi, Yemen, and its own soldiers in Iraq to create a three-pronged attack. While the Saudi government would have air superiority, it has no significant experience in quelling an insurgency (though Saudi has been successful in counterterrorism campaigns against al-Qaeda) and could prove more difficult if it was drawn out. This in of itself would be a win for the Islamic State, "remaining" sometimes is just as important as outright victory.

The biggest win for the Islamic State though would be becoming a real player in the Israeli-Palestinian fight. This would be easier said than done and would rely on a number of factors falling into place. In the past, the global jihadi movement in Palestine was more aspirational than a true force on the ground. In the aftermath of the Arab uprisings and with space filled by the movement in northern Sinai global jihadis have been able to make in-roads, albeit still a relatively small movement. Domestically, the continued failed governance of Hamas in Gaza and continued corruption and general illegitimacy that Fatah has as a result of perceived collaboration with Israel in the West Bank has also been helpful.

What could propel the Islamic State in the Palestinian arena is another Intifada. In light of the above wariness and failures by the status quo Palestinian political parties, there has been a rise in Salafism in both Gaza and the West Bank. Therefore, similar to Hamas' rise in the aftermath of both the first and second intifadas, it is possible that the consequence of a third intifada would be that the Islamic State would be able to carve a space out for itself, especially if it is perceived as the underdog punching above its weight and giving blows to the hated "Zionists."

If this came to fruition, it is possible that because the Islamic State is fighting Israel, it would lower the bar for support of the Islamic State due to a legitimate, but, at times, irrationally visceral hatred for Israel even if the group that is fighting this "resistance" or "jihad" against Israel has authoritarian tendencies, too. As a result, it is the hope of the Islamic State in the medium to longer-term that if it wins the Palestinians, it will subsequently then win the Muslim world.

Another way the Islamic State could gain "ungoverned" spaces or build up its capacities and networks is through creating breakaway groups of members that defect from al-Qaeda branches to new Islamic State "territories" in places like Syria, Yemen, Somalia, or North Africa. The recent successes on the battlefield in Iraq (and now again in Syria due to a shifting of new resources gained in the Iraqi offensive) and the announcement of the Caliphate, the Islamic State perceives that this could push more factions, individuals, or groups to join up with its cause and reject the "out of touch" leader of al-Qaeda Ayman al-Zawahiri.

Recently, in light of these Iraqi offensives, whether it is legitimate or through coercion, members and leaders within Jabhat al-Nusra in both the Deir al-Zour and Damascus region have defected, pledged bay'a to Baghdadi, and joined the Islamic State. There are also unconfirmed rumors that foot soldiers in both AQAP and Harakat al-Shabab al-Mujahidin, al-Qaeda's Somali branch, have some sympathies for the Islamic State. Thus far, we have already seen al-Qaeda in the Islamic Maghreb's Central Region officially splitting and supporting the Islamic State.

We have also seen some members and a leader in AQAP that went to Syria to fight that have since backed the Islamic State, too. All of those pledges of fealty occurred prior to the Islamic State's Caliphate announcement. Since then, the only relevant bay'a given was by a faction from within the Tehrik-i-Taliban Pakistan, a group known for its close ties to al-Qaeda, which itself had nine members defect to Baghdadi.

The Islamic State hopes this trend continues. The biggest potential tipping point would be for AQAP to switch sides since it is still rightly perceived as al-Qaeda's strongest branch. While AQAP's senior leadership has loyalty to Zawahiri and al-Qaeda, in part because of its leader, Nasir al-Wihayshi's mentorship under Usama bin Ladin in Afghanistan.

One thing to look for going forward is whether the large Saudi contingent that fought with the Islamic State in Iraq and Syria and then returns to Yemen to continue jihad with AQAP decides to make a power play against AQAP's senior leadership or attempts to fracture the organization and create a breakaway group while also taking members from AQAP with it.

One way that the Islamic State hopes any of these various potentialities comes to fruition is that it compels the West to focus more on its own homelands instead of security in the broader Arab world. This could be done through dispatching any number of the up to thousands of Westerners in its ranks to conduct terrorist attacks in the West. Thereby, creating a distraction for Western countries, while the Islamic State is continuing its hoped takeover of more territory and resources in the region.

As a result, it is a misnomer to think that it is an either/or policy for the Islamic State to only be interested in just state-building or terrorism. As we have seen with AQAP in the past, the Islamic State will likely be in the business of both.

For this potential plan to work out, though, the Islamic State will need to expand its support base beyond just its most hardcore following and address some of the skepticism and issues that top jihadi scholars like Shaykh Abu Muhammad al-Maqdisi have warned it about. Otherwise, all these aspirational ambitions will be for naught.

Archipelago of Provinces

This week, Abu Bakr al-Baghdadi, the leader of the Islamic State of Iraq and al-Sham, released a rare public message in which he declared the creation of several new "provinces" in various Arab countries. It was the first time that he and his organization have acknowledged groups that have pledged baya (religiously binding oath of allegiance) to the so-called "Islamic State" since the announcement of its "Caliphate" six months ago. The audio message offers insight into the group's expansion model and its plans for exacerbating religious tensions between Sunnis and Shiites beyond Iraq, Syria, and Lebanon. Whether Western governments want to admit it or not, the reality is that the Islamic State has expanded in a non-contiguous manner outside its base and now has authority over satellite groups and small amounts of territory outside Iraq and the Levant.

Since the caliphate announcement in June, a cacophony of different individuals and groups have pledged baya to Baghdadi. Yet in this week's audio message, he only recognized the annexation of jihadist elements in Saudi Arabia and Yemen, along with jihadist groups in Algeria (Jund al-Khilafah), Libya (Majlis Shura Shabab al-Islam), and Sinai (Ansar Beit al-Maqdis). He ignored non-Arab factions based in Pakistan, Indonesia, the Philippines, and elsewhere that have made similar pledges to him. This could suggest tighter links with fellow Arab jihadists, or that the organizations outside the Arab world are not ready for exploitation and growth.

Baghdadi also noted that his declaration entails "nullification" of the local groups in the five places mentioned above, as well as "the announcement of new wilayat (provinces) of the Islamic State and the appointment of wulat (governors) for them." While he claimed to annex these "territories," publicly available information indicates that only the groups in Libya and Sinai can legitimately claim to control land -- the validity of such claims in Saudi Arabia, Yemen, and Algeria remains to be seen.

That said, those groups that do have proven territorial control -- which are now being dubbed Wilayat Libya and Wilayat Sinai -- could follow the same economic model of sustainability that the Islamic State has pursed in Iraq and Syria over the past couple years. If they have not done so already, the Libyan and Sinai groups are prime candidates for fully grafting their jihadist networks onto the traditional criminal enterprise networks that have been used for trafficking, smuggling, and other black market activities over the years. Therefore, these two new "provinces" could have some level of viability, at least in the short term. Questions remain about whether this model can be employed by the Islamic State's new Algerian, Saudi, and Yemeni members, who do not seem to control any territory at this juncture.

In addition to declaring the annexations, Baghdadi made clear to his associates in Saudi Arabia and Yemen that it is time to start an overt military campaign against the rafidah, a derogatory term for Shiites that literally means "rejectionists." He also emphasized the order of priority, stating that jihadists in Wilayat al-Haramayn ("The Province of the Two Holy Places," meaning Saudi Arabia) and Wilayat Yemen should first target Shiites (including the Houthis), then the Saudi dynasty, and then finally the "Crusaders." In doing so, he formally clarified how the Islamic State perceives its enemies and its most immediate threat, while also illustrating its differences from al-Qaeda, an organization that has historically given precedent to fighting the "Crusaders" first.

If the Islamic State's followers in Saudi Arabia or Yemen follow through on this call for a campaign against Shiites, outsiders will be better able to measure the group's true influence and its level of command and control over those outside its base territory. Whatever happens, Baghdadi's message highlights his desire to continue projecting power in new areas. The Islamic State is staying true to its slogan of "remaining and expanding," in part to show the anti-ISIS coalition that while it may not have the same battlefield momentum it had this summer, it is still controlling territory in Iraq and Syria. For the group's leaders and adherents, this is a victory in of itself, supposedly highlighting how the will of God is on their side even as the world is against them.

In the end, the Islamic State's ability to expand its reach and its writ will depend on how successful this now-formalized annexation model proves to be. For now, and perhaps for the long term, this means the U.S.-led coalition will have to deal with a more complex threat environment.

New Haven in Libya

Two rival governments in Libya have fought an increasingly bloody civil war since last summer, as the world paid little attention. While they battled for control of the country's oil wealth, a third force—Islamic State—took advantage of the chaos to grow stronger. The beheading of 21 Egyptian Christians by Islamic State followers has finally drawn the global spotlight to the group's rising clout in Libya, which not long ago was touted as a successful example of Western intervention. The killings prompted Egyptian airstrikes on Islamic State strongholds in Libya and spurred calls for more active international involvement in what is fast becoming a failed state on Europe's doorstep.

The Libyan affiliate of Islamic State in Syria and Iraq has, in fact, been spreading its sway for months. First it established an area of control last fall in and around the eastern city of Derna, a historical center of Libyan jihadists. Recently, it also took over parts of former dictator Moammar Gadhafi's hometown of Sirte, on the central coast, setting up a radio station there and sending Islamic morality patrols onto the streets

All the while, the two rival governments of Libya focused on combatting one another, each supported by regional powers. Both preferred to largely ignore the influx of foreign jihadists forming new alliances with local extremists—and their unification under Islamic State's banner.

Libya isn't the only place outside Syria and Iraq where the extremist group has established affiliates, largely by absorbing homegrown jihadist groups into its project of world domination and religious war until t
he total triumph of Islam. There are also Islamic State "provinces" in Egypt's Sinai Peninsula, in Yemen, and in so-called Khorasan, a region straddling Afghanistan and Pakistan.

Islamic State's slickly produced video of the slaughter of the Egyptian Copts, concluded with the promse to conquer Rome, the historic center of Christendom. That threat is bound to reinforce existing pressure in countries such as France and Italy for a military intervention to stave off the complete collapse of Libya, which is just across the Mediterranean Sea from Italy.

"The situation in Libya has been out of control for three years," Italy's Prime Minister Matteo Renzi cautioned in a television interview after the video's release. "We shouldn't go from total indifference to hysteria." Libya has been unstable since Gadhafi's ouster and killing in 2011, but it descended into all-out civil war last summer.

One side is the old parliament, elected in 2012 and dominated by the Muslim Brotherhood and its allies. It includes militias from the conservative city of Misrata, a key force in the revolution against the Gadhafi regime. That parliament, known as the General National Congress, was replaced in last elections by another legislature, the House of Representatives, dominated by more secular and nationalist forces.

While the international community has recognized the new House of Representatives as the legitimate new authority in Libya, the GNC refused to accept its electoral defeat. Militias affiliated with the GNC drove the new administration out of Tripoli to the eastern city of Tobruk, triggering what soon became an all-out war that destroyed the Tripoli airport and valuable oil infrastructure.

As the West was distracted by Islamic State's blitz through Syria and Iraq last year, regional powers unleashed a proxy war in Libya. Egypt's President Abdel Fattah Al Sisi, who ousted the Muslim Brotherhood from power in his own country in 2013, threw his weight behind the Tobruk government, arming and assisting it. So did Egypt's regional allies, Saudi Arabia and United Arab Emirates.

Meanwhile, Turkey and Qatar - supporters of Islamist causes around the region -rallied behind Tripoli, as did Sudan. By then, however, it may have already been too late to stop Islamic State's spread, especially as the Tripoli administration has long played down the threat posed by Islamist militants.

Islamic State attacked the Corinthia Hotel in Tripoli, killing several foreigners and showcasing its ability to operate in the heart of the capital. Amazingly, the Tripoli administration's reaction to that outrage was to allege that the massacre was a provocation carried out by its Tobruk rivals and Egypt. Since then, most of the last Westerners in town left Tripoli.

The latest Islamic State attack, on the Coptic Egyptians, was intended to directly draw Egypt into the Libyan conflict, said Khalil al-Anani, an Egyptian scholar of Islamist movements at Johns Hopkins University. Mr. Sisi, whose takeover in 2013 was widely popular among Egypt's Coptic minority, has positioned himself as a defender of the country's Christians; He became the first Egyptian president to visit a Coptic church on Christmas.

But his task of thwarting Islamic State grows more complicated. His army already faces a deadly Islamic State insurgency in the eastern Sinai Peninsula, losing hundreds of soldiers over the past two years.

Ansar al-Sharia

Over the past two years, global attention has shifted to Syria and Iraq with the rise of Jabhat al-Nusra and the return of the Islamic State of Iraq and al-Sham (ISIS). However, nearly one thousand miles to the west, Ansar al-Sharia in Libya (ASL) has continued its work of facilitating a future Islamic state since the spectacular attack on the American consulate in Benghazi on September 11, 2012.

Initially, ASL launched a highly sophisticated program of dawa (outreach) which included the provisioning of social services both inside and outside of Libya. This has provided it with an avenue for local support. But since Libyan General Khalifa Haftar announced a major offensive against Islamist armed groups in eastern Libya in May 2014 (codenamed Operation Dignity), ASL has focused primarily on military action.

ASL's fortunes have dropped dramatically in the process, further exacerbated by the death of its leader, Muhammad al-Zahawi, confirmed in January 2015, and ISIS' intensification of its efforts to create a Libyan base independent of ASL since November 2014.

In many ways, ASL followed the model of Ansar al-Sharia in Tunisia (AST), viewing its outreach and social services campaign as an important part of establishing and building not only an Islamic society, but an eventual Islamic state governed by its interpretations of Sharia (Islamic law). In contrast to the Libyan government, which is often corrupt, incompetent, or extractive, ASL worked to convince the local population of its own competence and benevolence. Critically, this helped it win greater public support.

In addition to ASL's reach across Libya, from Benghazi, Tripoli and Ajdabiya to Sirte, Darna and the Gulf of Sidra, among other smaller locales, it has also operated abroad. Most notably, it has dispatched operatives to Syria, Sudan and Gaza to assist in humanitarian relief efforts. This has added a whole new layer to the meaning of global jihad and how various groups might try to engage populations outside their local areas of operation.

ASL has enjoyed a number of identities as an organization: On the one hand, it has been a charity, a security service, a health service and areligious education provider; on the other hand, it is also a militia, a terrorist organization and a training base for foreign jihadists. In recognition of this complexity, this analysis looks at the full spectrum ofthe group and teases out ASL's dawa campaign locally and globally; its hopes and future plans based off of its dawa literature on aqida (creed) and manhaj (methodology); its training of foreign fighters for the Syrian conflict as well as for the conflict with General Haftar; and, the rise of ISIS as a competitor.

In the aftermath of the Arab uprisings, most specifically in countries like Egypt, Libya and Tunisia where regimes were fully overthrown, the public sphere opened. These countries also represented a fresh start and laboratory for a new jihadi campaign in the wake of al-Qaeda in Iraq's (AQI) failures at controlling territory and instituting governance last decade.

For example, al-Qaeda leader Ayman al-Zawahiri thought that this new environment provided an opportunity "for dawa and informing…Only God knows for how long they [local governments and the West] will continue, so the people of Islam and Jihad should benefit from them and exploit them." In the same audio message, he further emphasized the superiority of Sharia over all other legal systems and laws. Zawahiri also endorsed the liberation of Islamic lands, opposed normalizing relations with Israel and underscored the importance of "cleansing thelands" of financial and social corruption.

In 2004, the foremost respected Sunni jihadi ideologue alive today, Abu Muhammad al-Maqdisi, wrote Waqafat ma' Thamrat al-Jihad (Stances on the Fruit of Jihad) in an attempt to steer the jihadi movement away from the abuses of his former student and AQI leader, Abu Musab al-Zarqawi.

In the book, Maqdisi examines the differences between what he describes as qital al- nikayya (fighting to hurt or damage the enemy) and qital al-tamkin (fighting to consolidate one's power). Maqdisi argues that the former provides only short-term tactical victories whereas the latter provides a framework for consolidating an Islamic state. Implicit is Maqdisi's emphasis on the importance of planning, organization, education and dawa.

The formation of ASL along with its sister organizations in Tunisia (AST) and Egypt (ASE) were seen as logical conclusions and implementations of Zawahiri's and Maqdisi's ideas. In short, these groups selected a dawa-first strategy instead of a jihad-first strategy. As a result, one of the main avenues through which ASL advanced its ideas was its social services programs. This cultivation of followers in a broad fashion – in contrast to the more vanguard-oriented organizations that have been involved in jihadism in a local, regional, or global capacity over the past 30 years – was seen as a new way to consolidate a future Islamic state.

At first, this approach appeared to forge a new and successful way forward for the jihadi movement, with an unprecedented number of individuals joining ASL and AST. Over the past two years, however, this dawa-first approached has backfired. Within a month of Abdel Fattah el-Sisi's coup d'état in Egypt in early July 2013, all of the key members of ASE had either been arrested or had been forced to link-up with Jama'at Ansar Bayt al-Maqdis' growing insurgency in northern Sinai. Still others had fled to Syria to join the jihad against the Bashar al-Assad regime.

Less than two months later, at the end of August 2013, the Tunisian government designated AST as a terrorist organization and proceeded to dismantle it via widespread arrests. As a result, some Tunisians left for Libya and joined up with ASL while others went to Syria and joined ISIS.

As for ASL, once General Haftar launched his war against them, it too mostly stopped conducting regular dawa. The dawa events it did sponsor were publicized after the fact and related to providing meat and food to the poor and needy during Ramadan, Eid al-Fitr and Eid al-Adha in the summer and fall of 2014.

Instead, much of what has been published by ASL since then has been related to the fighting with General Haftar's forces. Additionally, while still boasting of members in other cities, ASL has confined the vast majority of its military operations to Benghazi. And while ASL has not disintegrated like ASE or AST, its capacities have been severely degraded, providing ISIS with an opening in the fall of 2014.

At the height of ASL's campaign, it oversaw an extensive network of services inside and outside of Libya. In fact, it was involved in activities ranging from anti-drug campaigns, blood drives and food drives (including the slaughtering of animals on holidays for the poor) to Quranic competitions for children, housing projects for the poor, school cleanings, garbage removals and bridge repairs.

ASL provided such tangible services to the community as opening a medical clinic for women and children, an Islamic Center for Women, an Emergency Room and a religious school named Mirkaz al-Imam al-Bukhari Li- l-'Ulum al-Sharia. ASL also maintained security at the major al-Jala' hospital in Benghazi.

What made these efforts much more impressive was that ASL was not just acting independently, but was getting support and co-sponsorship from other local organizations. The blood drives were coordinated with the Benghazi Central Blood Center (CBC), for which the CBC even presented ASL with an award on July 25, 2013. ASL also coordinated lectures with the Social Security Fund's Benghazi Branch and cleaned roads in cooperation with the electrical company and Tajama' al-Qawarshah al-Khayri wa-l-Da'wai.

Moreover, the most successful program that ASL undertook was a vigorous anti-drug campaign together with the Rehab Clinic at the Psychiatric Hospital of Benghazi, the Ahli Club (soccer), Libya Company (Telecom and Technology) and the Technical Company. While in Sirte, ASL hosted a ten-day Quranic competition during Ramadan in association with the Office of Awqaf of Sirte, Radio Tawhid of Sirte, the Cleaning Services Company and the University of Sirte. Also during Ramadan, ASL assisted in a food drive that gained sponsorship from the Libya Company, Primera Gallery, al-Iman Foundation, Tajama' al-Qawarshah al-Khayri wa-l-Da'wai and the Faruq Center.

Beyond its local efforts, ASL launched a robust campaign abroad too, targeting Syria, Sudan and Gaza. ASL dubbed these overseas dawa efforts "The Convoy Campaign of Goodness To Our People in 'X-location.'" These efforts began in November 2012 when ASL sent aid packages to Syria and Gaza, including its dawa literature. The most sophisticated operation, however, came in response to the major flooding that hit Sudan in August 2013. An ASL team landed in Khartoum with five tons of medicine, twelves tons of grains and legumes and eight tons of children's milk in tow. The second delivery contained twenty-four tons of clothing and 1.5 tons of floor carpets for mosques. All of these items and packages were stamped or plastered with ASL's logo.

The level of aid in itself was outstanding, but the fact that it came from a global jihadi organization that had procured and delivered it safely to Sudan's capital testifies to the group's organizational capabilities as well as its possible ties to the Sudanese government.

The same types of questions apply to ASL's operations in Syria, and its potential ties to the Turkish state. In Syria, the campaign was called "Uplifting the Ummah, freedom from forced rule, Western dominance, and uplifted by the goodness, pride and dignity under the law of Rahman (one of the holiest of the 99 names of God within Islam)."

In late January 2014, ASL sent three tranches of aid, comprising slaughtered beef, flour and electric generators, to the rural Latakia towns of Salma and Kasab, among others. The effort in Syria illustrated a high level of planning and organization, since ASL had to gain access to local resources and grasp the human topography of the area. Lastly, also in late January 2014, ASL responded to an Israeli airstrike in Gaza.

The campaign was marketed as "We are over here in Libya and our eyes are on Jerusalem." ASL's contacts inside Gaza went door-to-door in the al-Nafaq neighborhood distributing cash-filled envelopes with ASL's logo to those "whose houses were damaged by the shelling of the Zionists." The speed of the campaign suggests the possibility of an ASL network in Gaza.

While impressive, these overseas campaigns represent the height of ASL's influence and power. Since the fighting with General Haftar has commenced, ASL has shown no signs of continuing its international campaign. Instead, it has shifted increasingly into self-preservation mode. Prior to discussing the war with General Haftar, however, it is important to highlight the ideological backbone of ASL, especially since its key points are part of the literature that ASL had distributed during its local and international dawa.

One of the most important pamphlets that ASL passed out during its dawa efforts educated individuals on its doctrine and agenda. ASL's core ideology has particular global jihadi underpinnings. First, there is immense emphasis on the tawhid (pure monotheism) of God, as "there is no other God, and there is nothing that can be revered like Him." The source of "interference or deduction" is the Quran, the "word of God Almighty," and the Sunna (actions and sayings of the Prophet Muhammad), which "sets out and explains the Quran."

Second, as the pamphlet makes clear, if a Muslim does not follow the literal authority of God, then he is branded or "excommunicated" as a kafir (unbeliever). Anyone who "calls for anything other than Islam," such as "democracy" or "secularism," manifests infidelity, or kufr, and is deemed "nugatory." The permissibility of takfir (excommunication) appears to stem from the institutional necessity to impose obedience through a set of actions and beliefs extracted and interpreted literally from the Quran and the Sunna.

Third, the pamphlet maintains that the theological mechanism to purget he Ummah (Islamic community) of kufr and to implement tawhid is military jihad. Jihad does not require a religious verdict set down by an imam because fighting the kufar (infidels) is "more obligatory in the world than adhering to the [Islamic] faith." Thus, waging jihad is considered a fundamental prerequisite to being considered a genuine Muslim.

If a Muslim wages jihad against the declared kufar, then ASL will not "accuse [that Muslim] of being a sinner."

Moreover, the "blood of Muslims is not haram," or forbidden, because there is no higher duty than jihad. The prioritization of military strength and discipline is the sine qua non of uniting the Ummah into one Muslim entity. Political parties, even Islamic ones, represent a pluralistic, democratic process, and therefore serve to "divide up the Ummah."

Ultimately, ASL aims to establish an authoritative, theological state based on Sharia to supplant the current laws and constitution. ASL's agenda appears to be local; namely, to fight rival militias in a war tocontrol Libya and to reform it into an Islamic state. However, the beliefs and theological justifications for violent action suggest a complete rejection of the current world order and constant conflict.

Another of ASL's pamphlets explains its issues with democracy in detail. Besides its focus on tawhid and the necessity of jihad, ASL has a deep aversion to democracy. The pamphlet's main argument is that "democracy" constitutes the antithesis to shura (council), or Islamic governance based on Sharia. There are three fundamental differences that make democracy and Islam incompatible: democracy is based on the "rule of the people" while shura is based on the "rule of God"; democracy enforces man-made laws forbidden in Islam while shura uses judicial ijtihad (independent reasoning) to make individual evaluations of cases in strict accordance with Islamic teachings; and, democratic systems are ruled by people while shura is ruled by God.

The purpose of the pamphlet is to delegitimize those Arab leaders who claim to be pious Muslims but govern and acquire political power through, or under the guise of, democracy. More importantly, by placing democracy and Islam in irreconcilable positions, ASL undercuts Islamic democratic parties, such as the Libyan Muslim Brotherhood's Justice and Construction Party, which seek to apply Islamic principles to public policy within a democratic framework.

For ASL, not only is "democracy" fundamentally incompatible with Islam, but it is also framed in its literature as an authoritarian system.

As the pamphlet makes clear, ASL directly associates the offshoots of liberal values found in many democratic societies, such as "lusts," "defamation" and "wine, clown-like behavior, songs, debaucherous behavior, adultery [and] cinemas" with the imposition of kufr institutions such as the Charter of the United Nations, the laws of the General Assembly and the "laws of [democratically-elected] parties."

Thus, the logic follows: if one does not engage in acts of lust and defamation, then one is deemed "extreme, terroristic and not tending towards world peace and coexistence." By imposing specific non-Islamic values on society and excluding Sharia-sanctioned law, "democracy" directly seeks to eradicate Islam. Moreover, elected assemblies and parliaments are built by "majority rule," a concept that "bears no relation to the Quran and the Hadith," and thus seeks to eradicate God-sanctioned rule. Lastly, ASL tars democracy with the failure of the Arab uprisings to bring about better governance, especially in Egypt, Tunisia, Jordan and Yemen. The lesson learned from those uprisings is that democracy is full of "provisions and deceitful illusions." Essentially, the pre-Arab uprising dictators and civil unrest that followed are the products of "democracy."

A third pamphlet that ASL has distributed among its supporters and would-be recruits is on how to handle interactions with police officers, should they be stopped in the street. This pamphlet provides talking points relating to the current Libyan system in order to sow doubts among the police and encourage defections.

ASL talking points include invoking God as one and the only arbitrator and source of governing authority, while the role of humans is emphasized as simply fighting" whatever governs that does not come from God." God, the ASL pamphlet argues, "will not rely on [humans] for governing," but simply to eradicate "evil" or anything that does not adhere to a literal interpretation of Islamic texts. By prosecuting criminals under Libyan civil code, policemen are actually "forcing people into kufr" because those people become subject to taghut (tyrants). The concepts of "policemen" and the "army" are not rejected, but only if the authorities "legislate" with Sharia.

A final ideological statement worth highlighting pertains to ASL's global outlook. While ASL has focused mainly on local issues, it does have a global dimension and is very much within the ideological milieu of global jihadism. ASL's statement in response to the United States' seizure of Abu Anas al-Libi, a Libyan wanted for his part in the 1998

East Africa embassy bombings, is emblematic of its global outlook. Ultimately, ASL argues that the United States is seeking to destroy Islam and impose its own culture, values and laws on Muslims and their lands. The U.S., called al-kufar, does this in three ways. First, it is "preventing the Muslims from establishing an [Islamic] state." Examples of this are coalition campaigns against the Taliban in Afghanistan and Islamists in northern Mali.

Second, the statement charges that the "war against and pursuit of jihad and the mujahideen," or "war against terrorism," is "at its essence a war against Islam." When intervening in other countries' affairs, the U.S. often targets "whoever they wish unsupervised and unaccountable" (an allusion to al-Libi, but more importantly the killing of Osama bin Laden without Pakistani consultation) while "violating holy sites and [Muslim]lands" (an allusion to Operation Desert Shield, Iraqi Freedom).

Under the pretext of fighting terrorism, the U.S. as the "decision-maker and leader of the world" is in reality attempting to impose its "unlawful assertions of 'superiority' over creation." ASL attributes Libya's chaos to the U.S. intervention and subsequent attempt to impose the "tyranny ofdemocracy," which is fully preventing the rule of Sharia. This aggression, arrogance and lack of respect for Muslims derives from the United States' kafir values of "murder and displacement" — a clear reference to America's history of slavery, troubled race relations and conflicts with Native Americans.

Third, ASL argues that "terrorism" is used by the U.S. as a label for those who do not adhere to their "democratic" agenda. In response, ASL calls for a mass campaign to "inform every Muslim of the goals of these belligerent states and their allies." The logic is that before being able and willing to wage jihad, the fighter must be indoctrinated with the belief that he is defending his religion and way of life. ASL urges Muslims to accept the scholar Ahmad Shaker's decree that "any cooperation with the British [or in the current case, the Americans], no matter how small, is tantamount to unbridled apostasy..."

Thus, for reasons already stated, Muslims must be in a constant state of war with the United States. In the context of Libya, ASL believes the country is suffering from "humiliation and disgrace" because it abandoned "governing with Islamic Sharia." By adopting a Western-style parliamentary system and not a Sharia-based one, the Libyan government is essentially "fighting Islam." Like the post-Saddam and post-Salih governments in Iraq and Yemen, respectively, post-Qaddafi Libya is attempting to adhere to Western standards of governance.

Indeed, while dawa has been ASL's main focus, it has also taken part in hisbah (enjoining right and forbidding wrong; usually connoting vigilante activities) and jihad. With regard to hisbah, ASL's Zahawi admitted that his group has been involved in the demolition of Sufi shrines and places of worship. Furthermore, ASL stormed the European School in Benghazi and confiscated books on the human body it deemed "pornographic," and thus contrary to Islam. Intimidated, teachers at the school blacked out those sections depicting the human body. In one video, members of Ansar al-Sharia in Sirte whipped some alleged transgressors of Sharia tens of times. Moreover, there have been numerous unsolved assassinations of security officials, government officials and civil society activists, many of which are suspected to be the work of ASL.

ASL's most well-known act of jihad is its attack on the United States consulate in Benghazi. Although there was no formal claim of responsibility, the ambiguous language used in the initial statement by ASL's spokesman, Hani al-Mansuri, suggests that some ASL members participated in the assault. As Mansuri carefully put it, "Katibat Ansar al-Sharia [in Benghazi] as a military did not participate formally/officially and not by direct orders." It is likely that some of ASL's local allies in other militias were involved, too.

On a more regional scale, similar to the Iraq jihad, Libya has become a training hub for those seeking jihad in Syria. In fact, most of those who train in Libyan camps – suspected in Misrata, Benghazi, the desert area near Hon and in the Green Mountains in the east – come from thecountries surrounding Libya.

There is increasing proof that ASL is training individuals to fight in Syria. On August 6, 2013, two videos leaked online of Tunisians who had been detained by locals in the Derna region and interrogated. Based on the information in the videos, the footage is likely from the late spring or early summer of 2012. It seems ASL was already actively training fighters for Syria, an ominous fact considering what transpired in Benghazi on September 11, 2012.

Furthermore, members of AST less interested in dawa are likely preparing and training in Libya in preparation for a potential insurgency or terrorism in Tunisia. For example, one Tunisian who had trained in Libya was responsible for an unsuccessful suicide bombing at a beach resort in Sousse, a city southeast of Tunis, in October 2013.

While hisbah and foreign fighter training has continued in the shadowsover the past few years, ASL's war with General Haftar has taken on a more public face, both in its messaging and online content dimensions. Since General Haftar announced Operation Dignity on May 17, thenature of ASL's public presentation has been more of a jihad-first than a dawa-first approach. In late May 2014, at the outset of the conflict, Zahawi held an off therecord press briefing in which he denounced General Haftar and labeled his offensive a crusade against Islam.

Zahawi's comments identified the United States, Saudi Arabia, United Arab Emirates and Egypt as backers of General Haftar, allowing Zahawi to allude to past outside interventions in Afghanistan, Iraq and Somalia and warn the United States against joining the battle. Zahawi struck a defiant tone, asserting that ASL was winning: "We thank God that we were able to defeat Haftar and we challenge him to attempt entering Benghazi again.

We warn him that if he continues this war against us, Muslims from across the world will come to fight, as is the case in Syria right now. The war would continue and Ansar al-Sharia would decide when it ends. "Ever since, ASL's propaganda has cast the residents of Benghazi as victims of aggression. For example, in a video dated May 31, 2014, one interviewee bemoans the destruction of his house and property, which had been shelled by General Haftar's forces. One month later, on July 29, ASL released a video telling the story of how General Haftar's army bombed the people of Benghazi while ASL stood in valiant defense of the city.

On August 7, ASL released footage of yet more destruction, with buildings burning and neighborhoods destroyed; on December 1, ASL publicized a series of pictures of burnt out apartments and homes in the Sabri neighborhood of Benghazi. The cumulative intent of thesemoves, of course, was to shape the war of public opinion against General Haftar.

Beyond fully mobilizing and militarizing ASL in Benghazi, the war united a number of Islamist factions under the banner of Majlis Shura Thuwar Benghazi (MSTB, the Benghazi Revolutionaries Consultative Council). On June 20, 2014, ASL, Raf Allah al-Sahati Brigade, February17th Martyrs Brigade, Libya Shield 1, and Jaysh al-Mujahidin announced their alliance. MSTB designated ASL's Zahawi as its leader, with Wisam bin Hamid of Libya Shield 1 as the military leaderand Jalal Makhzum of Raf Allah al-Sahati Brigade serving as the military commander.

To this day, MSTB remains a potent force, with its leaders releasing joint videos, as on October 5, when bin Hamid stated,"[w]e advise [Haftar's army] to return from what they are doing and that they repent to Allah the mighty before it is too late." Zahawi added, gleefully: "I congratulate our people in Benghazi on this great victory, and we wish to remain until we complete the phase we are in, and this is to control Benghazi, and God willing it will be safer for its sons and its people."

Since December 12, ASL has expanded its operations beyond Benghazi to Derna, in part due to its commitments with another newly-created umbrella organization. Indeed, ASL joined the Abu Salim Martyrs Brigade and Jaysh al-Islami al-Libi under the banner of MajlisShura al-Mujahidin Derna (MSMD, the Derna Mujahidin Consultative Council).

Unlike in Benghazi, ASL does not have leading positions in this alliance, highlighting its weaker position in Derna. Instead, the head of the Abu Salim Martyrs Brigade, Salim Dirby, leads MSMD with ASL's Sufyan bin Qumu positioned as a military commander alongside Yusuf bin Tahir of Jaysh al-Islami al-Libi. While in Benghazi the Majlis is fighting General Haftar, the umbrella in Derna in addition to fighting Haftar is also in direct competition with Majlis Shura Shabab al-Islam (MSSI), which pledged baya (fealty) to ISIS and its leader, Abu Bakr al-Baghdadi.

While Libya has become a key jihadi battleground, it has not exacted the same gravitational pull on foreign fighters as the conflict in Syria. However, Libyan training camps are now producing some fighters, initially intended for Syria, who are instead joining up with ASL or the Islamic State in Libya (ISL). The majority of foreign fighters in Libya are from the surrounding countries of Tunisia, Egypt, Algeria, Sudan and Morocco, but they also include some fighters from Palestine, Saudi Arabia and Yemen.

Similar to other conflict zones, most notably Syria, it seems that the upstart wilayat (provinces) that ISIS has "annexed" in Libya have recently drawn supporters from ASL. In part, this is due to the perception that ISIS is winning, has momentum, and is the "cool" jihadi group. Another likely blow to ASL is the death of Zahawi, which was confirmed in January 2015, even if he had been wounded and out of sight since late October 2014.

The quick rise of MSSI illustrates the changing nature of jihadism in Libya, but generally across the Arab world there has been a split between factions aligned with al-Qaeda and those closer to ISIS. MSSI publicly announced its existence on April 4, 2014, when masked members of the group took to the streets of Derna wearing military uniforms, driving pickup trucks and brandishing rocket-propelled grenade launchers, machine guns and anti-aircraft cannons.

They loudly proclaimed the imposition of Sharia. Until it formally announced allegiance to ISIS, MSSI was involved in such activities as security patrols and guarding the al-Huraysh hospital in Derna. They also publicized those who would "repent" to their cause, confiscated drugs and alcohol, and executed individuals.

In the lead up to ISIS formally "annexing" territory and turning MSSI into Wilayat al-Barqah, MSSI released a statement on June 22, 2014 in support of ISIS and Baghdadi. The statement was followed by a formal declaration of allegiance on October 3 that ceded MSSI's territory in Derna to the caliphate. In honor of the occasion, MSSI organized a forum at al-Sahaba mosque called khilafah ala manhaj al-nabawiyah (the Caliphate upon the methodology of the Prophet), a slogan used by ISIS over the past few years.

A month and a half later, Baghdadi released an audio message declaring the creation of new "provinces" in various Arab countries, including Libya. This conferred new legitimacy upon MSSI, which would operate within three Libyan provinces: Wilayat al-Barqah in the east, Wilayat Fizzan in the south, and Wilayat al-Tarabulus in the west. Highlighting the change, ISIS took control of MSSI's media operations.

Since then, ISL has slowly expanded its writ across different parts of Libya, executing and beheading members of General Haftar's forces along the way. Since the beginning of 2015, ISL has been involved in fighting in Benghazi, Sirte and Derna. It may also have executed two secular Tunisian journalists and killed twenty-one Egyptian Christian hostages in areas around Sirte as well as conducted a terrorist attack against the Corinthia Hotel in Tripoli.

While in Sirte and Derna, it has stepped up its hisbah patrols in local markets to ensure that they are not selling rotten or spoiled foods, confiscated hookahs (and closed stores selling tobacco since they view it as against Islam) and ordered stores to suspend sales during daily prayers. It has also conducted some dawa activities, the largest on November 25, 2014 under the motto of "The Caliphate upon the Manhaj [methodology] of the Prophet."

Additionally, it is also providing aid to the poor and needy and giving gifts and sweets to children in Benghazi in order to curry favor. In a move similar to Syria, ISL is now attempting to impose regulations on pharmacies and locals in the health industry. Of course, this shouldn't be interpreted as Islamic State taking full control of Libya, or even any of these cities, but it does highlight its growing presence and prestige.

These developments appear to be eroding ASL's legitimacy as well as its closely guarded and painstakingly manicured reputation. In response, in late January 2015 ASL began trotting out its new Islamic police force and Sharia court in Benghazi. Quite possibly, ASL feels compelled to compete openly with ISL, especially as it loses members to ISL.

This could lead to eventual violence between the two groups similar to what occurred between Jabhat al-Nusra and ISIS in Syria. As of now, there has not been any internecine jihadi fighting. In fact, there are rumors that ASL could pledge allegiance to ISL soon, especially in light of ASL's Sharia official Abu 'Abd Allah al-Libi pledging baya to Baghdadi.

Furthermore, can ASL sustain operations in cities beyond its Benghazi base? It is too early to tell, but if the current trajectory continues, ISL might swallow up ASL recruits outside of Benghazi and even make inroads within the city itself.

Jihadi organizations, including ASL, have always been nimble and adaptable; as we have seen with Jabhat al-Nusra, they have been able to survive the challenge from ISIS. For now, however, ASL faces an uncertain future and the prospect of cooptation by ISL or decline.

Islamic State and al-Qaeda in Tunisia

Over the past month, there are increasing signs that The Islamic State (IS) intends to build a base and set up a new wilayah (province) in Tunisia in the near future named Wilayat Ifriqiya, a medieval name for the region of Tunisia (as well as northwest Libya and northeast Algeria). This would challenge al-Qaeda in the Islamic Maghrib's (AQIM) Tunisian branch Katibat 'Uqba ibn Nafi's (KUIN) monopoly on insurgency and terrorism since their campaign in Jebel Chambi began in December 2012, opening another front in the broader AQ-IS war. As a consequence, outbidding between these two adversaries could lead to an escalation in violence, with Bardo National Museum style attacks becoming more common.

In mid-December last year, IS directed its first overt message to the Tunisian state and its people. Aboubaker el-Hakim (who went by Abu al-Muqatil in the video) claimed responsibility for the assassination of Tunisia's secular leftist politicians in 2013 -- "Yes, tyrants, we're the ones who killed Chokri Belaid and Mohamed Brahmi" -- thus confirming the Ennahda-led government's suspicions that he was involved. Beyond calling for more violence and for Tunisians to remember its imprisoned brothers and sisters, he also called upon the Tunisian people to pledge bay'a to Abu Bakr al-Baghdadi, to raise the banner of tawhid (pure monotheism) and to rip down the flags of Charles de Gaulle and Napoleon (alluding to the historically close relations between Tunisia and France).

This was followed on April 7th by Abu Yahya al-Tunisi of IS's Wilayat Tarabulus in Libya, who urged Tunisians to travel to Libya for training in order to establish and extend the writ of IS back at home. Only two days later, a new media account, Ajnad al-Khilafah bi-Ifriqiya (Soldiers of the Caliphate in Ifriqiya) Media Foundation, was created. While unofficial, it foreshadowed the targeting of Tunisia in much the same way the establishment of al-'Urwah al-Wuthqa (The Indissoluble Link) Media foreshadowed the pledge of bay'a given by Boko Haram to IS in March 2015.

Besides IS's claim of responsibility for the Bardo National Museum attack (which the government actually believes KUIN was responsible for), Ajnad al-Khilafah bi-Ifriqiya Media announced IS's first claim of responsibility for an insurgent attack in Jebel al-Meghila, near the town of Sbeitla. Additionally, Ajnad al-Khilafah bi-Ifriqiya Media claimed responsibility on April 22 for a separate attack in Jebel Salloum, in which one of its Algerian fighters was killed (signaling to Tunisians as well that other nationalities were within its ranks.) This was followed by IS official media disseminators, including Ajnad al-Khilafah bi-Ifriqiya Media, claiming responsibility for attacks in Tunisia on May 2, also in Jebel Salloum. This increasingly formalized approach suggests that the official announcement of a new wilayah may be imminent.

Although KUIN was first identified as a Tunisian cut-out for AQIM in December 2012 by then Tunisian Interior Minister Ali Larayedh, it was not until mid-January 2015 that the battalion publicly acknowledged the association. This pledge was reaffirmed by KUIN following the death of its leader Khalid Shaaib (Abu Sakhr Lukman) in late March and was an attempt to consolidate strength following false rumours that the KUIN might switch sides to IS. These rumors emanated in part from a statement by KUIN showing support for IS though there was no indication of bay'a. The need to distinguish between general support and a religiously-binding pledge of allegiance is vital -- AQAP released a statement in support of IS in Iraq after the fall of Mosul last year.

KUIN has also identified with Ansar al-Sharia in Tunisia (AST) when announcing martyrs, highlighting how some of its fighters are former members. AST has become largely defunct however, with members either being arrested, going abroad to fight and train in Syria and Libya, or joining up with KUIN followings its designation by the Tunisian government as a terrorist organization in late August 2013.

Since it first entered the public gaze, KUIN has remained obscure, maintaining a low-level insurgency with the Tunisian military for 2.5 years in Jebel Chambi. Members have also been arrested for attempted attacks in different cities of Tunisia as well as for weapons smuggling. More recently it has increased its online profile, at first through the Fajr al-Qayrawan Facebook and Twitter account and then Ifriqiya Media, a well-known non-partisan aggregator of online jihadi releases from all African-based jihadi organizations. Only this past weekend, KUIN created an official media outlet for itself called al-Fatih (the conqueror). Up until then, the main content it released showed pictures of its fighters, martyrs, training camps, graphics with quotes from the Qur'an and ghana'im (spoils of war) from its past operation in Hanchir Ettala.

While KUIN has been involved in a low-level insurgency for 2.5 years, it has not altered the status quo in Tunisia. Therefore, if IS attempts a full-scale terrorist or insurgent campaign in Tunisia, pressure on KUIN could mount and an outbidding scenario of escalating violence could ensue. It could also put more pressure on the Tunisian state, which has up to now been able to maintain control against jihadis since the revolution.

That said it is possible one or both organizations might attempt a large-scale attack that would gain a huge media audience, given the onset of tourist season. Moreover, in the aftermath of the Bardo National Museum attack, supporters of IS flipped the popular meme #IWillComeToTunisiaThisSummer in support of the Tunisian tourism industry on its head by showing off with bullets and weapons, intimating that they too would be coming to Tunisia this summer. Vigilance from both the state and the public, then, will be vital in maintaining order and diminishing the effects of violenc

The Islamic State in Sirte, Libya

While much of the focus on the Islamic State in Libya (ISL) has centered on its mid-June defeat in Darnah, over the past few months it has slowly built up its assets and capabilities in the country's Sirte district. In many ways, this effort is the first example of ISL fully resembling its ISIS parent in Iraq and Syria. Unlike in Darnah, where ISL originated, no other insurgent factions remain in Sirte to compete with the group. This is due to several developments: defections from the local wing of jihadist group Ansar al-Sharia in Libya (ASL), arrangements ISL has made with local tribes, and ex-Qadhafi loyalists from the late leader's hometown joining up with or acquiescing to ISL's rise in Sirte, in a manner similar to ex-Baathists in Iraq. As a result, Sirte could soon become the capital for ISL, equivalent to Raqqa in Syria and Mosul in Iraq.

Because ISL co-opted the ASL network in Sirte, convincing it to pledge baya (allegiance) to ISIS leader Abu Bakr al-Baghdadi in late fall 2014, it did not have to start from scratch when establishing itself in the area. Sirte was the first city in which ASL operated outside its base in Benghazi, beginning in late June 2013. For example, it put on a Quranic competition for Ramadan in July 2013, in association with the local Office of Awqaf, Radio Tawhid, the Cleaning Services Company, and the University of Sirte; a year later, it cosponsored a Ramadan dawa event with al-Baynah Foundation. This illustrated that ASL had been preparing to establish itself in Sirte ahead of time and had ties to key players within the city.

From that point forward, Sirte became ASL's second-busiest hub. The group was involved in a variety of governance, hisba (accountability), and dawa (proselytizing) activities in the area, at times extending them into other parts of the Gulf of Sidra region such as al-Nawfaliyah and Bin Jawad.

On the governance front, ASL provided security patrols in various neighborhoods and the University of Sirte, helped arbitrate issues between tribes and clans (including some from faraway Misratah), returned a stolen ambulance to a hospital, regulated traffic, and cleaned roads, among other things. In terms of hisba -- the system by which an Islamic "state" is entrusted with commanding right and forbidding wrong -- the group implemented the tazir penalty (i.e., corporal and other punishments left to the discretion of the authorities, as distinct from punishments set by the Quran) and confiscated and destroyed drugs, cigarettes, and alcohol.

It was also involved in providing iftar (breaking of the fast) tents and supplying presents to children during Ramadan, as well as giving lessons on how to circumambulate the Kaaba correctly during the Hajj in Mecca, passing out slaughtered sacrificial animals during Eid al-Adha, providing school supplies at the beginning of the school year, converting foreign workers to Islam, and conducting charity drives for needy families. All of this illustrates that when ISL began moving into Sirte, there was already a strong apparatus in place to exploit. The city now provides the perfect environment for ISL to build itself up in Libya.

ISL originated in Darnah in April 2014, when it called itself Majlis Shura Shabab al-Islam. After the Abu Salim Martyrs Brigade (former members of the Libyan Islamic Fighting Group) kicked the group out of Darnah in mid-June 2015, Sirte became the main priority for its state-building enterprise. Yet ISL had already been building up its presence in Sirte and other key cities in the district, including al-Nawfaliyah and Harawa. The group drew support from ASL defectors in Sirte as early as October 2014, but it did not act publicly inside the city until early January, from its base at the Ouagadougou Conference Center. Sirte was also the site where ISL members murdered Egyptian Christians in mid-February and Ethiopian Christians in mid-April.

ISL's campaign to seize full control of Sirte was jumpstarted on February 8, 2015, when it took over al-Nawfaliyah some ninety miles to the east. Apparently, ASL defectors provided logistical support for ISL members to enter the city; after securing it, ISL called for residents to pledge baya to Baghdadi and named Ali Qarqa (a.k.a. Abu Hamam al-Libi) as the town's new leader. This provided the group with its first true base in the broader Sirte district. Since then, it has focused on numerous activities in al-Nawfaliyah: conducting outreach forums; destroying cigarettes, alcohol, and caches of what ISL deems "sorcery materials"; distributing dawa leaflets; and training new soldiers.

The week after the al-Nawfaliyah takeover, ISL began making bolder moves in Sirte city, taking the radio station, the Wataniya television studio, the immigration center, Ibn Sina Hospital, the University of Sirte, and local government buildings. By then it controlled more than half of the city and had installed a local leader: Usamah Karamah, a relative of a former senior Qadhafi intelligence officer.

This led the Misratan faction called the Fajr 166 Brigade to launch a counter-campaign aimed at retaking the city, but the effort failed because many leaders back in Misratah were incredulous at the time that ISL had actually infiltrated Sirte and viewed the fight with Gen. Khalifa Haftar in the east as a higher priority. In late May, ISL seized al-Qardabiya Air Base and the Great Man-Made River irrigation complex; then, on June 9, it took the city's power plant, giving it complete control of Sirte. Afterward, ISL members began to loot and destroy the homes of local politicians.

The next week, ISL took over Harawa, halfway between Sirte and al-Nawfaliyah. This move consolidated the group's hold over a swath of territory stretching around 125 miles. ISL has shown little sign of governance activities in Harawa so far, focusing instead on handing out dawa leaflets and CDs, destroying cigarettes and other items the group deems haram (forbidden), distributing zakat al-fitr (charity given to the poor at the end of Ramadan), allegedly liberating a number of Egyptian Muslim prisoners kidnapped by "corrupted" bandits, and in one case arresting a thief.

ISL has also taken other towns such as al-Wushka (about sixty-five miles west of Sirte city) and Wadi Zamzam (105 miles west). The latter town extends into Misratah district, suggesting that wider fighting could emerge between ISL and the Misratans -- thus far they have only issued empty threats against ISL.

ISL's operations in Sirte have grown more sophisticated since June, surpassing even its original efforts in Darnah -- a situation abetted by its current lack of competition. Prior to June, the vast majority of its activities were limited to dawa and hisba: distributing literature, conducting forums, converting Christians, implementing tazir and hudoud (punishments for crimes against God that are based on the Quran and hadith, such as flogging, stoning, amputation, and execution), and demolishing shrines, among other activities described above.

After ISL's Darnah defeat and Sirte expansion, many members went west to help consolidate the group's control and governance efforts there. Although it still engages in dawa and hisba, ISL is now in the state-building stage -- it aims to show residents that life is continuing and that its presence has brought normalcy and stability. Similar efforts were seen last fall in Iraq and Syria, where ISIS members ostentatiously placed the group's black flag on lamp posts, erected dawa billboards throughout towns, conducted tours of different industries, highlighted the group's public works projects, and publicized photos showing the beauty and peacefulness of life in the so-called "Caliphate."

Likewise, ISL members in Sirte have shown off the city's landscapes, port, bustling markets, and fully stocked grocery stores. They have also decorated the entrance to the city with ISL flags, installed numerous dawa billboards, cleaned and decorated streets, provided zakat to the needy, visited Ibn Sina hospital, and toured local brick, aluminum, marble, and milk factories.

In another parallel to Iraq and Syria, ISL members have called on individuals to join the group's ranks via video messages issued under the aegis of "Wilayat Tarabulus," the so-called ISIS "province" encompassing northwestern Libya. In late January, Abu Umar al-Tawrigi called on his fellow Tuaregs to join the group and pledge baya to Baghdadi. In late April, Abu Muhammad al-Ansari stated, "Come to Libya. Our hearts and homes are open to you." In early June, Abu Dujana al-Sudani urged potential recruits to make hijra (emigrate) to ISL. And last month, Abu Hamza al-Masri reiterated these entreaties, asking legal scholars in particular to come help the group implement sharia.

ISL's seizure of Sirte has given the Islamic State a more sustainable base than its failed attempts in Darnah, as well as its first capital outside Iraq and Syria. Whether this leads to further territorial gains remains to be seen, especially given the various rivalries and areas of influence among Libya's many factions.

But ISL will become a far more formidable force if it is able to link its territory in Sirte district to the central Jufrah district, which has the Mabruk oil field and the town of Waddan -- a key supply line for Fajr between Misratah and Sebha districts and a pivotal crossroads for various criminal networks that ISL hopes to take over. The group is also attempting to co-opt more pro-Qadhafi tribes in the Fezzan region further south.

Meanwhile, ISL's consolidation has led ASL -- which still operates independently in Benghazi and to a lesser extent Ajdabiya and Darnah -- to focus more on service provision, dispensing justice, and security. This could lead to an eventual bidding war between the two rival jihadist groups. Whatever the case, it is important for U.S. policymakers and other parties to understand that while ISL did indeed lose in Darnah, it has emerged even stronger in Sirte.

The Tunisian-Libyan Jihadi Connection

It should have come as no surprise that Seifeddine Rezgui, the individual who attacked tourists in Sousse, Tunisia, more than a week ago, had trained at a camp in Libya. The attack represented the continuation of a relationship between Tunisian and Libyan militants that, having intensified since 2011, goes back to the 1980s. The events in Sousse are a stark reminder of this relationship: a connection that is set to continue should the Islamic State (IS) choose to repeat attacks in Tunisia in the coming months.

Although Ennahda did not explicitly call for individuals to fight against the Soviets during the Afghan jihad, militants in the mujahedeen were regularly involved in facilitation and logistical networks that brought Libyans to the region. Additionally, according to Noman Benotman, a former shura council member of the Libyan Islamic Fighting Group (LIFG) in Afghanistan in the 1980s, Libyans alongside Abdul Rasul Sayyaf, the Afghan leader of Ittihad-e-Islami, attempted to help the Tunisians create their own military camp and organization. This would not come to fruition until 2000, when future leaders of Ansar al-Sharia in Tunisia (AST), Tarek Maaroufi (based in Brussels) and Sayf Allah Bin Hassine (moved from London to Jalalabad, Afghanistan; also known as Abu Iyadh al-Tunisi), cofounded the Tunisian Combatant Group.

Following the Afghan jihad, many Ennahda members were exiled to Europe in the late 1980s and early 1990s by former president Ben Ali. While some returned home, the committed were drawn to the jihadi and foreign fighter networks that had spread across Europe, especially in Milan, Italy. Milan became a central hub for recruitment, logistics, and facilitation of foreign fighters going to the Bosnian war as well as assisting the Armed Islamic Group (GIA) in the Algerian jihad.

While the Egyptian Anwar Shaaban led the network, the group surrounding him was made up largely of Tunisians and Libyans, with some Algerians and Moroccans, working together. This milieu helped build interesting relationships among the individuals, along with other cells in Europe. One in particular was between Sami Essid bin Khamis, a future leader of AST, and the Libyan Lased Ben Heni, who was based in Frankfurt, who worked together to plan the 2000 Strasbourg Cathedral Plot (along with the London Algerian jihadi network).

Following 9/11, the successor group to the GIA in Algeria was the Groupe Salafiste pour la Predication et le Combat (GSPC; which would eventually become al-Qaeda in the Islamic Maghrib in 2007). In 2003, Nabil Sahrawi, the leader at the time, was attempting to regionalize the jihad beyond Algerian borders and emphasize recruitment from Tunisia and Libya. While the organization was still dominated by Algerians, the Tunisians and Libyans worked together in GSPC's "Zone 5," which was close to the border with Tunisia and under the banner of El-Fatah El-Moubine.

Because of this, there were a number of cases in the mid to late 2000s where groups of Algerians, Tunisians, and Libyans would get arrested together, either on the Algerian or Tunisian side of their respective borders. In many ways, this formation was a precursor to the now AQIM splinter group Katibat Uqba ibn Nafi (KUIN), based in the Chaambi Mountains on the Tunisian-Algerian border. Around the same time, GSPC networks in Algeria and remnant LIFG networks in Libya were providing logistics and facilitation to fighters going to Iraq in the mid-2000s to fight with al-Qaeda (the precursor to IS). There were a number of routes that Tunisians took to get to Iraq, but one was through the Libyan support networks, which was a reversal of the 1980s trend.

Here many relationships were forged, which would be important after 2011 since a number of Iraq jihad veterans then became involved with AST, Ansar al-Sharia in Libya (ASL), and then eventually the Islamic State in Libya. One such case was Abu Radwan al-Tunisi, from Bizerte, who came to Iraq via Libya and eventually died fighting the Badr Brigades.

Over the past four years, many of the prior trends continued and, at times, accelerated, in reaction to the opening up of Tunisian society and to Libya becoming a relative safe haven for foreign militants. AQIM continued to play a role, especially with smuggling weapons through Tunisia from Libya. Therefore, as with the last decade, a number of Tunisian and Libyan AQIM members have been arrested on Tunisian or Libyan soil, either together or by themselves, in relation to smuggling or plotting terrorist attacks set to occur on: May 2011, June 2011, February 2012, February 2012, December 2012, May 2013, May 2013, June 2013, May 2014, May 2014, June 2014, August 2014, August 2014, and August 2014. Then, in the fall of 2014, more people got arrested for similar reasons, except this time with relation to IS: September 2014, October 2014, December 2014, March 2015, and June 2015.

Besides the many arrests (of which many were likely not made public), there was also a strengthening relationship between Tunisian and Libyan militants through their sister organizations Ansar al-Sharia in Tunisia and Libya. ASL learned from the AST dawa model, with Tunisians providing assistance on how to implement it. There were already signs that Tunisians were training in Libya as early as the spring of 2012. These camps are likely where the original failed Sousse suicide bomber of October 2013 trained.

Within Libya, many attacks against Tunisian diplomatic facilities, such as against its embassy and twice against its consulate in June 2012, were connected with ASL. There is even the case of the Tunisian Ali Ani al-Harzi, who was recently killed in an American airstrike in Iraq fighting for IS. He was one of the ringleaders of the infamous Benghazi U.S. Consulate attack in September 2012, which is most associated with ASL.

Moreover, following the Tunisian government's designation of AST in late August 2013, those who did not quit the movement, get arrested, or join up with the jihad in Syria or with KUIN in the Chaambi Mountains, fled to Libya and ASL, including AST's leader, Abu Iyadh al-Tunisi. Further, as a result of the breakdown in AST, a short-lived integration between Tunisian and Libyan militant networks took place through the rebranding of AST to Shabab al-Tawhid.

Beyond the AST and ASL networks, since the fall of 2014, there has been increased Tunisian activity in Libya with IS. According to the Tunisian government, it is believed that up to 1,000 Tunisians are currently fighting or training in Libya. Even as dozens of Tunisians have died on the battlefield in Libya, a Tunisian was one of the attackers of the Corinthia Tripoli Hotel in late January 2015.

Additionally, a number of these Tunisian IS operatives have been dispatched back home and been involved in a spate of low-level insurgent attacks since early April 2015. Of course, most recently the two most high-profile attacks in Tunisia, first in March at the Bardo Museum in Tunis and less than two weeks ago at the beach resorts in Sousse, were all trained in Libya, at the same camps, by IS.

Therefore, with the continued Tunisian government security concerns as well as the difficulty in securing the Tunisian-Libyan border over the past four years, it is likely that we will see future IS attacks that emanate from or are connected with Libya. What we have seen already did not come out of nowhere; it has a history that stretches back decades and represents a problem too often ignored, taken lightly, or blamed on others by Tunisian officials prior to and after the 2011 revolution.

The Abu Sayyaf Group

The Abu Sayyaf Group (ASG) is the most violent of the Islamic separatist groups operating in the southern Philippines and claims to promote an independent Islamic state in western Mindanao and the Sulu Archipelago. Split from the Moro National Liberation Front in the early 1990s, the group currently engages in kidnappings for ransom, bombings, assassinations, and extortion, and has had ties to Jemaah Islamiyah (JI). The ASG operates mainly in Basilan, Sulu, and Tawi-Tawi Provinces in the Sulu Archipelago and has a presence on Mindanao. Members also occasionally travel to Manila.

2000, an ASG faction kidnapped 21 persons—including 10 Westerners—from a Malaysian resort, and, in May 2001, the ASG kidnapped three US citizens and 17 Filipinos from a resort in Palawan, Philippines, later murdering several of the hostages, including one US citizen. In June 2002, one of the two remaining hostages was killed in a crossfire between Philippine soldiers and the ASG. On 27 February 2004, members of ASG leader Khadafi Janjalani's faction bombed a ferry in Manila Bay, killing 116, and on 14 February 2005 they perpetrated simultaneous bombings in the cities of Manila, General Santos, and Davac, killing at least eight and injuring about 150. In 2006, Janjalani's faction relocated to Sulu, where it joined forces with local ASG supporters who are providing shelter to fugitive JI members from Indonesia.

In July 2007, members of the ASG and the Moro Islamic Liberation Front engaged a force of Philippine marines on Basilan Island, killing 14. In November

2007, a motorcycle bomb exploded outside the Philippine Congress, killing a Congressman and three staff members. While there was no definitive claim of responsibility, three suspected ASG members were arrested during a subsequent raid on a safe house. In January 2009, the ASG kidnapped three International Red Cross workers in Sulu province, holding one of the hostages for six months. Philippine marines in February 2010 killed Albader Parad, one of the ASG's most violent sub-commanders, on Jolo Island. In 2011, the ASG kidnapped several individuals and held them for ransom. In February 2012, a Philippine military airstrike against a terrorist encampment on Jolo Island killed senior ASG leader Gumbahali Jumdail, also known as Dr. Abu.In March 2013, the ASG released an Australian citizen the group had held hostage for fifteen months. In June 2014, Philippine authorities arrested senior ASG figure ASG Khair Mundos in metro Manila

The Taliban

The Taliban is a Sunni Islamist nationalist and pro-Pashtun movement founded in the early 1990s that ruled most of Afghanistan from 1996 until October 2001. The movement's founding nucleus—the word "Taliban" is Pashto for "students"—was composed of peasant farmers and men studying Islam in Afghan and Pakistani madrasas, or religious schools. The Taliban found a foothold and consolidated their strength in southern Afghanistan.

By 1994, the Taliban had moved their way through the south, capturing several provinces from various armed factions who had been fighting a civil war after the Soviet-backed Afghan government fell in 1992. The Taliban's first move was to institute a strict interpretation of Qur'anic instruction and jurisprudence. In practice, this meant often merciless policies on the treatment of women, political opponents of any type, and religious minorities.

In the years leading up to the 11 September 2001 attacks in the United States, the Taliban provided a safe haven for al-Qa'ida. This gave al-Qa'ida a base in which it could freely recruit, train, and deploy terrorists to other countries. The Taliban held sway in Afghanistan until October 2001, when they were routed from power by the US-led campaign against al-Qa'ida.

The Afghan Taliban's leader is Mullah Mohammad Omar, who was the president of Afghanistan during the Taliban's rule. The US Government is offering a $10 million reward for information leading to his capture.

The Afghan Taliban are responsible for most insurgent attacks in Afghanistan. In January 2014, the group staged a suicide and small-arms attack on the popular Lebanese Taverna restaurant in Kabul, killing 21 people, including three Americans, marking one of the deadliest attacks against Western civilians in Kabul since 2001. In a one-week span in March 2014, the Taliban conducted four high-profile attacks in Kabul city, culminating in a 28 March attack on a heavily guarded guesthouse in Kabul for employees of a US aid group. The targeted guesthouse was next to a Christian charity and day-care center that may have been the intended target. The next day, the Taliban conducted an attack on the headquarters of Afghanistan's election commission with rockets and automatic rifles, following an attack on the provincial election office earlier that week. On 20 March, the Taliban attacked Kabul's luxurious Serena Hotel, killing nine civilians who were all shot at point-blank range by four insurgents armed with small pistols smuggled inside.

Al-Nusrah Front

Al-Nusrah Front is one of the most capable al-Qa'ida-affiliated groups operating in Syria during the ongoing conflict. The group in January 2012 announced its intention to overthrow Syrian President Bashar al-Asad's regime, and since then has mounted hundreds of insurgent-style and suicide attacks against regime and security service targets across the country. The group is committed not only to ousting the regime, but also seeks to expand its reach regionally and globally. Initially, al-Nusrah Front did not publicize its links to al-Qa'ida in Iraq or Pakistan.

The Islamic State of Iraq and the Levant (ISIL) played a significant role in founding the group. ISIL predecessor organizations used Syria as a facilitation hub and transformed this facilitation and logistics network into an organization capable of conducting sophisticated explosives and firearms attacks. ISIL leaders since the beginning of al-Nusrah Front's participation in the conflict provided their facilitation hub with personnel and resources, including money and weapons.

During 2013, al-Nusrah Front and ISIL were consumed by a public rift stemming from ISIL leader Abu Bakr al-Baghdadi's April 2013 statement announcing the creation of ISIL and claiming the merger of both groups. Al-Nusrah Front and ISIL have strategies for Syria, and a public merger between them probably would have undermined al-Nusrah Front's autonomy in the country. In April 2013, al-Nusrah Front's leader, Abu Muhammad al-Jawlani, pledged allegiance to al-Qa'ida leader Ayman al-Zawahiri.

During early 2014, the rift between al-Nusrah Front and ISIL—in which ISIL has openly accused al-Qa'ida senior leaders of deviating from what it perceives as the correct jihadist path—has taken place not just on the ground but in social media as well. Al-Nusrah Front's leaders probably have learned lessons from members' previous experiences in Iraq and have sought to win over the Syrian populace by providing parts of the country with humanitarian assistance and basic civil services. Several Syria-based armed opposition groups cooperate and fight alongside Sunni extremist groups, including al-Nusrah Front, and are dependent upon them for expertise, training, and weapons. Al-Nusrah Front has managed to seize territory, including military bases and infrastructure in northern Syria.

The group's cadre is predominately composed of Syrian nationals, many of whom are veterans of previous conflicts, including the Iraq war. Thousands of fighters from around the world have traveled to Syria since early 2012 to support oppositionist groups, and some fighters aspire to connect with al-Nusrah Front and other extremist groups. Several Westerners have joined al-Nusrah Front, including a few who have died in suicide operations. Western government officials have raised concerns that capable individuals with extremist contacts and battlefield experience could return to their home countries to commit violent acts. An al-Nusrah Front attack in May 2014—the first known suicide bombing by an American in Syria—targeted regime personnel, highlighting the involvement of US persons in the conflict.

Ansar Bayt al-Maqdis

Ansar Bayt al-Maqdis (ABM) is the most active and capable terrorist group operating in Egypt. ABM shares al-Qa'ida's ideology and seeks the destruction of Israel, the establishment of an Islamic caliphate in the Sinai Peninsula, and the implementation of sharia. The group is based in the Sinai but since fall 2013 has expanded its operational reach into Egypt's Nile Valley.

ABM emerged in 2011 when it claimed responsibility for a cross-border attack into southern Israel from the Sinai. Since 2011, ABM has carried out additional cross-border attacks, launched rocket attacks against Israel, and repeatedly bombed the gas pipeline in the Sinai that supplies natural gas to Israel and Jordan.

Following the August 2013 crackdown by Egyptian security forces on those protesting the ouster of President Muhammad Mursi, ABM launched a campaign of attacks against Egyptian government and security targets. ABM since then has claimed responsibility for several of the highest-profile and sophisticated attacks in Egypt, including an attempted assassination of the Egyptian Minister of the Interior, the downing of an Egyptian military helicopter in the Sinai with a surface-to-air missile, and several deadly vehicle-borne improvised explosive device attacks against Egyptian security installations.

ABM for the first time demonstrated its willingness to target civilians when it claimed responsibility for a suicide bombing on a tourist bus in the Sinai in February 2014, though ABM described the attack as targeting Egyptian economic interests. ABM claimed responsibility for another suicide bombing in South Sinai in early May 2014 that injured Egyptian workers.

ABM has not made explicit threats against the West or Western targets in its official propaganda. However, the group views the West, and the United States in particular, as supporters of Israel and Egypt and expresses anti-Western sentiment in its rhetoric. Various social media accounts claiming association with the group have posted threats to US and other Western targets, although ABM has repeatedly denied a social media presence.

Egyptian security officials in late May 2014 claimed to have killed ABM's leader—whom they identified as Shadi al-Mani'—but ABM denied the individual was the leader of the group or that he had been killed by Al-Shabaab

The Harakat al-Shabaab al-Mujahidin—commonly known as al-Shabaab—was the militant wing of the Somali Council of Islamic Courts that took over most of southern Somalia in the second half of 2006. Despite the group's defeat by Somali and Ethiopian forces in 2007, al-Shabaab—a clan-based insurgent and terrorist group—has continued its violent insurgency in southern and central Somalia.

The group has exerted temporary and, at times, sustained control over strategic locations in those areas by recruiting, sometimes forcibly, regional sub-clans and their militias, using guerrilla warfare and terrorist tactics against the Somali Federal Government (SFG), African Union Mission in Somalia (AMISOM) peacekeepers, and nongovernmental aid organizations. As of 2013, however, pressure from AMISOM and Ethiopian forces had largely degraded al-Shabaab's control, especially in Mogadishu but also in other key regions of the country, and conflict among senior leaders has exacerbated fractures within the group. In 2013 al-Shabaab rivalries culminated in a major purge of opponents of deceased group leader Ahmed Abdi Aw-Mohamed.

Al-Shabaab is not centralized or monolithic in its agenda or goals. Its rank-and-file members come from disparate clans, and the group is susceptible to clan politics, internal divisions, and shifting alliances. Most of its fighters are predominantly interested in the nationalistic battle against the SFG and not supportive of global jihad. Al-Shabaab's senior leaders are affiliated with al-Qa'ida and are believed to have trained and fought in Afghanistan. The merger of the two groups was publicly announced in February 2012 by the amir of al-Shabaab and Ayman al-Zawahiri, leader of al-Qa'ida.

Al-Shabaab has claimed responsibility for many bombings—including various types of suicide attacks—in Mogadishu and in central and northern Somalia, typically targeting Somali government officials, AMISOM, and perceived allies of the SFG. Since 2013 al-Shabaab has launched high-profile operations in neighboring countries, most notably the September 2013 Westgate Mall attack in Nairobi and the May 2014 attack against a restaurant in Djibouti popular with Westerners. The Westgate attack killed 67 Kenyan and non-Kenyan nationals, and a siege continued at the mall for several days.

Al-Shabaab claimed responsibility for the twin suicide bombings in Kampala, Uganda, on 11 July 2010 that killed more than 70 people, as well as a June 2013 attack in Mogadishu on a United Nations compound, which killed 22 people. A February 2014 al-Shabaab attack on Somalia's presidential palace, Villa Somalia, involved a car bomb and armed assailants and killed 12 people, nine of them militants. In June 2014, an attack and siege in Mpeketoni, Kenya, killed nearly 50 tourists; although there was no claim of responsibility, al-Shabaab was widely believed responsible. There were other high-profile attacks in 2014 either ascribed to or claimed by al-Shabaab.

Ansar al-Sharia

Ansar al-Sharia groups in Libya emerged following the 2011 Libyan revolution. Their goal is to establish sharia and to remove US and Western influence from Libya. Ansar al-Sharia has nodes in Libyan cities that work with regional extremist groups to train, conduct attacks, and amass weapons. The term Ansar al-Sharia means "Partisans of Islamic Law."

Ansar al-Sharia in Benghazi (AAS-B) and in Darnah (AAS-D) were most likely involved in the 11 September 2012 attacks against US facilities in Benghazi that resulted in the death of J. Christopher Stevens, the US Ambassador to Libya, and three other US citizens. The United States designated AAS-B and AAS-D as Foreign Terrorist Organizations in January 2014. The groups are also suspected of involvement in attacks and kidnappings targeting foreigners, including the assassination of an American teacher in Benghazi in December 2013.

Muhammad al-Zahawi is widely recognized as AAS's amir and spiritual leader. He stated in a December 2013 news interview that the group continued to reject any form of government other than sharia and that the government should consult the Qur'an on all matters. Al-Zahawi publicly rejects any association between AAS and al-Qa'ida.

Ansar al-Sharia in Tunisia (AAS-T) was blamed for inciting the storming of the US Embassy in Tunis on 14 September 2012, and has since been designated by the United States as a Foreign Terrorist Organization. AAS-T remains intent on conducting attacks against Western interests in spite of increasing Tunisian security capability and counterterrorism operations. AAS-T attempted suicide attacks against two tourist sites in October 2013 and in 2014 probably has been plotting against Jewish targets and Western diplomatic missions in Tunisia.

Al-Qa'ida in the Arabian Peninsula (AQAP)

Al-Qa'ida in the Arabian Peninsula (AQAP) is a Sunni extremist group based in Yemen that has orchestrated numerous high-profile terrorist attacks. One of the most notable of these operations occurred when AQAP dispatched Nigerian-born Umar Farouk Abdulmutallab, who attempted to detonate an explosive device aboard a Northwest Airlines flight on 25 December 2009—the first attack inside the United States by an al-Qa'ida affiliate since 11 September 2001. That was followed by an attempted attack in which explosive-laden packages were sent to the United States on 27 October 2010.

The year 2010 also saw the launch of Inspire magazine, an AQAP-branded, English-language publication that first appeared in July, followed by the establishment of AQAP's Arabic-language al-Madad News Agency in 2011. Dual US-Yemeni citizen Anwar al-Aulaqi, who had a worldwide following as a radical ideologue and propagandist, was the most prominent member of AQAP; he was killed in an explosion in September 2011.

In August 2013, the US State Department temporarily closed several embassies in response to a threat associated with AQAP. Since then, AQAP has conducted a number of high-profile attacks inside Yemen targeting the Yemeni Government, including a complex, multistage attack in December 2013 against Yemen's Ministry of Defense that killed at least 52 people, and in February 2014 the group freed over two dozen prisoners after attacking Sanaa's central prison. Shortly thereafter the group released a video entitled "Drops of Rain," which depicted a large gathering of AQAP members operating openly while their leader threatened the United States. In May 2014, the US Embassy in Sanaa closed for a month due to a heightened threat from the group.

AQAP's predecessor, al-Qa'ida in Yemen (AQY), came into existence after the escape of 23 al-Qa'ida members from prison in Sanaa, in February 2006. Several escapees helped reestablish the group and later identified fellow escapee al-Wahishi as the group's new amir.

AQY in early 2008 dramatically increased its operational tempo, carrying out small-arms attacks on foreign tourists and a series of mortar attacks against the US and Italian Embassies in Sanaa, the presidential compound, and Yemeni military complexes. In September 2008 the group attacked the US Embassy in Sanaa using two vehicle bombs that detonated outside the compound, killing 19 people.

AQAP emerged in January 2009 following an announcement that Yemeni and Saudi terrorists were unifying under a common banner. The leadership of this new organization was composed of the group's amir, Nasir al-Wahishi; now-deceased deputy amir Sa'id al-Shahri; and military commander Qasim al-Rimi, all veteran extremist leaders. The group has targeted local, US, and Western interests in the Arabian Peninsula, but is now pursuing a global strategy. AQAP elements withdrew from their southern Yemen strongholds in June 2012, when Yemeni military forces under new President Abdu Rabbo Mansour Hadi—with the support of local tribesmen—regained control of cities in Abyan and Shabwah that had served as AQAP strongholds since 2011

Al-Qa'ida in the Lands of the Islamic Maghreb (AQIM)

Al-Qa'ida in the Lands of the Islamic Maghreb (AQIM) is an Algeria-based Sunni Muslim jihadist group. It originally formed in 1998 as the Salafist Group for Preaching and Combat (GSPC), a faction of the Armed Islamic Group, which was the largest and most active terrorist group in Algeria. The GSPC was renamed in

January 2007 after the group officially joined al-Qa'ida in September 2006. The group had close to 30,000 members at its height, but the Algerian Government's counterterrorism efforts have reduced GSPC's ranks to fewer than 1,000. The current leader of AQIM is Abdelmalek Droukdal, who has been in charge of AQIM since it was founded in 1998 as the GSPC.

AQIM historically has operated primarily in the northern coastal areas of Algeria and in parts of the desert regions of southern Algeria and the Sahel. Since the French-led military intervention in early 2013, however, the group has reduced its presence in northern Mali and expanded into Libya and Tunisia. AQIM mainly employs conventional terrorist tactics, including guerrilla-style ambushes, mortar, rocket, and IED attacks. The group's principal sources of revenue include extortion, kidnapping for ransom, and donations. In May 2009, AQIM announced it had killed a British hostage after months of failed negotiations. In June of the same year, the group publicly claimed responsibility for killing US citizen Christopher Leggett in Mauritania because of his missionary activities. In 2011, a Mauritanian court sentenced a suspected AQIM member to death and two others to prison for the American's murder.

AQIM since 2010 has failed to conduct the high-casualty attacks in Algeria that it had in previous years. Multinational counterterrorism efforts—including a joint French-Mauritanian raid in July 2010 against an AQIM camp—resulted in the death of some AQIM members and possibly disrupted some AQIM activity. In 2011, however, AQIM killed two French hostages during an attempted rescue operation, and in 2013 killed one French hostage in retaliation for France's military intervention in Mali. AQIM continues to hold five French, one South African, one Dutch, and one Swede hostage.

In 2012, AQIM took advantage of political chaos in northern Mali to consolidate its control there and worked with the secular Azawad National Liberation Movement (MNLA) to secure independence in Kidal, Gao, and Timbuktu for ethnic Tuaregs. The Islamic militant group Ansar al-Dine was formed to support the creation of an Islamic state in Mali ruled by sharia.

Since 2011, dissident groups of AQIM members broke away to form Movement for Unity and Jihad in West Africa (MUJAO) and al-Mulathamun Battalion and its subordinate unit al-Muwaqi'un Bil-Dima ("Those Who Sign With Blood") led by former AQIM battalion leader Mokhtar Belmokhtar. In August 2013 these groups merged to form al-Murabitun, ("The Sentinels"), and officially formalized the groups' ties; their stated goals are to "unite all Muslims from the Nile to the Atlantic in jihad against Westerners" and to curb French influence in the regio

Al-Qa'ida

Established by Usama Bin Ladin in 1988 with Arabs who fought in Afghanistan against the Soviet Union, al-Qa'ida's declared goal is the establishment of a pan-Islamic caliphate throughout the Muslim world. Toward this end, al-Qa'ida seeks to unite Muslims to fight the West, especially the United States, as a means of overthrowing Muslim regimes al-Qa'ida deems "apostate," expelling Western influence from Muslim countries, and defeating Israel. Al-Qa'ida issued a statement in February 1998 under the banner of "the World Islamic Front for Jihad Against the Jews and Crusaders" saying it was the duty of all Muslims to kill US citizens—civilian and military—and their allies everywhere. The group merged with the Egyptian Islamic Jihad (al-Jihad) in June 2001.

On 11 September 2001, 19 al-Qa'ida suicide attackers hijacked and crashed four US commercial jets—two into the World Trade Center in New York City, one into the Pentagon near Washington, D.C., and a fourth into a field in Shanksville, Pennsylvania—leaving nearly 3,000 people dead. Al-Qa'ida also directed the 12 October 2000 attack on the USS Cole in the port of Aden, Yemen, which killed 17 US sailors and injured another 39, and conducted the bombings in August 1998 of the US embassies in Nairobi, Kenya, and Dar es Salaam, Tanzania, killing 224 people and injuring more than 5,000. Since 2002, al-Qa'ida and affiliated groups have conducted attacks worldwide, including in Europe, North Africa, South Asia, Southeast Asia, and the Middle East.

In 2005, Ayman al-Zawahiri, then Bin Ladin's deputy and now the leader of al-Qa'ida, publicly claimed al-Qa'ida's involvement in the 7 July 2005 bus bombings in the United Kingdom. In 2006, British security services foiled an al-Qa'ida plot to detonate explosives on up to 10 transatlantic flights originating from London's Heathrow airport. During that same time period, numbers of al-Qa'ida-affiliated groups increased.

Following the 2011 death of Bin Ladin, al-Qa'ida leaders moved quickly to name al-Zawahiri as his successor. The group remains a cohesive organization and what is widely called al-Qa'ida's Core leadership continues to be important to the global movement despite leadership losses. Other jihadist groups, however, like the Islamic State of Iraq and the Levant (ISIL), have gained prominence and challenged the Core's global leadership.

Al-Qa'ida remains committed to conducting attacks in the United States and against American interests abroad. The group has advanced a number of unsuccessful plots in the past several years, including against the United States and Europe. This highlights al-Qa'ida's ability to continue some attack preparations while under sustained counterterrorism pressure and suggests it may be plotting additional attacks against the United States at home or overseas.

Moving forward into 2015, the group could seek to reconstitute the remnants of the group in Afghanistan. Al-Qa'ida's historical ties to Afghanistan make the country an attractive operating area, especially if the group can leverage its longstanding relationships with Afghan insurgents who supported it in the years preceding 9/11.

Imirat Kavkaz

Imirat Kavkaz, (IK, or Caucasus Emirate), founded in late 2007 by now-deceased Chechen extremist Doku Umarov, is an Islamist militant organization based in Russia's North Caucasus. Its stated goal is the liberation of what it considers to be Muslim lands from Moscow. The group, now led by Ali Abu-Muhammad, also known as Aliaskhab Kebekov, regularly conducts attacks against Russian security forces in the North Caucasus. In the period 2010-2011, it carried out high-profile suicide bombings against civilian targets in Moscow that killed dozens. IK maintains ties with militants from the North Caucasus fighting alongside groups aiming to topple Bashar al-Asad in Syria.

In the approach to the Sochi Olympic Games, Umarov on 2 July 2013 urged militants in Russia to target the Games, stating that Moscow "plan[s] to hold the Olympics on the bones of our ancestors, on the bones of many dead Muslims…and we mujahedin are obliged not to permit that." While there were attacks in Volgograd in the weeks before the event that killed more than 30 civilians, no attacks took place on site during the Games. The US State Department in May 2011 designated Imirat Kavkaz as a Specially Designated Terrorist group under Executive Order 13224.

The Islamic Jihad Union (IJU) is an extremist organization that splintered from the Islamic Movement of Uzbekistan in the early 2000s and is currently based in Pakistan's Federally Administered Tribal Areas. The IJU, which is committed to toppling the government in Uzbekistan, conducted two attacks there in 2004 and one in 2009. The IJU is also active in Afghanistan, where the group operates alongside the Taliban-affiliated Haqqani Network. The group has had particular success in recruiting German nationals and achieved international notoriety following the 2007 disruption of an IJU plot by the so-called Sauerland Cell to attack various targets in Germany. The US State Department in June 2005 designated the IJU a Foreign Terrorist Organization.

The Islamic Movement of Uzbekistan (IMU) is an extremist organization that formed in the late 1990s and is currently based in Pakistan's Federally Administered Tribal Areas. The IMU seeks to overthrow the government in Uzbekistan and establish a radical Islamist caliphate in all of "Turkestan," which it considers to be the Central Asian region between the Caspian Sea and Xinjiang in western China. The IMU has become increasingly active in the Taliban-led insurgency in northern Afghanistan, providing the IMU with a springboard for future operations in Central Asia. A known IMU spokesperson in a video message delivered to Radio Liberty's Tajik service claimed responsibility for a September 2010 ambush against a military convoy in Tajikistan. The IMU in June 2014 joined Tehrik-e Taliban Pakistan fighters in a deadly siege of Karachi International Airport that killed 37.

Boko Haram

Boko Haram, which refers to itself as "Jama'atu Ahl as-Sunnah li-Da'awati wal-Jihad" (JASDJ; Group of the Sunni People for the Calling and Jihad) and "Nigerian Taliban"—other translations and variants are used—is a Nigeria-based group that seeks to overthrow the current Nigerian Government and replace it with a regime based on Islamic law. It is popularly known in Nigerian and Western media as "Boko Haram," which means "Western education is forbidden" (the word boko is a holdover from the colonial English word for book). The group, which has existed in various forms since the late 1990s, suffered setbacks in July 2009 when clashes with Nigerian Government forces led to the deaths of hundreds of its members, including former leader Muhammad Yusuf.

In July 2010, Boko Haram's former second-in-command, Abubakar Shekau, appeared in a video claiming leadership of the group and threatening attacks on Western influences in Nigeria. Later that month, Shekau issued a second statement expressing solidarity with al-Qa'ida and threatening the United States. Under Shekau's leadership, the group has continued to demonstrate growing operational capabilities, with an increasing use of improvised explosive device (IED) attacks against soft targets. The group set off its first vehicle-borne

IED in June 2011. On 26 August 2011, Boko Haram conducted its first attack against a Western interest—a vehicle-bomb attack on UN headquarters in Abuja—killing at least 23 people and injuring more than 80. A purported Boko Haram spokesman claimed responsibility for the attack and promised future targeting of US and Nigerian Government interests.

Boko Haram's capability has increased in 2014, with the group conducting near-daily attacks against a wide range of targets, including Christians, Nigerian security and police forces, the media, schools, politicians, and Muslims perceived as collaborators. Boko Haram continues to expand its activity into neighboring countries and has claimed responsibility for the kidnapping of 11 Westerners in Cameroon since early 2013, raising the group's international profile and emphasizing the growing threat it poses to Western and regional interests.

Boko Haram's unprecedented levels of violence—including the kidnapping of 276 schoolgirls in Borno State, Nigeria, in April 2014—have brought international condemnation as well as collaboration on security initiatives by the United States, United Kingdom, France, African partners, and others as Nigerian and other regional security forces continue to try to oust the group from northeastern Nigeria and its safe havens throughout the area.

Hezb-e-Islami

Hezb-e-Islami, or "Party of Islam," is a political and paramilitary organization in Afghanistan founded in 1976 by former Afghan prime minister Gulbuddin Hekmatyar, who has been prominent in various Afghan conflicts since the late 1970s. Hezb-e Islami Gulbuddin (HIG) is an offshoot of that original Hezb-e-Islami, and is a virulently anti-Western insurgent group whose goal is to replace the Western-backed Afghan Government with an Islamic state rooted in sharia in line with Hekmatyar's vision of a Pashtun-dominated Afghanistan.

His group conducts attacks against Coalition forces, Afghan Government targets, and Western interests in Afghanistan. HIG is distinct from Hezb-e-Islami Afghanistan (HIA), a legal Afghan political party composed of, among others, some reconciled HIG members. HIG shares most elements of Taliban ideology and HIG insurgents cooperate with the Taliban in some parts of Afghanistan despite some ideological differences.

Hekmatyar and his deputies, Ghairat Baheer and Qutbuddin Hilal, continue to participate sporadically in negotiations with the Afghan Government. Hilal even ran for Afghan president in the country's April 2014 election. HIG, however, strongly opposes the proposed Bilateral Security Agreement with the United States and, after Hilal's failed presidential bid, boycotted the subsequent election run-off.

The group has conducted some widely publicized attacks during the past few years even while negotiations were under way. Most recently, HIG spokesman Haroon Zarghoon claimed responsibility for a suicide VBIED attack in Kabul on 10 February 2014, which killed at least two US civilians and wounded two other Americans and seven Afghan nationals. HIG was also responsible for a 16 May 2013 suicide VBIED attack in Kabul, which destroyed a US armored SUV and killed two US soldiers, four US civilian contractors, eight Afghans—including two children—and wounded at least 37 others. The attack marked the deadliest incident against US personnel in Kabul in over a year.

Jaish-e-Mohammed

Jaish-e-Mohammed (JEM)—also known as the Army of Mohammed, Khudamul Islam, and Tehrik ul-Furqaan among other names—is an extremist group based in Pakistan. It was founded by Masood Azhar in early 2000 upon his release from prison in India. The group's aim is to unite Kashmir with Pakistan and to expel foreign troops from Afghanistan. JEM has openly declared war against the United States. Pakistan outlawed JEM in 2002, and by 2003 JEM had splintered into Khuddam ul-Islam (KUI), headed by Azhar, and Jamaat ul-Furqan (JUF), led by Abdul Jabbar. Pakistani authorities detained Abdul Jabbar for suspected involvement in the December 2003 assassination attempts against President Pervez Musharraf but released him in August 2004. Pakistan banned KUI and JUF in November 2003.

JEM continues to operate openly in parts of Pakistan despite the 2002 ban on its activities. Since JEM founder Masood Azhar's release in 2000, JEM has conducted many lethal terrorist attacks, including a suicide bombing of the Jammu and Kashmir legislative assembly building in the Indian-administered Kashmir capital of Srinagar in October 2001 that killed more than 30. In July 2004, Pakistani authorities arrested a JEM member wanted in connection with the 2002 abduction and murder of US journalist Daniel Pearl.

In 2006 JEM claimed responsibility for a number of attacks, including the killing of several Indian police officials in Srinagar. JEM members also were involved in the 2007 Red Mosque uprising in Islamabad. Asmatullah Moavia, a militant currently associated with Tehrik-e Taliban Pakistan, split from the group after the Red Mosque incident because of disagreements over how to react to it. In 2009, Pakistani authorities detained several JEM members suspected of taking part in a 3 March attack on the Sri Lankan cricket team in Lahore.

In June 2008, JEM reportedly was working to resolve its differences with other Pakistani extremist groups and began shifting its focus from Kashmir to Afghanistan in order to step up attacks against US and Coalition forces. Rogue factions of JEM, in conjunction with other regional groups, may conduct attacks against Western interests in Pakistan as well as attack Pakistani Government entities.

JEM has at least several hundred armed supporters located in Pakistan, India's southern Kashmir and Doda regions, and in the Kashmir Valley. Supporters are mostly Pakistanis and Kashmiris, but also include Afghans and Arab veterans of the Afghan war against the Soviets. The group uses light and heavy machine guns, assault rifles, mortars, improvised explosive devices, and rocket-propelled grenades in its attacks.

Jemaah Islamiyah

Jemaah Islamiyah (JI) is an Indonesia-based clandestine terrorist network formed in the early 1990s to establish an Islamic state encompassing southern Thailand, Malaysia, Singapore, Indonesia, Brunei, and the southern Philippines. Its operatives, who trained in camps in Afghanistan and the southern Philippines, began conducting attacks in 1999. The network's existence was discovered in late 2001 after Singaporean authorities disrupted a cell that was planning to attack targets associated with the US Navy.

JI is responsible for a series of lethal bombings targeting Western interests in Indonesia and the Philippines from 2000-2005, including attacks in 2002 against two nightclubs in Bali that killed 202 people; the 2003 car bombing of the JW Marriott hotel in Jakarta that killed 12; the 2004 truck bombing of the Australian Embassy that killed 11; and the 2005 suicide bombing of three establishments in Bali that killed 22. A JI splinter group led by Noordin Mat Top in July 2009 conducted suicide bombings at two hotels in Jakarta.

Southeast Asian governments since 2002 have arrested more than 300 suspected terrorists, significantly degrading JI's network. Thai authorities detained the network's operations chief in 2003. Indonesian police killed JI's most experienced bombmaker in 2005 and arrested its two senior leaders in mid-2007. Malaysian authorities arrested two senior JI operatives in Kuala

Lumpur in early 2008 and in April 2009 recaptured fugitive Singapore JI leader Mas Selamat Kasteri, who escaped from his Singaporean prison cell in early 2008. Indonesian police in September 2009 killed Noordin Mat Top.

Since 2009, JI has been overshadowed by the activities of its splinter groups and other Indonesia-based terrorists, some of whom are experienced operatives previously affiliated with JI; others are convicted terrorists who completed prison sentences and have since resumed their activities. Indonesian terrorist Umar Patek—arrested by Pakistani authorities in Abbotabad in January 2011 and repatriated seven months later—was convicted in June 2012 for his role in the 2002 Bali bombings and sentenced to 20 years in prison. In November 2012, Philippine security forces killed senior Indonesian JI leader Sanusi.

Lashkar-e-Tayyiba

Lashkar-e-Tayyiba (LT), also known as Army of the Righteous, is one of the largest and most proficient of the Kashmir-focused militant groups. LT formed in the early 1990s as the military wing of Markaz-ud-Dawa-wal-Irshad, a Pakistan-based Islamic fundamentalist missionary organization founded in the 1980s to oppose the Soviets in Afghanistan. Since 1993, LT has conducted numerous attacks against Indian troops and civilian targets in the disputed Jammu and Kashmir state, as well as several high-profile attacks inside India itself. Concern over new LT attacks in India remains high.

The United States and United Nations have designated LT as an international terrorist organization. The Pakistani Government banned LT and froze its assets in 2002. In June 2014, the US Treasury Department imposed sanctions on two additional LT leaders and the US State Department amended the Foreign Terrorist Organizations and Specially Designated Global Terrorist designations for LT to include four additional front organizations. In April 2012 two senior LT leaders were designated by the US State Department Rewards for Justice program.

The Indian Government has charged LT with committing the 26–29 November 2008 attacks in Mumbai, in which gunmen using automatic weapons and grenades attacked several sites, killing more than 160 people. Pakistani authorities have detained and are prosecuting several LT leaders for the Mumbai attacks. David Headley, an American citizen who acknowledged attending LT training camps, pleaded guilty in March 2010 to scouting targets for the Mumbai attacks. On 21 November 2012, India executed the lone surviving Mumbai attacker—Ajmal Kasab, a Pakistani—after the Indian Supreme Court upheld his death sentence. India has accused LT of involvement in other high-profile attacks, including the 11 July 2006 attack on multiple Mumbai commuter trains that killed more than 180 people, and the December 2001 armed assault on the Indian Parliament building that left 12 dead. Afghan and US officials have blamed LT for the May 2014 attack on the Indian consulate in Herat, Afghanistan.

LT's exact size is unknown, but the group probably has several thousand members. Elements of LT are active in Afghanistan and the group also recruits internationally, as evidenced by the arrest in the United States of Jubair Ahmed in 2011, Headley's arrest in 2009, and the indictment of 11 LT terrorists in Virginia in 2003. LT maintains facilities in Pakistan, including training camps, schools, and medical clinics. In March 2002, senior al-Qa'ida lieutenant Abu Zubaydah was captured at an LT safehouse in Faisalabad, suggesting that some LT members assist the group.

LT coordinates its charitable activities through its front organization, Jamaat-ud-Dawa (JuD), which spearheaded humanitarian relief to the victims of the October 2005 earthquake in Kashmir. JuD activities, however, have been limited since December 2008 by the UN's designation of the group as an alias for LT. During the 2010 floods in Pakistan, JuD and an affiliated charity, the Falah-i-Insaniyat Foundation (FiF), were widely reported to have provided aid to flood victims. In 2014, JuD and FiF were providing relief to internally displaced persons in Pakistan who fled from Pakistani military operations in the Federally Administered Tribal Areas.

Lashkar-e-Jhangvi

Lashkar-e-Jhangvi (LJ) was founded in 1996 as a militant offshoot of Sipah-i-Sahaba Pakistan, a Deobandi and anti-Shia group that emerged in the mid-1980s in reaction to class-based conflict and the domestic Pakistani Shia revival that followed the Iranian revolution. LJ seeks to transform Pakistan into a Deobandi-dominated Sunni state, and primarily targets Shia and other religious minorities.

Akram Lahori is the leader of LJ but in 2002 was arrested, later convicted of sectarian killings, and is currently incarcerated. Lahori officially remains LJ's amir and Malik Mohammad Ishaq, one of LJ's founding members, is believed to have taken command since his release from prison in 2011. According to Pakistani media reporting, LJ consists of at least eight loosely coordinated cells spread across Pakistan with independent chiefs for each cell. At least seven of these cells—Lashkar-e-Jhangvi Al Alami, Asif Chotoo group, Akram Lahori group, Naeem Bukhari group, Qari Zafar group, Qari Shakeel group, and Farooq Bengali group—are active in Pakistan's largest city, Karachi. Many are linked to al-Qa'ida and Tehrik-e Taliban Pakistan (TTP) but still recognize Ishaq as the head of LJ. In particular, LJ cells also often coordinate with TTP factions in Karachi when targeting law enforcement agencies and Shia.

LJ collaborates and has overlapping membership with other Pakistan-based radical Sunni groups including al-Qa'ida and TTP. Pakistani authorities suspected LJ collaborated with these groups in the 2009 attack on the Pakistan Army General Headquarters in Islamabad and in several attacks in 2010 targeting Pakistan's Criminal Investigation Department. LJ members reportedly also have been linked to a number of high-profile kidnappings and killings of Westerners in the region, such as the 1997 killing of four US oil workers in Karachi, the 2002 kidnapping and execution of US journalist Daniel Pearl, the August 2010 kidnapping of the son-in-law of the former Chairman of the Joint Chiefs of Staff Committee, and the August 2011 kidnapping of a US citizen that was later publicly claimed by al-Qa'ida.

In 2013, LJ claimed credit for some of the most deadly sectarian attacks in Pakistan's history. In January, a billiard hall in Quetta, Balochistan Province, was hit by two blasts, first by a suicide bomber and about 10 minutes later by a car bomb, killing 92 people and injuring more than 120, mostly Shia. In February, explosives hidden in a water tanker exploded in a crowded market in Hazara town, a Shia-dominated area on the edge of Quetta. The blast killed 81 people and wounded 178, stoking anger and frustration among Shia at the authorities' inability or unwillingness to crack down on LJ. The group, with al-Qa'ida, also claimed responsibility for a June suicide attack in Quetta against a bus carrying Pakistani female university students. A female suicide bomber was one of the attackers, and at least 25 people were killed, which included a follow-on assault on a nearby hospital

Tehrik-e Taliban Pakistan

The Taliban is a Sunni Islamist nationalist and pro-Pashtun movement founded in the early 1990s that ruled most of Afghanistan from 1996 until October 2001. The movement's founding nucleus—the word "Taliban" is Pashto for "students"—was composed of peasant farmers and men studying Islam in Afghan and Pakistani madrasas, or religious schools. The Taliban found a foothold and consolidated their strength in southern Afghanistan.

By 1994, the Taliban had moved their way through the south, capturing several provinces from various armed factions who had been fighting a civil war after the Soviet-backed Afghan government fell in 1992. The Taliban's first move was to institute a strict interpretation of Qur'anic instruction and jurisprudence. In practice, this meant often merciless policies on the treatment of women, political opponents of any type, and religious minorities.

Tehrik-e Taliban Pakistan (TTP) is an alliance of militant networks formed in 2007 to unify opposition against the Pakistani military. TTP's stated objectives are the expulsion of Islamabad's influence in the Federally Administered Tribal Areas and neighboring Khyber Paktunkhwa Province in Pakistan, the implementation of a strict interpretation of sharia throughout Pakistan, and the expulsion of Coalition troops from Afghanistan. TTP leaders also publicly say that the group seeks to establish an Islamic caliphate in Pakistan that would require the overthrow of the Pakistani Government. TTP historically maintained close ties to senior al-Qa'ida leaders, including al-Qa'ida's former head of operations for Pakistan.

Baitullah Mehsud, the first TTP leader, died on 5 August 2009, and his successor, Hakimullah Mehsud, died on 1 November 2013. TTP's central shura in November 2013 appointed Mullah Fazlullah as the group's overall leader. Fazlullah is staunchly anti-Western, anti-Islamabad, and advocates harsh tactics underscored by his ordering the November 2012 attempted assassination of education rights activist Malala Yousafzai. TTP since 2008 has repeatedly publicly threatened to attack the US homeland, and a TTP spokesman claimed responsibility for the failed vehicle-bomb attack in Times Square, New York City, on 1 May 2010. In June 2011, a spokesman vowed to attack the United States and Europe in revenge for the death of Usama Bin Ladin. A TTP leader in April 2012 endorsed external operations by the group and threatened attacks in the United Kingdom for its involvement in Afghanistan.

Al-Murabitun

Al-Murabitun, which seeks to "unite all Muslims from the Nile to the Atlantic in jihad against Westerners" and "liberate Mali from France," according to the group's public announcement, was formed when veteran jihadist Mokhtar Belmokhtar in August 2013 merged his al-Mulathamun Battalion with Al-Tawhid Wal Jihad in West Africa (TWJWA). The merger formalized an already close relationship between two of the most active terrorist groups in North and

West Africa. The two groups—both offshoots of al-Qa'ida in the Lands of the Islamic Maghreb (AQIM)—conducted numerous attacks against Westerners in North and West Africa prior to their merger, including the January 2013 attack on the I-n-Amenas gas facility in Algeria that killed nearly 40 Westerners, including three Americans, and a joint operation in May 2013 in Niger simultaneously targeting a French uranium mine and a Nigerian military barracks.

French CT operations have killed at least four senior leaders and dozens of rank-and-file members of al-Murabitun—including its titular leader, Abu Bakr al-Masri—in Mali since November 2013, possibly preventing the group from carrying out a high-profile attack in the region. However, al-Murabitun has conducted small-scale but lethal attacks against UN targets in Mali and remains the most potent threat in the Sahel because of Belmokhtar's anti-West agenda and vast network of extremists. In its initial announcement, the new group pledged allegiance to al-Qa'ida senior leadership and its commitment to the philosophy of jihad put forward by Usama Bin Ladin, suggesting a focus on anti-Western attacks, and in two separate statements in 2014 the group reaffirmed its allegiance to Ayman al-Zawahiri and restated its intent to continue to attack France and its allies.

Al-Mulathamun Battalion and its subordinate unit, al-Muwaqi'un Bil-Dima ("Those Who Sign With Blood"), led by Mokhtar Belmokhtar, splintered from AQIM in fall 2012 due to leadership disputes. Belmokhtar has a long history of jihadist activity in North and West Africa dating back almost two decades. He fought with the mujahidin in Afghanistan as a teenager and trained with al-Qa'ida, where he lost an eye mishandling explosives. By the late 1990s, Belmokhtar seized control over lucrative trans-Saharan smuggling routes, reportedly earning millions by trafficking cigarettes.

Tawhid Wal Jihad in West Africa (TWJWA), also known as the Movement for Unity and Jihad in West Africa (MUJAO), was founded in late 2011 as an offshoot of AQIM and has coordinated terrorist attacks across North and West Africa. Since the French-led intervention in Mali began in mid-January 2013, TWJWA has conducted a majority of the attacks targeting French and African forces in the vicinity of Gao and Kidal, using suicide bombings, vehicle-borne improvised explosive devices, and landmines.

Al-Murabitun, an Arabic phrase meaning "The Sentinels," invokes a medieval dynasty of the same name—known in English as the Almoravids—that originated as a religious and military movement and whose nomadic founders emerged from present-day Western Sahara in the mid-11th century. The Almoravids ruled much of northwest Africa and southern Spain for nearly 100 years, professing a rigorous Islamic creed and imposing a strict form of sharia on the peoples they conquered.

Jund al Khilafa

Jund al-Khilafah was previously a faction of al-Qaeda in the Islamic Maghreb, the Al Qaeda affiliate in North and West Africa. AQIM grew out of Algerian Islamist groups that had fought in the 1990s Civil War. Abdelmalek Gouri (who would later lead Jund al-Khilafah) was formerly the "right-hand man" of Abdelmalek Droukdel, who was the leader of AQIM. Gouri was also part of an AQIM cell responsible for suicide attacks on the government's headquarters and the UN compound in Algiers in 2007. He was also behind an attack in Iboudrarene in April 2014 that left 11 Algerian soldiers dead.

On 14 September 2014, the leader of al-Qaeda in the Islamic Maghreb (AQIM) in the central region, Khaled Abu Suleiman (nom de guerre of Abdelmalek Gouri), announced in a communique he was breaking allegiance with al-Qaeda and took an oath of allegiance to the leader of Islamic State of Iraq and the Levant, Abu Bakr al-Baghdadi. He was reportedly joined by an AQIM commander of an eastern region of Algeria. He claimed that other members of AQIM had "deviated from the right path" and declared to al-Baghdadi 'You have in the Islamic Maghreb men who will obey your orders."

A new armed group calling itself the "Soldiers of the Caliphate in Algeria" has split from al-Qaeda's North African branch and sworn loyalty to the group calling itself the Islamic State (IS), fighting in Syria and Iraq. In a communique released, a regional commander of al-Qaeda in the Islamic Maghreb (AQIM) said he broke away from the group, accusing it of "deviating from the true path".

Gouri Abdelmalek, nom de guerre Khaled Abu Suleimane, claimed leadership of the splinter group, and was joined by a AQIM commander of an eastern region in Algeria. The "Soldiers of the Caliphate in Algeria" is the latest group to break with AQIM and side with Baghdadi, after veteran Algerian jihadist, Mokhtar Belmokhtar's group, "Those who sign in Blood" pledged allegiance to the IS group.

But experts say the announcement will not have a major operational impact on the ground as AQIM has been focused on the Sahel region rather than OPEC member Algeria.

Jund al Khilafa, or "Soldiers of the Caliphate," claimed responsibility for the beheading of French tourist Herve Gourdel last year. Since the beheading, the group has reportedly suffered severe setbacks from the Algerian military. Late last year, the government said that it killed the leader of Jund al Khilafa and several other members of the group. In May, more than 20 members were killed in an ambush in Bouira province. The new emir of the Islamic State branch in Algeria was killed in that ambush.

The report of Abdelmalek's death comes roughly three months after Jund al Khilafa -- a small Islamist group formerly linked to al Qaeda -- published a video showing the beheading of Gourdel in what the group said was a display of support to al Qaeda's rival ISIS.

Gourdel, 55, was hiking in central Algeria's Djudjura National Park when he was abducted in September. Jund al Khilafa, having just declared allegiance to the Islamic State in Iraq and Syria (ISIS), then published a video of Gourdel's beheading on September 24.

The video was titled, "A message of blood for the French government." The group said it was responding to an appeal by ISIS spokesman Muhammad al-Adnani to kill "the spiteful and filthy French" because of their support for military action against the group in Iraq.

A video message showing the execution was designed to resemble beheadings carried out by ISIS, as were the words of one of the militants, who said: "Let the French people know that their blood is cheap for their President, and it is the same as you made the blood of the Muslim women and children cheap in Iraq and Sham (Syria)."

The Algerian government called the beheading an act of "criminals," and French President Francois Hollande said at the time that Algeria's Prime Minister assured him he would do the utmost to find the killers. Algerian army launched its attack in Isser after tracking what it believed was "a dangerous terrorist group driving a vehicle" in the city, the Algerian defense ministry said. Abdelmalek was later confirmed as one of the three that the army killed.

Gourdel was just one of the Westerners to be beheaded by an Islamist extremist group this year. Since mid-August, ISIS has beheaded American journalists Steven Sotloff and James Foley, British aid worker David Haines, British aid convoy volunteer Alan Henning, and American aid worker Peter Kassig.

Ansar Dine

Ansar Dine is a paramilitary terrorist group of insurgents based in Northern Mali but operating throughout the country to impose Sharia law. Their primary operations are against the Mali military and opposing rebel groups. In 2012 they captured the caravan town of Timbuktu and imposed strict Islamic law on a previously moderate and tolerant society. In the global war on terrorism, they are associated with the Islamic groups AQLIM, National Movement for the Liberation of Azawad (MNLA), al Qaeda in the Lands of the Islamic Maghreb (AQIM), and the Tuareg Rebels.

Background

Iyad Ag Ghali is a 54 years old Malian. He is the leader of Ansar Dine. From the region of Kidal, northern Mali, Iyad Ag Ghali is a Irayakan, family of the Ifoghas. It is in Libya, however, where he made his debut in the early 1980s: in his early twenties he chose to join the Islamic Legion of Colonel Gaddafi

In Libya, Ag Ghali manages to get noticed. He was sent to Lebanon to fight the phalanges and Christians, according to some sources, aside from some shooting in Chad, in the course of the 1980s, before returning to Mali when the "Guide" declares the dissolution of the Legion.

Ag Ghali is disappointed, but soon found another cause to champion, becoming one of the leading figures of the Tuareg rebellion: it was he who, at the head of the Popular Movement for the Liberation of Azawad (MPLA), attacked the town of Menaka, June 28, 1990. Six months later, the Tamanrasset agreements were signed under the auspices of Algeria, brought an end to the fighting, but the rebels were deeply divided.

Ag Ghali founded the Popular Movement of Azawad (MPA), which brought together the most moderate Tuaregs, he didn't hesitate to confront his former companions and sometimes to allied with the Malian army... His military superiority isn't doubted. For many Malians he is the one that brought peace to the North in the late 1990s.

Gradually, the man got in to contact with radical preachers like the Pakistani Jamaat al-Tabligh ("association for preaching"). In 1999 Iyad Ag Ghali has changed: he stopped shaking hands with women, made his wife wear a veil and spends most of his free time in mosques. Surprising? Not so much. This radicalization is associated with a strong anti-Western sentiment, sharpened in training camps in Libya. In addition, the economic crisis has pushed many Malians, both sedentary and nomadic, into the arms of religion.

In 2003, Ag Ghali is involved with the fundamentalist cause, but not Jihadism: he said to be hostile to terrorism and suicide bombings. This "state of mind" makes him the ideal intermediary to negotiate the release of hostages held by Islamic Salafist Group for Preaching and Combat (GSPC). Thus, in August of the same year the government in Bamako asked Ag Ghali to intercede with Abou Zeid for European tourists kidnapped in Algeria – which he did with success.

Three years later, in May 2006, the anger is brewing again in Northern Mali. Tuareg accuse the authorities of failing to meet their commitments. Ag Ghali meets with President Amadou Toumani Toure (ATT), but negotiations fall short. He then approaches Ibrahim Ag Bahanga, another great figure from irredentist Tuareg, who died in August 2011. Algeria is again involved, obtains the signature of new agreements for peace (the Algiers Accords, signed in July 2006) and, as in the previous uprising, Ag Ghali traded his fighting uniform for a uniform of a man of peace.

Ahmada Ag Bibi

Ahmada Ag Bibi and Iyad Ag Ghali know each other for a long time. In the early 1990s already, they both were in the People's Movement of Azawad (MPA). Ag Bibi is a great activist for the Tuareg cause, but that does not stop to soak in more obscure cases and to be linked to negotiations for the release of Western hostages. In Ag Bibi's address book there are bandits, smugglers, politicians in Bamako and Algiers, and even members of several intelligence services (he was a member of the parliamentary committee Defense and Homeland Security). Also he was the chairman of the parliamentary group for Mali-Algeria friendship and in November 2011 he accompanied the former colonel in the French army, Jean-Marc Gadoullet, to negotiate for the release of Abu Zayd AREVA and VINCI hostages.

When the North rised again in January 2012, Ag Bibi joined the MNLA and Ansar Dine, driven by both realism and friendship towards Ag Ghali. He is not attached to secularism, but believes, as the Ansar Dine diplomat Alghabass Ag Intallah, in negotiating "peaceful solutions" and could therefore be the man to talk to. "Only Algeria can play a role of mediator between the parties to the conflict," he said.

Ag Mohamed Najim, another veteran of the Islamic Legion who Ag Ghali cordially detests, is therefore preferred. This is a slap for Ag Ghali but he didn't mind. He created his own training group, Ansar Dine. Probably he hoped to cause dislocation of MNLA, which weaknesses he knows so well the. At the same time, Ag Ghali also renounced to become the successor of the amenokal (traditional leader) of Ifoghas, the old Intallah Ag Attaher preffered his son, Alghabass Intallah Ag. Again, the bitterness is strong, but he cannot afford to openly confront the patriarch.

It is better to deal and work hand in hand with Ag Intallah, who is highly respected in the region. Ag Ghali holds his hand in June 2012. The MNLA is dying, and now it is Ansar Dine which discuss with the mediator of the Economic Community of West Africa (ECOWAS), President Blaise Compaoré of Burkina Faso. The former soldier of Gaddafi is now recognized as a key player in the Malian crisis. If he distanced himself from the Salafists, as incited by foreign diplomats, he might even become an ally. Moreover, if he considers that direct confrontation with AQIM can serve his ambitions, he will not hesitate to turn against its current "partners". Abou Zeid, Mokhtar Ould Mohamed Hamada and Belmokhtar Kheirou know better than anyone else.

Alghabass Ag Intallah

Originally Alghabass Ag Intallah isn't a warlord. As a member of the National Assembly, he is especially the son of the powerful Ifoghas chief and his designated successor – a line that allows him to benefit from many contacts into the Persian Gulf, including the royal family of Qatar. When the Tuareg rebellion broke out in January 2012, he first ranked alongside the National Movement for the Liberation of Azawad (MNLA) – though always advocated for dialogue with Bamako – then rallied Ansar Dine. Ag Intallah is not a fanatic, and his choice is probably more pragmatic – the fragmentation of MNLA is unequivocal – ideologically. Today, Ag Intallah is the political face of Ansar Dine, it's ambassador. He is the one who is received by the mediator of the crisis, the Burkinabe President Blaise Compaore. Iyad Ag Ghali knows too much for having interest in linking his fate to reign Ifoghas.

ISIS Foreign Fighters from Europe

In the summer of 2012, the first reports emerged of so-called "foreign fighters" (FF) leaving their country of origin or habitual residence to join the Syrian uprising against the Assad regime. Since then, the number of these "travellers" to the Syrian, and more recently, Iraqi battlefields has grown significantly: From September 2014 to September 2015 alone, the number of FF reportedly doubled and reached 30,000 combatants coming from 104 countries.

Some countries are directly affected by the FF issue by foiled or successful attacks, others by being transit countries or departing bases for non-national fighters. While the phenomenon of FF is not new, the sheer size and widespread origins has given the phenomenon a whole new dimension.

Experts and government officials have increasingly warned of the potential security threat this phenomenon might pose to Europe and beyond. Europol, for example, cautioned that FF returning from the battlefields could use "their training, combat experience, knowledge, and contacts" to carry out terrorist acts in the EU.4 Academic researchers and think tanks have confirmed this security threat, and also point out the psychological and social problems that returning FF might pose to themselves and their direct environments.

The past years have seen several attacks connected to FF. These include the January 2015 attacks on the headquarters of the satirical newspaper Charlie Hebdo, and the subsequent attack on a kosher supermarket in Paris, as well as an earlier attack by a French national, who had allegedly spent several months fighting in Syria before carrying out an assault on a Jewish museum in Brussels in May 2014.

But it was not until the tragic events that unfolded on the night of 13 November 2015 in the streets of Paris that fears of a large-scale attack involving groups of returnees from Syria/Iraq were painfully confirmed: At least seven of the perpetrators were alleged to have fought with the so-called "Islamic State" (IS). The most recent attacks in Brussels on 22 March 2016 only seem to underscore the deadly relevance of foreign fighters.

Austria

By September 2015, 230 identified individuals had left Austria for Syria/Iraq; 130 FF were still in the conflict zone and at least 34 had deceased. More recent open-source information points to estimates of up to 300 FF from Austria. According to the Austrian Ministry of Interior (MoI), the number of returnees may exceed 70 persons. In the course of a parliamentary inquiry conducted in March 2015, the MoI affirmed that seventeen women had left Austria as of 9 February 2015 for IS-controlled territory; some of whom were under eighteen at the time of their departure.

While the 2014 Annual Report for the Protection of the Constitution noted that the Austrian FF have no homogenous background, the US Country Reports on Terrorism (2014) point out that people departing from Austria were predominantly of Chechen, Turkish, and Balkan origin. Austrian news agencies further noted that most Austrian FF are second-generation immigrants of Chechen origin. The age range of FF is between 18 and 35 years.

Belgium

Most recent estimates from both official and non-government sources range between 420 to 516 individuals who have travelled to Syria/Iraq since 2011, making Belgium the EU MS with the highest number of FF per capita. An estimated 180–260 FF remain in the conflict zone; 60 to 70 have been killed, mostly in combat. Between 55–120 individuals had returned, and 50 tried to leave but were stopped (yet, these 50 are still included in some counts).

Regarding the profiles and composition of the Belgian FF contingent, Peter Van Ostaeyen provides detailed numbers in October 2015, indicating that 47 of the 516 are female, around 6% are converts, the age of 202 Belgian fighters varies between 14 and 69 (with an average of 25.7), that of the 266 individuals whose origin is known, most come from Brussels (101 of whom 24 from Molenbeek), Antwerp (72), Vilvoorde (28), and Mechelen (14); that 79 individuals can be linked to the group Sharia4Belgium which seems to have inspired many young Belgians to leave for the Levant; that at least five persons are fighting in pro-regime ranks, that at least 112 (but most likely more) are fighters/members of IS, and that around seventeen (but most likely many more) are fighting with Jabhat al-Nusra (JAN).

Bulgaria

According to the Bulgarian MoI, "[c]urrently there is no confirmed information regarding participation of Bulgarian nationals or foreigners staying in Bulgaria in terrorist activities of armed groups in Syria and Iraq". According to open-source information consulted by ICCT, up to ten Bulgarians are estimated to have travelled to Syria/Iraq.

Denmark

According to the Danish Security and Intelligence Service (PET), at least 125 people have left Denmark to travel to Syria/Iraq since January 2011, with a quarter deemed to still be in the conflict zone. At least 27 have died abroad, some while committing suicide attacks. While the majority of the Danish contingent joined IS, PET estimates that "a small number, including Kurds and Shiites, has gone to the conflict zone in Syria and Iraq to fight militant Islamist groups or other armed opposition groups".

With regards to the characteristics of the FF originating in Denmark, PET affirms that the majority are Danish citizens, but with very diverse ethnic origins, including ethnic Danes. Ministry of Justice (MoJ) officials note that "the individuals that leave Denmark to join IS are mainly young Sunni Muslim", including "a number of converts". Women are estimated to constitute 10% of all those who went to Syria. In its 2013 threat assessment report, PET warned that "the group that has left for Syria is younger and more varied than those who left for Afghanistan, Iraq, and Somalia".

PET assesses that the individuals who have left Denmark are mainly affiliated with Islamist circles in cities such as Copenhagen, Aarhus, and Odense and half of the returnees are part of Islamist circles. Public sources point to the fact that at least 22 FF came from the port city of Aarhus and attended the Grimhojvej mosque, which has refused to denounce IS. Lastly, PET assesses that just under half of the individuals who have left Denmark for the conflict zone have been involved in crime.

With respect to the motivations of those willing to leave and join armed groups in the conflict zone, PET points to a wide range: "Some wish to help their fellow Muslims in Syria and do humanitarian work. Others wish to fight the Assad regime. For some the establishment of an Islamic State in Syria is a priority and they may be motivated by achieving what they regard as martyrdom. Finally, maybe there are some who go to Syria in search of excitement and adventure".

France

It is estimated that more than 900 individuals had left France for Syria/Iraq by October 2015. Overall, the number of radicalised French nationals or residents involved in jihadist networks, but not necessarily having travelled to Syria/Iraq, is estimated to be close to 2,000.

By November 2015, an estimated 570 FF were still in the conflict zone, of whom close to 200 were female; about 140 had died (including approximately ten in suicide attacks), and 246 had returned. In addition, it is estimated that 85 minors are involved in jihadist networks and ten are in Syria/Iraq. Regarding affiliation, it is estimated that about 75% had joined IS and 25% JAN.

As with other countries, there is no typical profile of a French FF. FF are known to come from all regions and socio-economic environments. While many French FF are young men with a pre-existing criminal record, there is also a growing contingent of women and even entire families who aim to settle permanently in the Caliphate. Converts represent 23% of the French FF contingent.

France's national terrorist threat system, the Vigipirate Plan, has two levels and one sub-level (vigilance, reinforced vigilance, and attack alert). The response to the ICCT questionnaire – which was returned prior to the Paris attacks – stated that the main threat to France was home-grown terrorism and the phenomenon of FF as a whole. The Paris area has been on the highest level since the January 2015 attacks, with the level throughout the country being raised to the same level following the November 2015 events.

Germany

The German MFA estimates that by July 2015, more than 720 individuals had left the country to fight for or otherwise support terrorist groups in Syria/Iraq. In October, the Federal Prosecutor General put this number at 750, with The Soufan Group (TSG) referring to 760 German FF by November of the same year. According to the MFA, more than 30% is believed to still be in the conflict zone, with 250 having returned. Approximately 100 have died, including at least twenty as suicide attackers.

Regarding the profile of FF, 40% hold only German citizenship, 20% hold dual nationality (German and another), and 40% left from Germany but are not German citizens. The female proportion stands at 20%. Five percent were under the age of eighteen when they left and the majority of those who have left are younger than 30 years of age. Twelve percent are believed to be converts to Islam. Most of those traveling come from North Rhine-Westphalia and Hesse, though a "large number of travellers also come[s] from Berlin, Bavaria and Hamburg". Additionally, many German FF are believed to have either been unemployed or in the low-paid/skilled employment sector prior to departure. Two-thirds were known to the police prior to departure.

Regarding possible motives for FF to travel abroad, the German MFA, while referring to a 2014 study on 378 radicalisation cases, noted "the interest of FF to live in a true Islamic area and to fight for this or other Islamist goals or otherwise support the Islamist cause". The study also noted the relative speed with which individuals radicalise, often in less than 12 months.

According to the NCTV, by 1 November 2015, around 220 individuals had left the Netherlands "for jihadist purposes", with 40 returnees, 42 deceased and 140 remaining in Syria/Iraq. Most of those killed were members of IS, and all of them male, resulting in a proportionate increase in the percentage of females within the whole FF contingent.

Publicly available information about the background of Dutch FF is scarce. Some initial research indicates that the majority are male and under the age of 25. The majority have lower or lower-middle class socio-economic backgrounds, low-to-medium levels of education and limited chances on the labour market. Dutch FF were raised in both traditional religious immigrant (Moroccan, Somali, Antillean, Turkish) families, as well as in ethnically Dutch settings. Many have been exposed to crime and drug abuse in their immediate social circle; some have had a traumatic experience in their life in the period prior to travelling to Syria/Iraq.

Some are deeply frustrated about their own societal position or that of their ethnic group, feeling that they did not have a future in the Netherlands or any way to improve their position. There is a notable cluster of Dutch FF stemming from The Hague, but also other towns, such as Delft, Zoetermeer, Gouda, and Arnhem.

A final point of interest is that mental-health conditions may also play a role among the group of Dutch FF. In a study among 140 (potential) FF, whose files were cross-referenced with police databases, it appeared that "individuals with histories of behavioural problems and disorders are overrepresented".

Spain

The Spanish MoI reported in November 2015 that 139 FF had left Spain, and 25 individuals had returned. According to a report published in the same month by Fernando Reinares and Carola Garcia Calvo, there are an estimated 120 Spain-linked FF. Ten percent of those who went to Syria from Spain were female.

Reinares and Calvo183 also reconstructed the profiles of twenty Spanish residents that had travelled to fight with jihadist groups in Syria before 2014. Eleven of the twenty are Spanish citizens, while the remaining nine are Moroccan nationals living in Spain; most lived in the Spanish enclave Ceuta in North Africa, but also in Girona and Malaga. The majority are between their mid 20s and early 30s; they were mostly married and with children; and were low-skilled, (un)employed workers as well as students at the time of their departure. Several were already known to the police (especially in Ceuta) and implicated in drug trafficking. Out of the 20, at least three young Muslim Spanish nationals residing in Ceuta became suicide bombers.

UK

According to the UK Office for Security and Counter-Terrorism (OSCT), approximately 700 individuals had left for Syria/Iraq since January 2011, of whom 315 are currently in the conflict area, over half returned, and approximately 70 died. The total number is below the latest TSG estimate which indicates 760 FF as an official count in November 2015. The OSCT further reported that the majority of UK FF have joined IS, and that a majority holds British citizenship.

Most FF are between 18 and 30 years of age, although the average age is reducing. Almost all are Muslim. The OSCT stated that it is not possible to deduce one unifying motivation for all FF, and that multiple underlying factors play a role, mostly related to a weak social status that makes individuals vulnerable to IS' message(s), including through the Internet and social media. Yet, in 2013, Maher concluded that "many of those travelling to Syria as foreign fighters are male; in their twenties, of South-Asian ethnic origin, with recent connections to higher education, and with links to individuals or groups who have international connections".

Italy

According to the Italian MoI, 87 FF departed from Italy between 1 January 2011 and late October 2015. Fifty-seven are allegedly in the conflict zone and eighteen have died. The response of the government also indicated that fifteen FF had joined IS, two had joined JAN, and seven had joined other opposition forces including the FSA.224 The Italian Defence Minister noted that only twelve FF had Italian passports, with six also holding another (dual) nationality.

Basic Characteristics of FF

Although there is not one typical profile of a European FF, some key characteristics can be identified. Based on this research, FF today are mostly young men between the ages of eighteen and mid-to-late twenties, with some countries reporting that between 4% and 10% of FF are under eighteen,263 whereas in four countries in Eastern and Southern Europe, the FF contingent is older, with more than 50% being over 30. The proportion of females in the total FF contingent varies between 6% and 30%,264 with some countries indicating that the number has grown in recent months.

Little data could be found on the marital status of all (i.e. male and female) departed FF. However, information from five countries indicates that around half are married, whereas one Southern European country had a majority of unmarried FF.

On the basis of the data available for nine countries accounting for over 30% of the total contingent, most FF originate from large metropolitan areas or peripheral suburbs. The majority of German FF come from cities, for instance from Berlin and Hamburg. It is notable that many FF originate from the same urban neighbourhood. This is the case for example in Aarhus, Copenhagen, and Odense in Denmark, as well as Gothenburg in Sweden, and Brussels or Antwerp in Belgium, or Delft, Zoetermeer, Arnhem, and The Hague in the Netherlands. This seems to indicate that there are already-existing (extremist) networks in these areas, that a circle of friends radicalises as a group and decides to leave together, or recruits those friends remaining at home while already in the conflict zones.

The number of converts to Islam among FF is significant. In the case of two Eastern European countries, this percentage reaches 100% (note, however, that the total number of FF in each of these countries is below five). For MS with higher numbers of FF, the research illustrates that between 6% and 23% of FF are converts; 12% in the case of the German FF contingent. Another example of the importance of converts is the composition of a group behind a foiled terrorist attack in Barcelona in June 2015, where five out of the eleven captured IS sympathisers had converted to Islam from either atheism or Christianity.

Other data was less conclusive. For example, there is a significant variation when it comes to the national background of departees. In two Western European countries, the majority hold a nationality other than the one of the country where they departed from; whereas in another Western European country the inverse trend can be observed, with the majority of FF holding at least the citizenship of the country of departure (or dual nationality).

In certain cases, strong links to previous criminal activities were found, for instance, in the case of France, Austria, and Slovenia. While, for two countries, none of the FF had a prior criminal record, for five others, between 24% and a "majority" had been convicted for criminal offenses. It should also be noted that in some EU countries, persons who left for Syria/Iraq were linked to pre-existing Islamist circles back home.

For instance, in the case of Denmark, some FF "are affiliated with known Islamist circles [...] in Copenhagen and other major cities". In the case of Luxembourg, all those who left had previous links to Islamist networks. In one Northern European country, the percentage of those linked to Islamist circles reached 85%.

Lastly, ICCT also aimed to find out whether FF (have) had mental-health problems. From the data provided by only three MS, between 0 and up to 20% of FF fall within this category.

From Activism to Violent Action

The Wide-Range of Motivations of Foreign Fighters Based on the information collected through the ICCT questionnaire, FF motivations to depart include a wide variety of push and pull factors: Solidarity with other "fellow Muslims" abroad (in Syria mostly, and especially during the early stages of FF travel), the fight against the Alawite Assad regime in Syria, the desire to live in a territory ruled by Islamic law, alienation and social exclusion felt in Europe, as well as the desire to conduct jihad. For some, the search for excitement and adventure play a role, as does peer pressure and the prospects of life in the caliphate, such as marriage and housing. At least one response to the ICCT questionnaire mentioned the relative ease of travel to Syria/Iraq by land as a motivating/facilitating factor to undertake the journey to the conflict zone.

Other sources indicate that FF' motives could also relate to more politically-oriented factors, such as EU MS' foreign policy (past or current military engagement against armed groups close or affiliated to IS or al Qaeda) or EU national integration policies allegedly alienating Muslim groups.

Both the data gathered for this study and academic literature emphasise a new generation of foreign combatants, different from the Afghan "Holy warriors" and "hardened jihadists", "galvanized by hateful religious and political ideologies [... and] determined to turn the global tide against the 'infidel' regimes".

The three previous generations of FF show differences with this generation in terms of socio-economic and educational background, battlefield experience, age range and motivational factors. This so-called fourth generation of FF, can, according to Coolsaet,271 be split up in two main groups: The first group builds on pre-existing social relations and their travel is "another form of deviant behaviour, next to membership of street gangs, rioting, drug trafficking and juvenile delinquency". Joining IS then offers a "thrilling, larger-than-life dimension to their way of life". The second group, however, showed no previous deviant behaviour, or specific distinction from their peers.

Key features of this group is the absence of a future and feelings of exclusion, and their "search for belonging and a cause to embrace". This difference is largely related to the different role religion seems to play as a motivational factor for EU FF compared to previous generations.

Contrary to previous waves of FF who departed for Afghanistan, Iraq, or Somalia, today's cohort appears to be younger and less educated in Islam and, in the words of Oliver Roy, "more radicals than Islamists". As pointed out in a recent paper, most young Sunni Muslims became susceptible to fundamentalist interpretations of militant Islam after they found it difficult to integrate into European societies due to cultural, religious and social differences.

The psychology literature on the FF phenomenon confirms this assessment: "The perception of grievance drives the search for a violence-justifying ideology, not the other way around".

The language of jihad then only legitimates the grievance, offering a designated culprit and a direct justification to fight the wrong, whether that is poor integration, real or perceived marginalisation, relative deprivation, or discrimination. As such, the decision to make hijra "to the land of Islam" may be less of a religious obligation than an emotional response to a feeling of injustice in their home societies, or what French novelist Erick Orsenna calls "the breeding ground of hopelessness" following the Charlie Hebdo attacks.

Although much is still unknown about the underlying grievances of radicalisation and the trigger that pushes people over the edge to the extent that they support the violent cause of organisations such as IS or JAN, it is important to stress that evidence so far does not seem to support the notion that religious conviction is the initial push factor in most cases, even though it does play a role as a pull factor exploited by recruiters, and as a legitimation of the violence later on in the process of radicalisation.

Patterns of Radicalisation

This research, through questionnaires and open-source material, disclosed a wide variety of radicalisation patterns with radicalisation taking place in various environments, such as within the family, within friendship groups, and in mosque or prison communities. In a study on AQI, it was indicated that FF overwhelmingly joined the jihad via sympathisers networks (33.5%) and personal social networks (29%). The role of social media was also noted as significant in several responses to the ICCT questionnaire. With approximately 46,000 Twitter accounts operating on behalf of IS, social media represents a powerful instrument in IS propaganda. Online extremism expert J. M. Berger notes that "many, perhaps most, potential recruits first learn about ISIS from the media, only then seeking it out on social media".

The radicalisation process appears to be the result of a combination of individual and context-related factors. Notwithstanding the heterogeneity of EU FF' backgrounds, various analyses and reports emphasise socially vulnerable profiles, mainly composed of marginalised and single individual or cliques, youth in transitional stages of their lives, who discreetly radicalise, "under the radar", and in a relatively short period of time. The youngest perpetrator of the Paris attacks, for instance, allegedly went from smoking and